THE
LAST
POOL

THE LAST POOL

Upstream and Down
and Big Stony

by Howard T. Walden 2d

illustrated by Milton C. Weiler
introduction by Sparse Grey Hackle

CROWN PUBLISHERS, INC., NEW YORK

Inquiries should be addressed to Crown Publishers, Inc.,
419 Park Avenue South, New York, N.Y. 10016.

Library of Congress Catalog Card Number: 72–84316

ISBN: 0-517-500353

Printed in the United States of America

Published simultaneously in Canada by
General Publishing Company Limited

To the memory of
STEPHENSON B. WALDEN

Books by Howard T. Walden 2d

Upstream and Down, 1938 and 1946
Big Stony, 1940 and 1947
Angler's Choice (ed.), 1947
Familiar Freshwater Fishes of America, 1964
Native Inheritance: The Story of Corn in America, 1966
Anchorage Northeast, 1971
The Last Pool—Upstream and Down and *Big Stony,* 1972

Table of Contents

Foreword

I wrote the original manuscripts of *Upstream and Down* and *Big Stony* in the 1930s. In the decades since, changes of great import have occurred. Many trout waters of the Northeast have been redesigned by natural forces—floods, storms, ice. Many more have been altered by man; some, indeed, including two or three brooks I wrote about in *Upstream and Down,* have been obliterated by man. Their once profound meaning to me lives only in my memory; the joy of fishing them is forever denied to the present and future generations.

Among other changes of these decades, certainly insignificant changes by any standards other than my personal ones, are my own ideas about trout fishing and about writing. Preparing the original texts of *Upstream and Down* and *Big Stony* for this new edition I encountered many passages which seemed unrepresentative of my thinking today. Some, particularly in *Upstream and Down,* bespoke tactical theories or hunches I no longer hold; others concerned the writing itself. These I have attempted to amend as I see them now with much older eyes.

The spirit, however—the heart and philosophy of trout fishing I tried to express in the originals—is for me steadfast. I have endeavored to keep that, in this new volume, as I have felt it since I began to fish, more than six decades ago.

Howard T. Walden 2d

Palisades, New York
April 20, 1972

Acknowledgments

The author acknowledges his gratitude to:

The Sportsman, formerly of Boston, Mass., for permission to reprint the sections "Old Timer," "Places," and "Downstream after Dark" in *Upstream and Down.*

Outdoors, formerly of Boston, Mass., for permission to reprint "Old Glory's Trout" in *Big Stony.*

Field & Stream, New York, N.Y., for permission to reprint "Midwinter Night's Dream" in *Big Stony.*

The author also salutes

The memory of the late Gene Connett and Waldron M. Ward, Jr., of the Derrydale Press, New York, who first published *Upstream and Down* and *Big Stony* in 1938 and 1940.

Frank J. Lowe, formerly of the Derrydale Press, who arranged for the republication of these books by The Macmillan Company, New York, in 1946 and 1947.

Milton C. Weiler, whose art is proof against the erosions of time and who has graciously allowed his illustrations for the original books to be used in this volume.

Nick Lyons, of Crown Publishers, Inc., New York, without whose editorial wisdom, tolerance, and guidance this book could not have been published.

And Sparse Grey Hackle who needs no introduction to trout anglers but whose Introduction of this volume so brightly honors it.

Introduction

This is a confession of envy of the enjoyment that the reader newly come to these Walden fishing books will experience; an affirmation of my own joy, remembered over the more than thirty years since I first read these classics; and a prediction that the newcomer to *Upstream and Down* and *Big Stony* will read and reread this volume from time to time with the same enjoyment I have derived from my own perusals.

Only books like these survive as pinnacles of angling literature, timeless and unchanging, because they deal with those fundamentals of angling that also are timeless and unchanging—the fisherman and the fish. Books that deal with tackle and tactics and the endless, trivial detail of "how-to-do-it" proliferate like weeds and like weeds perish. They become out-of-date and are superseded as greenheart is displaced by bamboo and bamboo by glass fibers; as hair gives way to silk and silk to plastic filaments; as silkworm gut is superseded by nylon monofilament; and as the native brook trout yields his haunts to the European brown.

Walden does indeed write briefly about tackle in *Upstream and Down* but from the standpoint of its impact on the fisherman himself as Opening Day approaches. "In March the solid habits of a winter melt down the gutters of temptation," he warns, and describes the fisherman's downfall once a display of colorful new tackle has lured him into the store.

"A few irresponsible casts" with some offbeat gaudy fly after a long day's diet of sober, efficient Hare's Ears and Cahills will "prevent angler's scurvy," he says. And when, after describing his extravagant purchase of a new reel, he adds, "and every angler knows the vice-presidential function of a trout reel," he reveals himself as a thrifty angler; a careless one who strips in line to lie about (and alas, sometimes beneath) his hobnailed shoes instead of playing his fish properly off the reel; and one who like me has had long and unrewarding experience with vice-presidents.

Big Stony has a finely written, sensitive delineation of three-dimensional characters in an unusual plot; but besides, it is a collection of fishing stories and reminiscences—colorful, graphic, fascinating, skillfully written, and basically what the fisherman best loves. One hears them at the Long Table of The Anglers' Club and in the streamside lodges of the Brooklyn Flyfishers, the Tuscarora, the Beaverkill, the Big Bend, the DeBruce Fly Fishing (to which Howard and I both belong), the Brodhead Hunting & Fishing, the Parkside, and half a hundred fishing clubs more. The dedicated angler can never get enough of this good talk, these engaging stories, and will find it difficult indeed to put down this book before finishing it.

The first, original editions of *Upstream and Down* and *Big Stony* are scarce and hard to find, for the books attained their status as classics on a combined total of only 1,500 copies. The present volume now offers what will be to many literate anglers newly come to the sport their first opportunity to read the books an earlier generation remembers and admires. I envy them.

SPARSE GREY HACKLE

xiv

Upstream and Down

The Spark Is Kindled 1

The exact date of my first trout fishing escapes me but I would say that the year was 1910 or earlier, placing the experience in that time of life when all of one's perspectives have a form and color so fresh and fragile they cannot endure into later years.

The fishing was hardly spectacular. It was worm fishing in a small brook that meandered through woodland and meadow not more than three miles from home. The trout averaged seven to eight inches; a ten-incher was a prize; a lunker of twelve inches or over was extremely rare but not unknown.

The brook was typical of many others in that part of northern New Jersey yet it remains in my memory as the most individual, the most alluring of all water I have known. I came to know it as I knew my backyard. I could travel a straight line through dense woods and arrive upon any one of the brook's ten or twelve likelier pools. I knew where each spring rill fed the main stream and where each slough of slack water backed into the damp woods. Several fallen trees crossed it to facilitate an angler's passage upstream or down; some of them partially dammed the current or diverted the channel, creating ideal trout holes. Those little pools and pockets were difficult indeed to fish and threatened the loss of a hook among the roots of their deep dusks, but they were the abiding places of the native brook trout, and a worm dropped carefully by a hidden angler would often evoke an immediate strike.

The stream took its source five miles north of our town, flowed south four miles and east two more, emptying into a broad tidal river. In the course of its journey it wandered through open meadow and deep woods, flowed into and out of two ice ponds, and in its lower reaches skirted the backyards of another town. During our pretrout era the stretch between the two ice ponds was our favorite water for sunfish, shiners and an occasional bullhead. For some time we did not fish the reaches opposite and below the town; the water there had a perceptible murk of pollution and a suburban setting quite at odds with our angling ideals.

For even a longer period we avoided the water above the upper ice pond. In retrospect I can muster only a few flimsy reasons for this neglect. The upper brook was farther from home but the added distance would scarcely have deterred us. Perhaps because it was smaller it seemed to hold little promise. And since none of us had ever taken a trout below the upper ice pond we could assume none was above it. Our habitual area had its known potentials of fish and it sufficed us. As if we were an Indian tribe we marked for ourselves, subconsciously and without ever speaking of it, the established boundaries of our domain. To stray beyond them was a matter of consequence; when at last it occurred to one of us it was not casually acted upon, alone, but placed before the clan as a project for collective judgment.

The plan to fish the stream below the town was conceived in a mood of reluctant experimentation, induced by reports of great catches of sunfish and shiners at the "Railroad Pool," an abnormal widening of the stream below a railway trestle. Here, in a two-hour, after-school session, we took fifty or sixty shiners and sunfish, on bits of dough mixed with cotton. These averaged appreciably larger than the fish of our smaller pools upstream. We went back to the Railroad Pool again and again, fishing this unlovely water to the neglect of the crystal coilings and shady glades of the upper brook. And inevitably we began to know a sense of guilt though for a while none of us confessed it. Our repeated sallies to the Railroad Pool and our frequently gluttonous catches hinted at some shameful preference for the grosser, meat-in-the-pot aspects of angling. A reaction was overdue.

There came a day when I knew I was surfeited with the Railroad

Pool and its easy fish. I would leave that place for good and all and head north for my fishing—not immediately north, in the water we knew so well, but far up, above the second ice pond where none of us had ever fared. This bit of unorthodoxy, broached as usual to the partners, was received with mingled expressions of amazement, skepticism and scorn. I would get nothing up there. The brook was too small; no one ever fished it in those parts. No one ever bothered, they said, with that undersized rill whose water in my imagining came quiet and dark out of the deep woods above the second ice pond as if colored by the somber shade and mystery of its uncharted forests.

Its reputation of not being "bothered with" might well have made it all the more alluring to me. But indeed I had heard, some time before and in so remote and vague a fashion that I had scarcely given the tale credence, that it *had* been bothered with. A boy I knew (he was not a fisherman) advised me that a boy he knew (also not a fisherman) had seen a man emerge from that wilderness above the upper ice pond, late one afternoon. The man had carried a very slender rod; over his shoulder hung a willow creel in which three extraordinarily beautiful fish reposed on damp moss. These fish, it seemed, were larger than the average run of shiners and sunnies, were without scales but were decorated with brilliant markings—bronze-green, mottled backs, brightly spotted sides and yellow-orange underparts.

Up to that time, I had never seen a trout. But I had seen pictures of trout, and the description of these three fish, disjointed and third-hand as it was, tallied with the pictures. Yet it was not conceivable that trout could inhabit our brook. One had to go to the fastnesses of Canada or Maine to catch trout. And further, they were not a boy's fish. You graduated to trout, eventually, from the sunfish-and-shiner school. It was a man's business, like driving a car; there was something preposterous even in my serious consideration of it.

Thoughts like these almost battered down the small persistent hope that kept me headed upstream after leaving my companions at the Railroad Pool. The way was long and it led by all of that water I knew so well. The temptation to pause at some of these deep holes was strong; fishing water never looks so inviting or so surely potential as when from some necessity you pass it by unchallenged. The day was gusty and cool, past the first week of June, a day of alternate brilliance and shadow as the rent fabric of clouds hurried east across the sun. The water of my stream was by times sparkling and dark: in the lee of an old stump it was quiet as a summer dusk, but a long meadow stretch of the brook built up a respectable sea in the wind and was traversed incessantly by the hurrying dark tracks of the gusts.

I crossed the brook above the lower ice pond, negotiated the length of a pasture, passed the swimming hole—deserted in this blustery chill—and headed north through a grove of hardwoods until I reached the upper ice pond.

An east-west road, little used in that remote year, crossed the upper end of the pond. Immediately north of the road the brook was narrow and aimless in a small area of lush meadow; and then, abruptly at the limits of this little lea was the wall of the woods. It confronted me like a challenge; I could imagine that lofty timber marching unimpeded to the shores of the Arctic.

I stood for a moment on the little bridge where the road crossed, looking north, looking hard at that looming and dusky barrier of the woods. It looked back at me with no expression, or perhaps with all expression, threatening and beckoning at once. I saw it as the whole of nature and in its countenance all that nature ever had offered man.

After a moment I went ahead, north. Beyond our accustomed reservation at last, I was glad of the narrow path that went in my direction. I followed it across the little field north of the road and with it entered at last the deep woods. The path went its way; the big trees stood aside in deference to its narrow progress; it had courage and persistence and seemed to know what it was about, and I drew a measure of confidence from its manifest reliability.

The crown of this forest seemed enormously high, remote from its roots as if detached, as if it were a veil of dark clouds over the world. It moved ceaselessly aloft as the wind tangled in its infinite patterns, giving a play of sifted inconstant light to the path and lower trunks and ferns and all that grows in dampness and deep shade. The continuous drone of the lofty wind seemed to insulate these lower strata in a stillness. There were close low dogwoods,

4

witch hazel, aspen and beech; and in this green gloom they lived in a breathless taut suspension of motion. Skunk cabbage and ferns, and last year's leaves, and the rotted litter of a century's fallen trees gave off a smell that seemed a perceptible vapor, the very odor of life, an emanation from the striving of a myriad minute organisms and the tiny stretching of countless roots, and the yielding of earth to this microscopic push of growth.

As I went along I felt the strangeness of my presence on the path, as if I were invading some profound privacy of the woods. But the woods were persistent in keeping their secrets intact. One does not readily get at the inner quick of nature. I traveled the path in a stillness but I realized, after a while, that the stillness was traveling with me. It was as if all that small swarming activity of growth was suspended as I passed, to be resumed when I had got safely by. The woods quieted as I approached, like April peepers in a pond. The ever-present hush was like the still shyness of children before a passing stranger. A murmuring would start up again behind me—I felt rather than heard it—and I was sure the same murmuring lay ahead.

I forgot, almost, that I had come to fish. The path in its northward boring had slanted gradually west and down. There was a rift in the ground growth at my feet and a whisper barely audible in the profound quiet. The brook was there, black below some overhanging ferns, talking to the roots of an oak as it went by. In this sudden confrontation I looked hard to make sure of the brook. And being more than ordinarily curious as to brooks, I lay on my stomach and peered down through the rifts in that complicated lower jungle. Doing so I was surprised at the volume of water under my eyes. A beam of sunlight sharply illumined the extreme secret bottom of the pool, two feet down in the convolutions of black roots. The light hovered there a moment, showing me a patch of sand and a sparkle of iron pyrites, and then the light was gone with the ceaseless motion of the forest crown. I waited for its return, peering into the liquid twilight, and gradually my eyes defined the elements of this deeper gloom. Close under the bank was the imponderable dusk of the roots; out beyond that the vague bottom of sand and pebbles. For all I could see this microcosm contained no life. Such shapes as were in it were still, as if they had been there forever: waterlogged sticks, a stone or two, blurred as shadows. The intensity of the unaccustomed focus strained my eyes. As I was about to turn away, the faintest imaginable movement arrested my gaze, directed it again to the dark floor of the stream. I couldn't be sure—it might have been some caprice of a labored vision—yet I could have sworn that one of those longish blurred shapes had moved. "Moved" is scarcely the word: the change was barely perceptible and was not a movement of the whole object but only of its downstream end.

Peering down through the gloaming of the pool I saw again that gentlest shadow of a motion. There was no doubt of it now: the lower end of that shape stirred from side to side in the current like a flag in a zephyr.

The sunbeam returned, miraculously, as I watched, suffusing the pool with its radiance, giving the dark water a misty luminosity. But it was enough. In the soft amber glow I saw the fabulous reality of the trout. Then again the pool was dark.

My focus had not wavered during the alternate lightening and darkening of the pool but now I perceived that my trout was gone. I had not seen it move away and shall never know how it accomplished its exit. It dematerialized, merely. It might have been a figment of the sunbeam that revealed it, coming and going with the light, some solar precipitation visible, as the iron pyrites were, only in the full sun.

At this moment, I think, my respect for the *fontinalis* was born, and probably the same moment saw the close of that semester which had been concerned with the sunnies and shiners of the lower stream. The sunbeam had given me a sort of diploma.

In my fishing that afternoon I was successful beyond my most extravagant hopes; more successful, indeed, than on many ventures over the same water in later years. Whatever gods presided over that windy forest rewarded me, perhaps, for humility, a sense of reverence in their temple and a quietness along its dusky aisles. My awe in their whole show was surely manifest; I could be glad that only they were present to see my hands tremble as I assembled my three-piece, hardware-store bamboo.

I went downstream to begin fishing, having some shadowy notion of sacrilege in exploiting the spot which had shown me the trout. The brook followed a devious course, as if deliberately lingering in this woodland. I crossed and recrossed it, clambered over windfalls, and occasionally, at some bend where the water was dark and deep, paused to drop a worm into the slow-curling current. Nothing occurred for some time, beyond the challenge of the fishing itself in the succession of pools I had never seen. Later I came to know them well but on that young and avid afternoon each seemed to question me anew, presenting its strange problems.

When long continued, fishing that is unproductive of fish immerses the angler in the routine rhythms of his progress and the handling of his rod. The anticipation of a strike becomes almost nonexistent, so deeply is it sunk beneath the mechanics of fishing.

In this state of lapsed alertness I had my first strike from a brook trout. I have a clear memory of that little run of water. The brook here effected a straight cleavage of the banks for twenty feet, a precocious riffle, swift and sun-flecked, achieving a miniature roar over its pebbly bottom and building four-inch waves toward its downstream end. A child riffle, true in all respects to riffle type. Later I saw grown ones, in the Esopus and the Neversink in the early season, where the pebbles were boulders and the waves nearer to two feet, and they were the same except in degree. And this one came at length to a pool, as do most riffles, great or small. It was a deepish cavity of still water beneath the overhanging branches of an oak. The worm coursed down the little rapid, entered the green-shaded stillness. A flash deep in that shadowed amber brought me alive. My rod had a simultaneous reaction: it bent its overstout tip a full six inches toward the water. The line between reel and first guide went taut in my left hand. The ensemble of rod and line was convulsed with the living resistance at the far end.

Nothing like this had ever happened to me. No sunfish or shiner had ever charged my bait with such unexampled ferocity or felt half as strong as this fighting fish felt now. I knew it was a trout and I knew that I must land it. There must be no bungling here; all else in my life might fail but the act of this moment must succeed.

I can remember a conscious effort to be calm as I led that fish up the little rapid, trying to temper my pressure, to strip in line just fast enough to keep it taut. The trout came to me slowly; presently its whole identity was surging there in the shallows a rod's length away. In seconds more it was on the bank. I killed it the quick way —the backward bend of the head—laid it on a bed of moss and sat on the bank to look at it. This was a full moment, flooding warm with victory. But it held something else to prevent any smugness in triumph. I hadn't foreseen it but it was there. (It has followed me always along every stream I have fished and caught up with me each time I have taken a trout from its element and killed it.) The trout seemed to me then, in some voiceless idiom of thought, a crystallization in the flesh of all the changing character of a running stream: the suavity of deep water, the dusky stillness of a pool, the gay abandon of a rapid and the play of light and shadow over them all. It might have been born, I thought, of these patterns of nature rather than the processes of eggs and fertilization, as if some secret chemistry of beauty had precipitated this form out of shadow and white sun, clean sand and mossy stone, roots and the derelict leaves, the ease of the backwater and the high strife of the central current. Here was the essence of the stream itself, before the trout began to fade in death, in its colors and clean fair lines, the immaculate continuity of head and body, body and tail.

I went on downstream in the aging afternoon, keener now as one is always keener after his first fish. The stream widened gradually; a tributary came in from the west and piled up a sand bar at the confluence, a long sun-illumined shallow hurrying over the white bottom. It was a glaringly exposed water but in its center a trout lay over the bright sand. I saw it from afar, saw that it was larger than my first. Approaching on hands and knees I put the worm gently fifteen feet upstream and let it go down while I trembled for the anticipated strike. It came, violent in the shallow water. I hit back but there was a little slack. My line came back to me and beyond, weightless, entangling itself in the streamside foliage. The water continued indifferently over the white empty sand as if nothing had happened. I might have imagined a trout had been there.

But farther down, in a pool almost large enough to swim in, I took a ten-incher from an infinite maze of roots. My line was taut here and I drew out the fish the way the worm had gone in, with never an inch of slack. The struggling weight amazed me as the trout came up; it was much the biggest fish I had ever caught. But my day was not yet at the crest.

By now I thought I had come a good distance from the starting point and light ahead through the trees confirmed me. The clearing was there, perhaps a hundred yards downstream, then the short stretch of meadow brook, and below that the ice pond.

Every bend of this little stream was a surprise, so dense was the June foliage that shielded its secrets. The edge of the woods was closer now but the trees marched up to that edge in mass formation and the forest gloom was still as deep. Thus I came all at once upon a wood road, a bridge across the brook, and below the bridge a pool of much greater dimensions than any I had fished this afternoon. The wood road was overgrown and innocent of ruts; the bridge was far gone in decay, sagging to the eternal stream. A big spider moved out of sight into the black underparts of the tumbled structure. The water here was dark and fast, finding its way through the soft wreckage, complaining at the obstruction. One of the old boards, pivoted on a single nail, swung back and forth in the current in a slow changeless routine. On the downstream side the brook freed itself from the tangled ruin and spread deeply and wide. The black central current was effervescent with bubbles that rose and floated away under the towering forest.

The size of the pool and perhaps some aura of the deep past that hung over the ruined bridge gave me the conviction that an outsize trout was there. The strong current below the bridge had its way with the worm; I took line from the reel and let the stream have it through the guides. The stream might have taken all of it had not something else been equally greedy and intolerant of the patient ways of streams. The worm had gone half the length of the pool when I perceived that although I was still paying out line, the far end had not only ceased its down-current drift but was actually coming back upstream, toward me! That seemed in keeping with the dark mood of the place: something of the sort was rather to be expected in this ancient glen which had been so long apart from the world that it had forgotten about physical laws. But I did not quite succumb to this witchery of perverted principles. I gathered the yards of curving slack until I came up short against the vibrant, deep-boring body of the trout. It turned downstream, presenting its full strength to my startled calculation, and I knew that this was by far the heaviest fish my rod had ever known. Doubtless my tactics were indelicate and too greedily swift, but they sufficed. A landing net would have been needed had I been using a fly rod appropriate to this encounter, but my instrument was a stout bait rod with the action of a small derrick. It brought in that trout as if leering at its courage. The fish was well hooked. I stepped down from the bridge, beached the trout on an arc of sand, hauled it several feet up the shelving bank and killed it with a stone.

Laid out on one of the old boards of the bridge, with the two others dwarfed beside it, it took my six-inch ruler twice and an inch over. A thick deep fish, it mounded up on the board, an extravagant pile of beauty which at the moment I could not believe.

I sat there on the bridge for some minutes looking at the big one and its lesser kindred of the upper stream, and listening again to that quiet voice which has nagged me many times since. It tells me that to kill a trout is to wound myself.

Then I wrapped the three fish in the large emerald leaves of a streamside plant and bore them back to the Railroad Pool where my colleagues were still taking shiners from the dull water. They looked at me and my trout and back at me, in a still wonder, as if I and my fish were new arrivals from Mars. They took down their rods in silence; one told me afterward that he had left his string of shiners on the bank. But they were not long in defeat. There were many questions, and before we reached home their own first trout were as good as caught.

We did have sense enough to restrain ourselves, realizing even then that this little stream was not inexhaustible and that only the miracle of its seclusion had kept it in trout. We took an oath of secrecy and established certain private rules based upon our ideas of conservation. We set bag limits which, in the light of experience, were dictated by an unwarranted optimism, for on very few occasions did any one of us take more than two trout from those upper waters.

In time we acquired better tackle and possibly more skill, but often we returned empty-handed. I recall no single day to compare with that first afternoon and only one subsequent trout to match my big one of the pool below the ruined bridge.

Inevitably the stream became known. Strangers found it in the deep woods; cars parked on the roadside at the upper ice pond. The

State became interested and made yearly plantings of brown trout and rainbows. The fishing improved—in the opinion of those who cared little about the decline of the wild native trout or the ravishment of that dusky privacy which had been the little brook's intrinsic charm.

I would not go back to it now. When I last saw it, many years ago, a new bridge had replaced the ancient ruin at the lower pool. The road that passed over, cleared and tidy, had the flinty look of ambition as if it hoped to be a suburban street before long. The ranks of the forest had been thinned and harsh sunlight had flooded in upon the secret cool dells. Water once black under the dripping fern banks was now exposed all the way down, bright with sun and with emptiness. The brook was doomed. Life there had reached its peak and passed over. One who had seen it when it hummed with the joy of its abundant life could see now that it was dying, that it knew the feel of the cancer of progress.

Fishermen 2

A tendency to classify people into groups or clans or families has often no further excuse than the fact of a mutual fondness for some specialized endeavor. Some of us who go to the streams, lakes and oceans with rod and line are perhaps a little tired of owning to brotherhood in the "great angling fraternity." The fact that Smith and Jones both fish is no more a sign of fundamental kinship between them, no more an earnest of sympathetically beating hearts than is a common liking for turnips.

Smith is a convivial soul, never happier than when plenty of his friends and plenty of the friendly fluids are at hand. Since some of Smith's associates like to fish—or what they speak of as such—and since the opportunities for steins on the table and a good song ringing clear are not untrammeled at home, Smith and his fellows have taken to steins on the afterdeck and a good song ringing clear across the Sound. Fishing? It is. Each has a rod, reel and the rest—good tackle, too—and occasionally some to-do is raised when one of the rods boats a specimen larger than the common run. That is fishing enough; it might be difficult to say that fishing is not the raison d'être but merely a low by-product of Smith's marine excursions.

But it is not much like Jones's fishing. Jones is apt to leave his friends at home when he takes his rod with him; indeed some say

13

that Jones goes fishing to get away from people. Jones has a way of getting up before daybreak and being off in his car in the limpid dawns of May and June. If you essay to follow Jones you will need good tires for you may not be long on the concrete highway. Jones has a penchant for the narrow traffic-free routes that thread the hills and valleys of the obscure townships. Following Jones could be an eye-opener to folk who think no natural beauty is left within a hundred miles of the metropolitan district. Jones is likely to bring up at last by an old plank bridge spanning a dark torrent in some narrow gorge. Rhododendrons choke the banks of this little stream, hemlocks are rooted in the sandstone shelves on either side, laurel glimmers up the shady slopes. On one of the planks of the bridge is a carven heart and initials—L.H. & A.R. '08. That is about all in the way of signs. If billboards were anywhere near, Jones would not have led you to this spot.

Watch him now. His rod is a delicate thing, about three ounces and six feet, a specialized instrument for his small-stream work. His handling of it is of comparable fineness. Watching Jones cast you realize at once that he has been doing this thing for a long time, long enough to be beyond any concern with the petty exactions of technique. Apparently his subconscious being is taking care of the rod and of the waders which find their precarious way up the slippery floor, for his eyes are intent upon the water and the drop and drift of his fly. But if you know him well you know that all of this action does not completely absorb Jones. Another part of him is alert to register the little asides in the drama of his day. A pair of wood ducks angles over a pool ahead, a mink vanishes around a distant rock, a tanager is a momentary vivid accent. Beyond these lesser overtures is always the immemorial backdrop of trout fishing. And these, no less than the possible weight in his creel at dusk, are what Jones drove all the miles for.

Thus Jones's fishing, and Smith's. And yet a mutual acquaintance will tell himself that he must get Jones and Smith together. Both fishermen—how they would hit if off!

But if all fishermen are not brothers all trout fishermen may at least be distant kin. There is identity of motive here despite a wide diversity of method. Whatever your purpose is in going to the stream it is fundamentally the same as mine. I am not sure what your purpose is; nor, in fact, what mine is. But I know what each is not. If we wanted mere size in our fish we would go to the lakes for bass or to the deep sea for tuna. If we wanted a lazy day out of doors we would still-fish from a boat or a pier or a Sound reef. If we cared for convivial companionship we would scarcely go alone or, going with others, separate immediately at the stream not to rejoin until dark.

All of which impinges upon the too simple and pat. So complex a business as the human ego is not easily dissected and card-indexed. But the fact that a single sport can appeal alike to freckled country kids and to men of prominence in the learned callings— and to a hundred levels of humanity in between—is a fact to meditate upon. If we look at a few of these we might start with the most elemental of all trout fishermen.

THE BAREFOOT BOY

I mean the general run of kid anglers, shod or unshod, who are of farm stock or the kindred lineage of the small towns. Here is the simplest of the angling organisms, related to the whole of trout fishing as the amoeba is related to the sum of biology. He is the complete fisherman with no frills, the embodiment of first principles in angling, the only fisherman in America who can fish without the aid of pockets. A pole, a string, a hook, a can of worms. A hook, not a bent pin: the bent pin is a bucolic legend perpetrated by irresponsible writers who should know better. One simply does not see any bent pins in the equipment of the most untutored trouter extant. Bent pins are no good as angling hardware and, anyway, eyed Sproats, Snecks and Carlisles can be had for a few cents in the country stores.

Equipped thus, the barefoot boy's chances of consistently catching trout are not to be enthused over. There is a superstition abroad that the practical stream knowledge of the farm fisher boy is tantamount to fish sense (which is close to genius) and that the hickory pole, twine, eyed hook combination often succeeds where the finest fly-fishing tools fail miserably. That superstition belongs to the

15

nonangling public and is meat for certain comic-strip artists who cannot tell a night crawler from a Whirling Dun.

But if the kid's reputation is spurious his destiny is perhaps noble. Conceivably this suntanned lad is the guardian and trustee of the next fifty years of American wildlife. His collective numbers can conserve our future fish and game, save our streams from industrial poisons, keep our state and national forests green and sweet. In his tough little hands rests much of the hope we may have for the continued integrity of trout fishing.

But he doesn't know it now. He is out to catch trout in his own way, and he is certainly the most sublimely uninhibited and unimpeded of all that tide of anglers which flows upstream and down from April to August. Such sporting ethics as he has—and they are not wanting—are instinctive and undisturbed by any Nietzschean speculations as to good and evil. His fishing code is well defined in the clear air of boyhood, his principles unclouded by the maturer sophistries of sportsmanship. To him there is nothing unethical in his preference for worms rather than flies. Worms will catch trout and cost him nothing; flies will cost a good deal and be unmanageable with such tackle and skill as he owns. His stream manners are beyond reproach. I have not known him to parade through the pool I am casting over or to make any undue racket on the stream, an admirable restraint considering the natural ebullience of his years.

He is a pretty fair fisherman, after his fashion, and he knows the brook near home as many a mature angler will never know it. Yet his legendary precocity is unlikely to "clean out" his home stream. A good many trout will elude his #4 Sproat and his worm only to fall to your Quill Gordon or my light Cahill.

Let him grow and he will be a great fisherman someday. Meanwhile he is a picturesque ornament upon our waters and as good an augury for the future as I can think of offhand.

OLD-TIMER

Mill and I had finished our sandwiches and sat smoking our pipes in the high noon. An angler was coming into sight around the bend

downstream. At a hundred yards it is not easy to distinguish features and form yet we could see at once that this noonday adventurer was neither kid nor novice. He was full of years and full of experience. Thigh deep, he poled himself in midcurrent with a five-foot staff, braced himself against it and cast across and upstream. Here was a thoroughgoing angler with a simple and effective system. He would fish every yard of water fifty feet above him, plug ahead with the staff to within ten feet of the previous casts' limits and repeat the routine. There was a slow inevitability about him; he drew nearer to us as the hand of a watch draws nearer the hour. For some minutes we regarded him intently, without speaking, and as he wore along upstream we knew we were watching a stylist. An inbred and ancient grace was implicit in his casting. The rhythm never varied; the man and the rod were as one, as if the rod were a physical extension of the man. The back cast was exquisitely timed; the interval of pause might have been clocked a hundred times without the variation of a tenth of a second; the throw drew easily forward, shooting the fly far and true to the full length of line and leader where it hovered for a motionless instant before settling to the water. There was not the semblance of a jerk, not the minutest interruption of this oiled routine.

Our eyes were fixed upon this all-unconscious exhibition—he was completely unaware of a gallery—and something akin to a hypnotic spell fastened on us there in the heat and stillness of the noon. Such casting was scarcely credible, and yet we were looking at it. I thought, as he came closer, that here was the product of many influences: of inherent skill, of years and years of application, and of something else, the high devotion of the artist to his art. I could see his face now and I thought it showed some quiet light of elation. It was not smiling but it seemed supremely happy with what could have been the happiness of mastery. I watched his face, relieved thus to divert my attention from the intolerable perfection of his casting, and saw it to be deep-scored with life. The expression did not change; it was as constant as the backward and forward rhythm of his arm and body. It was still in its mold after something had broken at last the iteration of that physical routine.

For now, for the first time since he had rounded the lower bend, one of his forward casts did not come back.

In my protracted spell of admiration and wonder I had forgotten that the old man was actually fishing for trout. He had not forgotten it, however, or forgotten what to do in the event of the present contingency. For he had struck and hooked what appeared to be a heavy deep-fighting native while I had been intent upon his face. An alertness for the strike had been there all the time, ready and waiting. The impeccable mechanics of his casting had not disturbed this nice adjustment, this essentially human equilibrium of nerves.

But now in the higher pitch of the battle the machine seemed again dominant. Here was merely another functioning of the machine: playing a trout differed from casting a fly only as the action of a motor in high gear differed from its action in low.

I remember how that trout went away, sounding for the rocky caverns of the west bank. The water was deep there, black under its surface of slow suds, a broad eddy backing away from the main current. The trout had allies in this submarine grotto: roots and rocks and the sunken litter that piles in every deep still pocket of a stream. Freedom was there if the trout could reach it. But the old man knew it as well and he was keeping the fish off. Coaxing it away, as it were. What impressed me throughout that struggle was its gentleness and absence of haste. I had at no time the feeling that tackle was being strained. The old man steered the boring fish away from the haven it sought in the deep eddy, back into the central current and across to a clear run of water over the sandy bottom of the east side. The fish turned downstream now, racing with the current and gaining slack. I held my breath. But the old man negotiated the stripping in of line, and the reeling of the stripped slack, as he had all else. The operation seemed so casual and unhurried as to be almost contemptuous and yet so effective that the trout came abreast on a line that held only inches of slack and went past, downstream, against pressure again.

At this juncture I thought, for the first time, of the five-foot staff. I had come to accept it subconsciously—it had been so unobtrusive in all the exercise of casting and of playing the fish—but now I realized that some sort of shift must be made as the old gentleman turned to face the battle downstream. The stick had been wedged into his right armpit, sloping behind him and braced against a rock to hold his slight figure in the current.

This, I thought, would be a delicate and perhaps dangerous maneuver. But while I considered offering assistance the thing was done. It was disappointingly easy, indeed it was no maneuver at all but a mere pivoting of his body in a semicircle, using the staff as a sort of axis for the turn without moving its lower end, so that now he had his prop before him instead of behind. It looked easier this way and the thought occurred to me that, far from being concerned at the necessity of turning he was actually relieved by it and glad of the opportunity! The whole affair was of a piece with the rest of his show, so facile that it seemed he must have some elemental affinity with the water itself.

The fight wore along, drew itself out to an exorbitant length, verged almost upon boredom. The trout had every fair chance to escape and yet it had none. That gentle inexorable pressure wore it down, turned it again and again on the apparent edge of escape. There was a feebleness in its rushes now and I knew that only one result was possible. I almost turned away, but there was still the business of landing, the handling of rod, net and staff with two arms. The old chap would drown the fish, perhaps, in the swift water below. And then, a little beach on our side would do for the rest.

But no. He was bringing the trout in now, but not up through the central channel. The fish had worked over toward the eastern shore and from there the old gentleman brought it home, yard by yard, a crosscurrent job through quiet water. No thought of drowning here. With ten feet of leader still off the end of his rod the old man picked up his staff in his left hand, waded slowly toward the shallow east shore, tossed the staff upon the bank, took the net with his now free left hand, drew the unresisting fish over it and lifted him clear.

Seventeen or eighteen inches, I guessed. I could see the orange underbody gleam in the sun.

I looked at Mill and he looked at me, and although we didn't speak I knew him to be thinking as I was, that the thing had been too perfect, too lacking in any element of uncertainty. But the final act was still to come. The old man put the rod under his arm, stooped and wetted each hand in the stream, one at a time, shifting the net from one hand to the other. Then, with the net handle under the other arm, he grasped the trout in its meshes, released the fly from its mouth and returned it very tenderly to the water. A slow ripple spread away toward midstream and disappeared.

He looked up then, seeing us for the first time. An odd questioning expression, mixed with a sort of dismay, came over his face. "Never saw you at all," he said. "And I'm sorry—if you were resting this pool."

"We were resting only ourselves," I said, "until you came in sight downstream. Since then we've watched a great show, and I guess we both want to compliment you on it."

It sounded somehow awkward and I thought the old gentleman was perhaps a touch embarrassed. He looked away for a moment. Then he said, "In sixty-nine years of this thing one gets quite a bit of practice. And perhaps," he added, "kills too many trout. These days I release nearly all. Maybe a mistake on this one—he's big enough to do some harm. But damn, he gave me a nice go."

"Sixty-nine years of 'this thing,' " Mill remarked sometime afterward. "That would make him about eighty, if he started when he was about ten."

The old chap waded across to the east bank, paused to change his fly and entered the stream again with his staff. The casting recommenced, caught up the accustomed rhythm; the machine was again in low gear, the hand of the watch drew away from the hour. He inched his way upstream, the current knifing around the slight brown-clad figure that diminished slowly in the noontime sun until it was gone around the far bend. Something almost fateful was in his inexorable creeping progression. It would stop when the stream stopped, not before; it would cease when the banks closed in upon him in the far upper rills, when at last he had no water ahead to aim his fly at.

One could think about his fishing philosophy and conclude that each bend of the stream, opening a new vista, was an extension of life for him. He was, in a sense, deathless, so long as he had another bend to go around and could hold his curiosity in what lay beyond it.

But one day—and it could not be far off—there would be the last bend, the last problem of water, rocks, wind and sun. And his own errorless mechanics would meet him then face to face, the perfect functioning of physical law.

THE SCIENTISTS

There may be few such artists with the rod as the old gentleman we watched that noon. But there are others whose fishing is equally effective as judged by comparative creel counts over the course of a season.

Some of the scientists, for instance.

Whether or not your trout-fishing scientist possesses a degree (and often he doesn't) he is a combination of entomologist, meteorologist, stream student and bookkeeper, and this odd mix of talent often brings the difficult trout to his net.

First of all, this fellow knows his bugs. And you are fortunate indeed if you are one of his acquaintances. You had better respect his passionate traffic with insects and take his tips, for he is a man to put your faith in. . . . "Well, what fly this time?" is a good question to ask, some evening as he rigs up. Ask it casually if you will—as if you were making conversation instead of pointedly seeking advice, for conceivably you do not care to acknowledge his superior acumen—but ask it. Then mark his answer and make a mental note of the weather at the time. He will probably say, "Can't tell until I see the stream," but he may add, "Think maybe a Pale Evening Dun will take 'em." He has the offhand manner of all true authorities. Perhaps the day has been windless and warm, thickening toward late afternoon with a high humidity and an imminence of rain. Remember all this, and the next time you fish in this sort of weather be sure you have a few Pale Evening Duns in your box.

Or it is a cloudy afternoon with signs of clearing and a dying wind toward dusk: the sort of evening that will be brilliant and breathless under a red sunset, auguring a warm day for tomorrow. You or I may not know that this will bring on a hatch of some mayfly or other, but he does. His notebooks, or his immaculate card-indexed mind, tell him it has happened thirty-six times out of forty-three in the past five seasons. Hence a little while before the first feeding trout of the evening breaks the surface with its broad flanks this fellow is already busy with a March Brown, anticipating the tastes of the waiting fish. The trout expects this fly to be on the water and its appetite is edged for this special morsel. At least, such is the theory. Then give it to him, reasons the scientist, and give it to him early. While I fool around with a Cowdung or an Adams or merely wait to see what sort of hatch it will be he is calmly starting a hatch of his own. And when the real hatch arrives, confirming his over-ture as usual, he already has two or three trout in his creel, overanx-ious beauties who swiped food off the table before the dinner bell rang. And these two or three may effect the difference between success and failure for the evening. For once well underway the real hatch, if prolific enough, will minimize the chances of taking even one trout. I have seen the dusk so full of mayflies and the stream surface so incessantly broken by rising trout that my single artificial offering had, mathematically, about one chance in ten thousand of being taken. Someone said that trout, like common stocks, should be bid for before the rise begins.

This fellow's success in the field of entomology is predicated upon his ability as both meteorologist and stream expert. What the flies will do in any given hour depends largely upon the season, the weather, the water and the geography, especially the last. Flies, like humans, have developed different customs and traditions in differ-ent parts of the trout country. The west Jersey mayfly may exhibit the same behavior, under like atmospheric conditions, as its cousin on the Brodhead but the same species may show manners of an-other sort on the streams of Vermont.

Hence the trout-fishing scientist plays his best ball on the home grounds.

A knowledge of the water is important. To take a trout in the twilight or near dawn is no remarkable feat; most of us can do this by ordinary diligence. How different to take a good one in the bright hard hours of the high sun. The extra notch of ability is needed here, the uncommon knowledge, the degree of stream lore not possessed by the rank and file. On certain days in the summer even this superior talent may avail nothing. A trout holed up for the heat of the day can be almost invulnerable to any temptation on or near the surface. But even now it may possibly be coaxed *if you can find it.* The problem, indeed, is chiefly one of location. You will not find your fish in any old pocket of deep and shaded water but rather in some pool where a cold spring rill, unseen by many, trickles into the stream. Such places are known to your scientist-angler; if the stream is familiar to him he has observed every feeder rill and every spring, and also (for purposes of avoidance) every pool without benefit of a cold-water tap. In the seasons long gone and in his off-season explorations he has noted such details and filed them away in his notes or the proper pigeonhole of his mind. And if the stream is new to him he is constantly on the lookout for these apparently insignificant findings, eternally studious of the stream bed and the lay of the surrounding land. Little of a riparian nature eludes him. In his first mile of fishing he will learn more about that mile than many a native, dwelling nearby, has learned in a lifetime. And what he learns is to him far greater riches than those little asides which delight others—the surprise of a sudden woodcock or the eye's chance caress of some rare flower of the upland meadow. The woodcock and the flower may be gone tomorrow—they are speculative gains—but the spring is a fixed asset. It will be there tomorrow and hopefully for years, cooling a pool on many a shimmering summer noon. And the studious angler will be there again and again, taking a trout from those depths. Meanwhile his less observant fellows have plodded past the same spot, weary and with empty creels, resigning themselves to another day too hot for fishing.

This is the sort of fact that finds entry in the record books of the ultrascientific. A map, of perhaps inartistic but accurate execution, shows the tiny spring estuaries along with all manner of equally priceless information upon the structure of the stream: depths and shallows, riffles and pools, windfalls and undercut banks, boulders and backwaters, wooded and meadow stretches. Closely associated notes, tabulated perhaps in ruled columns under the head of "Experience," record dates, weather, time of day, number of trout caught, size and species, flies used, quality and extent of hatch. An average struck from these voluminous data may well predict the success or failure of the next venture upon any given and indexed water. (Perhaps the end of trout fishing will be marked by the feeding of such things into a computer!)

These two advocates—the artist and the scientist—are surely among the elite of trout fishermen. The former is a disciple of pure form. His quest for trout is incidental to his pursuit of a perfection of style in his fishing, and perhaps for this reason he is prone to release many fish that come to his net.

The angling scientist, on the other hand, is a disciple of knowledge, that specialized sort that will put a trout in his creel. If any discern here the taint of a meat-in-the-pot reason for his learning let me add that I have known a few of his kind and have noticed that they, too, release many a good trout. After all, the purpose of trout fishing is, or should be, to catch trout if not to kill them. The scientist's methods are legitimate. On many a fishless day I have wished they were mine.

THE PURIST

Here is another fisherman who embraces a pure ideal. If one sees again an apparent distortion of objective, a veering away from the plain purpose of catching trout for its own sake, I can only suggest that the purist's goal seems to me as worthy as any.

Purism, in trout fishing, used to be exclusively an English institution. It seems typically a by-product of an ancient culture, a way of fishing in consonance with other aspects of a leisurely and graceful mode of life. Perhaps it has faintly the odor of decadence. Fishing only the rise, and only with dry flies, is such a refinement of angling as almost to remove it from the category of fishing. It can be at times, on the eastern waters of the United States, chiefly an exercise of walking the banks with an occasional interlude of casting, for on certain days and hours scarcely a trout will break the surface.

On the chalk streams of southern England the purist fares better with authentic rises occurring more frequently and lasting longer than on the eastern waters of the United States. Natural conditions, no doubt, had much to do with the Englishman's adoption of purism. Yet one surmises that the Briton's different feeling for sport is a factor. Sport is one of his old traditions, as old as his literature and architecture and ways of trade. These have a quality of quietness, an antique dignity and grace. Perhaps the primitive lust to kill underlies even the Englishman's dry-fly purism, the original soil feeding the old roots, but the flower seems infinitely removed from that murky genesis. Some centuries of cultivation have been needed to produce this bloom.

We in America have not had the centuries. A nation still so close to pioneering that some of its citizens' grandfathers knew fishing not as a sport but as a means of survival can scarcely be expected to turn out purists en masse. That a few are to be met with in the course of a season on eastern streams is perhaps as good a sign as any of our civilization's coming of age.

HOGS

It would be charitable to attribute the occurrence of the fish hog to the same close heritage of necessity. Less than two centuries ago the more fish a man could catch the longer his family would be full-bellied and content. Trout swarmed in the streams and rills, bag limits were unthought of and all the year was the open season. "Sportsmanship" and "fishing ethics" were phrases that might have been unearthed from a few dusty and recondite tomes imported from England—phrases perhaps meaningful to a scholar on the more civilized eastern seaboard but of no import whatever from ten miles inland to the dim Indian frontiers. A man fished when and where he could and with the deadliest means at his disposal.

That was but a few generations back and possibly we have not quite lived it down. In this era of synthetic put-and-take fishing for hatchery stockees, bag limits have lost some of their conservational meaning. Yet they still acknowledge a level of gluttony, both as to numbers and size of trout, and perhaps too many fishermen pride themselves on "getting the limit."

These men are not necessarily scoundrels. I had at one time a neighbor for whom I cherished a high regard, a gentleman whose convictions upon all the important isms of life were leavened with a nice yeast of small amiabilities. He was a garden putterer, a gentle soul with animals and children, and a nongushing lover of the rural delights. Yet he once showed me a newspaper photograph of himself and another fish hog holding between them a string of fifty (count 'em) trout, the least of which had weighed nearly a pound. The caption, an imbecility in the approved tradition, reported this catch as the work of a single morning. The other hog was radiant with a beastly sort of virility; my neighbor looked as if he were trying not to be ashamed of the trout, his partner, himself and the whole piece of ostentatious excess.

He was of course ashamed of all these but he confided to me that probably he would do it again if the opportunity offered. He would not submit to a photo again but he might catch as many, or almost as many, and he might take the same henchman for company because this fellow knew where they were. Speculation as to the overall effect on fishing if he and everyone else persisted in such wholesale massacre had not fretted his conscience. *He* had done it only once. But I gathered, from some inquiry, that his sense of proportion had been violated. He mentioned something about "the beauty of restraint."

I concluded that he was not really dangerous and that one more such surfeit would precipitate a curing reaction.

In so large a "family" a few black sheep are inevitable. Fortunately their offenses seem no longer to be condoned and even openly glorified. The daily press, once notoriously guilty of popularizing hoggishness, has largely mended its ways, aware of the trend of public thinking. The same seems true of those former predators, the resort advertisers, the ballyhooers of the wilderness. The sporting magazines, long hostile to the fish hog, could help the cause substantially by refusing advertisements featuring oversized bags.

NOBLESSE OBLIGE

The victim of the old-master complex is a different sinner from the plain fish hog and not to be condemned to quite so deep a hell. The fellow with a reputation to uphold—and it is a poor community that does not boast at least one superfisherman—simply must make his bag. His reputation is quite apt to be deserved, being based upon many past feats of prowess. In consequence he feels obliged to bring home the limit each time he goes astream. Anything much under the limit would be plainly a betrayal of his public.

These champions are indigenous not only to the small hamlets and middling cities of the trout country. Many a well-groomed party from the metropolitan infernos, migrating north on the heels of the vanishing ice, includes one fisherman of a supercraft. He was high rod last year and the year before and he will be high rod this year. That much is conceded; anything else would be a preposterous upset, an overturn of sacred tradition. With that premise established, the party can go on and enjoy itself. The second, third, and fourth rods can bask in their comparative glory (or busy themselves with irrelevant matters) when the creel counts are made at the end of the day. After all, there are philosophic compensations for creels which contain much air. It is not all of fishing to fish, as we have read in many places.

Often these urban "old masters" are young chaps—fortyish or less. They are not distinguishable from their partners by any difference of gear or singularity of demeanor. Looking closely, though, you may discern a faint but assured, hardy-perennial arrogance. You will not find it in the long winters of the marketplace. But now, hieing north with the geese, it begins to respond again to that ancient urge which quickens the blood of men and the sap of trees in the springtime. The winter in town may have been a long and persistent failure, a winter to kill the spirit of any businessman. But that commercial frost is melting now in the warm sun, and in its place blooms again that flush which betokens the rare and certain scent of victory. For there is one place, still, where this fellow's singular skill will prevail. And as he gets farther and farther north, nearer and nearer that one element which is his very own, he is thawing out at last, smiling a little to himself in that unobtrusive, slightly arrogant way.

He can scarcely be blamed for this or for coming off the stream with the limit at the end of the first day. Some measure of success is the due of every man. And arrayed against all the denouncements of human greed are the facts of State breeding and stocking, and the facts of minks and watersnakes and snapping turtles and mergansers who throw back no trout under six inches and beside whom the most masterful angler may be little better than a tyro.

Hoggishness in any form is a case primarily for one's conscience. There are still some anglers who will feel guilty after the fourth or fifth trout. Among the skilled veterans not a few are civilized enough to be untempted by the reputations accruing to "high rods." These admirable souls know supremely how to fish but their skill is ever shy of evidence. They will enter the kingdom of heaven, that noble tribe. They will fish, free from any injunction of conscience to put back a trout they want to keep, in the supernal dusks when the mayflies come out over the Elysian pools.

SHE

She comes under the head of "fishermen" and, a long way off, she looks like one. This resemblance, indeed, is in exact ratio with her distance from the eye of the beholder. At twenty miles she could barely be distinguished from the octogenarian of this chapter; at twenty feet she would be seen as she is.

Which is what? The perfect anomaly, maybe, or perhaps merely the typical woman in another anomalous role, making herself still truer to type. The female character is exalted to the extent of its success in evading category, and by this token the woman trouter is the most thoroughly female woman of all.

There are any number of reasons why she should not fish. Her legs are made neither for boots nor for waders. Her natural grace, if any, is not the grace that flows from arm to fly rod so surely and easily as to make the rod seem a sentient thing of nerves and tendons, with some anglers practically an extension of the body and personality of the man. Neither is her grace of locomotion such as to carry her smoothly over the slippery rocks and waterlogged windfalls of the stream bed. Her feet lack the nice manly facility of coping with obstacles. A man slips easily along, upstream or down, sidestepping here, purposely sliding there, letting his subconscious mind do the navigating while his attention is on the cast. It is a careless but effective technique that most women will never know. Their feet balk, recoil, flinch at the rugged obstructions of the bottom. A man wading upstream from one point of vantage to the next is not wholly engrossed with the mere act of wading. His feet are taking care of themselves while his arm is occupied with a series of false casts to dry the fly and his eyes are searching the water for any sign which may betoken a trout. The woman wades, and that is occupation enough for the moment. . . . No, I do not mean *all* women.

In fishing the wet fly downstream a man may wade a hundred yards of fast water, casting as he goes, without a break in the routine, without a single recourse to the solid bank or the anchorage of a mid-channel boulder. This downstream drift can be thrilling, an elemental progress like no other species of locomotion known to man, and he feels that he is sharing the stream's own elemental power. But that thrill is denied to one who cannot forget her feet while wading.

And then there is a thing called stamina, another reason why most women should not pursue the *fontinalis* and its cousins. Despite the delicacy of its instruments, trout fishing is one of the strenuous sports. Of course exercise can be geared to one's capacity for punishment. A woman can take an hour or two along a pleasant stretch of grass-banked stream but that doesn't prove trout fishing a diversion for the feeble and senile. By and large it is a sport for the hardy and the strong. In the course of a season it presents plenty of situations to challenge a superior quality of muscle.

But the reasons a woman should not fish seem pretty well balanced by the reasons she does. Love of costume is one, and its close relative, desire for social distinction, is another. However lavish the wardrobe it is incomplete without the smart outfit for fishing. A new world of opportunity opens here to the astute designer, and he is not slow to grasp it. For the trout stream is a most special arena and the fishing ensemble must be unique from head to foot. If a woman's legs are inhospitable to boots and waders the resourcefulness of the fashion virtuoso is happily challenged. Waders "created" especially for women—waders that hobnob with the adjective *chic* in the swanky ads—are among his sartorial triumphs. And if even these will not restrain the feminine bulges, why then, forget waders. "For the woman who prefers to be lightly and smartly shod we have developed the 'cruiserette.'" It is a thing as feminine as a dancing slipper, and about as useful on the average run of trout water. But never mind that. The more elegant couturiers are above the coarse exactions of boulders and sunken snags. Somewhere is a stretch of club water with rustic bridges across it and banks close-cropped as any fairway, and here the "cruiserette" can disport itself without courting ruin to its every fashionable stitch.

The hardihood complex, the desire of women to be as men, is probably another motive. If it is responsible for such phenomena as Wellesley crews and Channel swimmers it may well account for an odd fisher girl here and there.

But perhaps there is another reason why women fish for trout. Perhaps they like it. I have known one or two who could have only this upright impulse behind their genuine zest for the sport. One, in particular, left a vivid and windblown, glorious picture in my memory. She came down a long wash of heavy water on an afternoon in April. A northerly was at her back, a man's wind, and the gray air was active with snow. One or two wisps of golden hair escaped from under a rakish and nondescript hat and blew out before her in the gale. She was coming on, down the middle of that boisterous freshet and casting as she came, casting a couple of wet flies while the ice formed in her guides, casting with a methodical practiced rhythm and yet with something of ecstasy, the sheer physical elation of high action. She was part of the sweeping wind, the snow and the tumultuous stream.

"What luck?" I called as she came opposite.

"Just one," she answered, flinging the words upon the wind. "But not bad."

The casting was interrupted a moment; her left hand deserted the frozen line to reach into her creel and draw out a rainbow of probably better than a pound. Then she returned to the gale and the snow and the gusty exaltation of her casts.

Gear 3

If no tackle-store windows flaunted their blandishments in March the good old virtues of thrift and prudence would be more firmly lodged in the national temper. March is not only a mad month in its own right but the month just prior to the new trout season, and the tackle-store windows suddenly remind us of it all.

In March the solid habits of a winter melt down the gutters of temptation. On a fateful noonday in March the once resolute structure of your hiemal character will be tested and found rotten. For months you have led an upright and circumspect life, defending your stronghold against the onslaughts of the winter and the wolves. And now as you walk along a city street to lunch you fall to congratulating yourself as much as you dare, without getting smug about it, upon your victory over winter. You consider with a sense of affection the fuel man and the doctor who supplied ammunition to your fortress in the dark days—and their charges for same. The bright bitterness of spring is in the air. Winter is dying, vaporous, in the streets. As always, you mourn a little the passing of that season you had dreaded. It has given you something that no summer can bestow, a triumph over odds.

And then you come to that window. A large pane of glass with a lot of multicolored gadgets behind it. . . . That's right, fishing. Always some shock of surprise is in that annual discovery. You knew of course that the season was somewhere ahead but these tackle-store people had got the jump on you—they had gone and looked at the calendar and found out how close it was.

Fishing. . . . Here it is, spread before you again. Another year. The city street and the shapes of gray masonry fade to the outer limits of thought. A greenness grows upon the city, the gray-green of April woods; the raucous unrest of the street dies out of your ears. In the spacious stillness the brook at your feet whispers and talks, running toward June. Low in the damp alders a pair of blackbirds mutter over their building plans.

That old HDH of course—the enamel had begun to crack last July. And always some new flies and leaders. Your mind goes over the dusty inventory of the past season. A wader had leaked in its left leg, a creel was going senile, a dry-fly oil bottle had held about two drops on that hot afternoon last August when you folded up for another year.

You go inside.

Of all arrays of merchandise none is so irresistible at just this season when the angler stands at the gates of April, May and June. Here is the lovely paraphernalia of trout fishing—poems in bamboo and silk, feathers and pigskin. Rods stand in long racks, resting on their butts, pointing up straight as arrows and seeming astrain for the stream, rods lithe and clean as athletes, long able rods for dry-fly work in big water, delicate shorter wands for the little brooks, dark aristocrats wound in dull greens or grays only at the guides, gayer fellows of many colors. Reels of austere simplicity for trouting, spools of a stark efficient beauty, wide of diameter but narrow athwart, their dark satin ashine in the glass counters. Silk and nylon lines in coils, tapering from fat lustrous Cs to the lean Hs, lines of rich browns, tans, creams and the silver-green of stream water. Leaders of the color of an April mist and of the amber translucence of mountain streams in the iron country, short ones with dropper loops and the tapered nine- and twelve-footers, stout of butt, attenuating to 4X at the tip.

And flies. On the long counters the swarms have come to rest. In tray after tray they are neatly assorted: flies of a feather, too, flock together in the tackle stores. A soft blur of color, a pattern of their opulent hues extends ten feet along the counter like an oriental mat, the tone modulated by the very brilliance of its individual

34

parts. Your old friends are here, the veteran and tried campaigners: the Coachmen, Cahills, Hendricksons, Quill Gordons, Hare's Ears, Olive Duns, Pale Evening Duns, Catskills, Cowdungs, March Browns, Montreals and Lady Beaverkills, and the various fanwings, bivisibles and spiders, and the rarer ephemerae for your gambling moments, the Red Tags, Greenwell's Glories, Silver Sedges, Tupp's Indispensables, Alexandras, Pink Ladies, Yellow Sallys and the Fancies of Wickham and Flight. What names, and what connotations! Mention any one of them and some fishing landscape will form itself in your mind's eye. A June dusk at the railroad pool below Phoenicia, the Esopus black in the deepening twilight, black and fast and murmuring up to your waders, and the air full of fireflies and the threnody that begins with the summer darkness.

And the lesser items of equipment, the light sails of a trouter's rig which give his outfit the stamp of the connoisseur: fly boxes in dull aluminum or plastic, leader pouches and fly books bound in pigskin (with your initials put on while you wait), leather-bound creels, collapsible landing nets, waders and short jackets and vests multipocketed, ponchos, hats for sun and rain, oilskin clothing of a soft greenish outdoor color, and the small essentials such as leather holders for oil bottles, atomizers for spraying flies, fly extractors, gadgets for dressing lines, gut snippers, amadou and spring scales.

The thaw that is sending winter out of the land reaches at last to your wallet. How amazing that all tackle stores are not successful! Is there a problem of sales resistance? Can this business be like ordinary forms of merchandising, such as selling a man a necktie or a lawn mower? For the tackle people do not sell the dull stuff of necessity—or, rather, the stuff of dull necessity. A distinction is there, since fishing is a *bright* necessity. One wonders, with Omar Khayyam, what the vintners buy.

A man's annual stock-up trip to the tackle store is hardly less engaging than his first day astream. He who will shop all over town to save a few dollars on a suit of clothes will blow that money on a trout reel, and every angler knows the vice-presidential function of a trout reel. When I was a kid I bought one, a "Featherlight" (only the ancient will remember it) for one dollar and I used it for a decade. Not long afterward I bought another for nine dollars, a fairly fat price for a trout reel in that long-ago year, but I could excuse it on a number of counts. A new rod, bought the year before, needed a more fitting companion, and I had a vague intention gradually to acquire some nice tackle anyway, and besides I liked the looks of this implement, and furthermore I should of course have two reels since I had in that year two lines. When my small private voice asked me how I figured nine dollars' worth of material and workmanship going into one single-action spool to hold my surplus line I could only answer that other and bigger wastrels had given twenty-five dollars and more for a trout reel and had bought not one at a time but two or three. As these things work out, the one-dollar reel balanced perfectly on my only rod and had a soft well-bred click, while the more expensive job overburdened the butt end of the rod and had a click that was a fair imitation of a machine gun.

Despite the eagerness of anglers to give up a winter's savings for these baubles the tackle people will tell you they *do* encounter sales resistance and other commercial hazards. They talk about seasonal demand, and the danger of overstocking this and that, and the need to sense a popular "number" in advance, and periods of inertia.

The people engaged in it are not all poets. Yet a few hardy souls are left, gallant merchants of fishing gear who love their wares as a boy loves his toys. These, I have noticed, have stayed in business. Once, late of a spring evening, I talked with one of them in the back of his store. It was at the close of a day in the season of "peak demand," sales had been good and he perhaps felt expansive. We got around to the subject of the right advertising for fishing tackle.

"The only advertising I shall ever need," he said, "is advertising that will get them *in* here. Once *in* here"—and he indicated with a sweeping gesture his galaxy of offerings—"all this lovely stuff—"

He had no need to tell me that all his "lovely stuff" would sell itself. He was a fisherman; he had bought tackle in other stores before he had one of his own. And he was right. You cannot gild *those* lilies.

The reason for the diversity of tackle is the diversity of men. Your rod, no less than your shoes, should fit you. Yours is the high privilege of whipping it about in the tackle store before you buy, yours the right to feel its power, its action and balance, the affinity of its nerves with the nerves of your wrist—all the physics of its motion and its poise that will make it, for you, a source of delight or an instrument of torture through a long day of casting upwind.

There is of course too much tackle or too many varieties of every kind of tackle, particularly of flies. Man's underrated love of beauty has been chiefly responsible for the demand but his lack of courage and conviction must share the guilt. Most of us are timid souls in this matter. The possibility that only six fly patterns will ruin a day for us whereas three dozen will assure success is too weighty for any but the strongest wills.

Still, getting beyond sixes and dozens into the hundreds, no excuse but an aesthetic one can account for the extravagant swarms which descend each spring upon the tackle counters. Although a few ancient patterns such as the Red Ibis, Grizzly King and Silver Doctor never had natural counterparts in the insect world, the early conception of the trout fly was as an imitation of a natural bug. That was a legitimate enterprise until all the trout-stream insects had been imitated. Then, since nature would not oblige by evolving new flies to be copied, man set about creating them for himself, giving us a new hatch each season. These spurious bugs, I suppose, are counterfeits of some which nature ought to have coined. Spurious or no, some of them are at times successful in taking trout and thus are justified to practical men. To other than practical men, who compose maybe 50 percent of all trout fishermen, no such sanction is necessary. Let the philosophy of practical ends go hang its back-cast in a honey locust tree. What they want in their flies is a nice variety of colors. Interior decoration for the fly box is one of the popular though unpublicized arts. (There exists among anglers a kind of tacit agreement to blink this dilettantism and perhaps it should not be mentioned at all.)

Pocket-size fly boxes for a single day's fishing can hold three to five dozen flies. Doubtless this is one of the stratagems of the tackle makers since expert opinion holds that no more than one dozen patterns are necessities to the man who is after trout. (Of course one expert's favorite dozen differs in its components from that of another.)

But most fly boxes are kept full. If that proves anything it proves merely that the tackle makers' little conspiracy is successful. But it poses a question: what sorts of flies occupy all the space? The answer depends upon the angler: the truly disciplined has only his dozen reliable patterns but he carries five of each while the gambler and aesthete has five dozen patterns but only one of each. Others, the great majority, are somewhere between. Usually the gambling type will hedge a little rather than plunge utterly. He will have two or three Quill Gordons, two or three Cahills, just in case. Bravado is all right in its way but there is no sense in ruining the day by a hung-up backcast that loses the one fly they are taking.

Once I met a man on the Neversink who told me he had ten dozen flies—five dozen dry, five dozen wet, all working capital, ready at hand. "Let me see them," I said, avidly. As a lover of the rare specimens possibly I could trade off a few duplicates and get something choice. He drew a dry-fly box from a pocket, a wet-fly box from another pocket and opened them. Each contained a uniform company of sixty Coachmen, varied only as to white and dark wings. The color guild would unanimously have blackballed that low unimaginative dullard. I can add that he was catching trout, however.

But he was missing something else. The bright nonessentials, the decorative gewgaws among flies which delight the childish heart of the angler as bright beads delight the savage, have their function. The fact that most of them have never taken a trout and that some, indeed, have never even bounced upon a riffle only enhances their speculative value. One can never tell what they *might* do. A trout caught on one of these beauties seems worth three taken on such a professional killer as the Coachman. There comes a time in a fishing day when the angler's inclinations are balanced aright for the gambling chance. He is sitting on a rock in mid-current, changing flies; he glances over his extravagant collection and if he has been methodical all day with such deadly species as the Hare's Ear and Cahill he may welcome a few irresponsible casts with, say, an Alexandra. It is like a strawberry sundae after a solid week of pork and beans. These bright bits of tinsel, these mere collectors' items, prevent angler's scurvy.

Even if true that a bare dozen fly patterns will catch all the catchable trout in all the streams, how many anglers, indeed how many flytiers, will be thus confined? Let the flytiers experiment ad infinitum. The rarest gem of their coinage may one day earn its

niche even among the killers as, coasting down some dark pool, it coaxes a two-pounder from the depths.

Winter is the time to overhaul your gear. The autumn is too close to the past season. You put away your trout tackle in the late summer; your appetite for fishing is sated and the gulf between you and spring is too great to be bridged by anticipation. Autumn is the nadir of the trout-fishing cycle.

The turn of the new year looses the first definite fishing impulse. The days are still buried deep in winter but they can be counted, now, to April, and the sun is on his way north. January holds a breathless promise, the incredible possibility of a new spring. There comes an evening when you take your rod from its incarceration and assemble it. You had almost forgotten you had a rod, but in holding it now, in feeling again its familiar temper the coming season has edged a little closer.

The tackle box is next. It is enough to fix the necessary mood, and the inevitable sequence is the dragging forth of all your gear. The evening—one or several—assumes the clean dimensions of any planned enterprise. In this annual interval you take your inventory and become engaged with peaceful things—winding silk, rod varnish, ferrule cement.

Somehow I usually find less than I had anticipated in the way of necessary repairs. And annually this has disappointed me a little. One can hardly be expected to haul out all his tackle in the dead of winter and then put it back again, unchanged. If one finds no loose windings on his rod it should be ethical to loosen one or two. Fishing gear, like all other stuff we buy, is certainly no better than it ought to be. But good rods seem exceptionally durable. I am fishing in these years with a rod which has known at least twenty seasons. Its ferrules are still intact; only two guides have had to be replaced. It has a slight bow in one tip joint but it will still throw a fly into the teeth of a brisk summer westerly. Perhaps an angler's pride and affection, as well as his bank balance, will keep him using a rod after it should be pensioned off. But making due allowance for this, good rods if well cared for are extraordinarily long-lived.

Looking closely, however, you will find work enough for a winter's evening or three. Ferrules and tips that remained tight through weeks of casting can lose their affinity for the bamboo in the inactive darkness of a closet. Guides can loosen though their windings seem sound as ever, the lid of a creel can slip its moorings, leaders can become brittle in the steam heat and the elastic of your net acquire a sullen stiffness.

In the long evenings the comfortable sense of ample hours is an asset to any workmanlike job. You can take it easy with fishing tackle while the snow rustles against the windowpane, knowing it will take nature quite a while to perform the slow chemistries of her annual liquidation.

In these tasks some fishermen find diversion equal to that of fishing itself. Indeed I know one or two perverted zealots who hold that tinkering with tackle is better than fishing with it. Winter is the climax of their angling year, the spring and summer chiefly important as a means of wearing out tackle against next winter's repairing orgy. This may be a left-handed philosophy, a crazy rearrangement of means and ends. Maybe not.

Even we who hold that repairing tackle is less fun than repairing to the stream with tackle must concede much to the former. These little jobs justify January, thaw the frozen memories of past Aprils and give an impetus to the next one. Spring is definitely started once you get out your gear for the annual audit.

Methods 4

"What fly today?" is a classic question in trout fishing, probably because it is easy to ask and difficult to answer. It voices what is foremost in a man's mind as he contemplates the water; it asks in three words for the key to the day's success.

But the issue is hardly so vital as it seems. You look at the signals nature is flying: the presence or absence of a hatch, the height and speed and color of the water, and something else, maybe sensed rather than seen, which gives the water the dry-fly look, or doesn't.

Having observed these phenomena and being of quick decision and resolute will, you tie on a fly you have a measure of faith in. I commonly fish with two such forthright souls but I am not of so staunch a kidney. Choosing the starting fly is to me a difficult business. My open fly box presents its assorted temptations. The slate-winged Coachman is perhaps the arch seducer of the lot. In any sort of weather and at any time of day, save possibly the deep dusk, that fly is handing out a cogent sales talk. "If you want trout, here I am. If you want to fool around with all this riffraff—" I have heeded that line quite often and been glad; I have ignored it and been, if not sorry, skunked. Early in the morning it has a special appeal to my acquisitive sense and similar gross impulses. There is a tonic value in landing a good trout in the first few minutes of play. I want that trout badly: catching it eliminates the possibility of a blank, saves the day at once from complete failure. . . . Give the Coachman his chance, take one fish anyway and then divert yourself if you will with the more chancy patterns. That sort of dreary reasoning shapes in my mind as I contemplate the fly box preparatory to the first cast.

The choice is difficult but not complicated, despite the fact that some four dozen flies are sitting there begging for attention. The Coachman or not the Coachman, that is the question. If not the Coachman then I can play a kind of eeny-meeny-miney-mo with the rest. A simple decision. But by the time I have made it Mill and Arch are usually assembled and knee-deep in trout water. Neither of them, indeed, is above netting a trout while I am still pondering the rococo interior decorations of my fly box.

And then there is the question as to fishing upstream or down. If you are alone the answer is easy: it is compounded of your natural preference and the architecture of the stream. You can fish a dry fly upstream in most water but certainly not all. Trout water has a way of confounding the nice theories. The textbooks tell you to fish upstream with the dry fly and that is the logical procedure on ideal casting water. But how much water is so neatly classified? Every stream has pools and riffles where you will cast downstream or not at all. Here is a likely, troutish run where smooth water glides deep between low overhanging branches on both banks. Upstream are wadeable shallows and a rift in the jungle to accommodate your backcast but downstream no such facilities are afforded. The only way you can fish that water is to cast from above it with a long but slack line and let the current take care of the rest. The current is master of that situation. It will straighten the curving slack and doubtless effect a hideous drag. (A wet fly or nymph is better here.) But if you are momentarily in the favor of the gods it will float your fly, dragless, over the dark desirable regions of the stream and take up most of the slack before the strike, if any, occurs. This is perhaps too much to ask. Often in such desperate fishing the strike occurs far too soon, while still the yards of curving slack lie written on the surface. More often no strike rewards you for all your pains. But you may count it a moral victory if you get a fly into such a place at all, and get it out again whether or not a trout is attached. These places are the graveyards of trout flies.

The decision for upstream or downstream fishing is complicated by the presence of a partner, particularly so if he has an opposite preference to yours. Meeting for lunch means retracing steps, and the casual encounters when in "going around" each other you stop for a comparison of notes must be forgone.

But once you are fairly launched on your day the choice of a fly and the direction of your progress seem of minor import. If successful early you are proved right in your choice of everything. Or so it seems. An early fish gives you a confident outlook upon the entire day. A trout on the first cast is the worst sort of luck of course, meaning, according to believers in the occult, that you will get no more today, but a trout taken in the second or third pool or riffle is a good omen. This is a normal kill, a result not of luck but of sound planning.

Or again, so it seems. For an hour may go by without another rise and then the fly that seemed so right becomes suspect. It may be the wrongest fly you can use. Doubts can sometimes swarm thicker than mayflies and confidence evaporate faster than the stream itself in the sunny shallows.

Inevitably, now, you will change, and you might as well find at once a comfortable windfall or boulder.

Changing the fly can be anything from a master stroke in tactics to an excuse to stop for a smoke. It can impart new hope, new anticipation: anything *may* happen with a different fly. The infinite possibilities make it worth the trouble. (It *is* something of trouble, especially at dusk. I never could tie the Turle by the sense of touch alone.) But perhaps nothing in all of trout fishing is nearer to pure futility than repeated changes on a day essentially a dud. The way really to enjoy changing flies is to change when you're catching trout.

Changing not only flies but methods, i.e., dry fly to wet fly or nymph, may have a sound reason such as an abrupt change of weather or the sudden subsidence of surface-feeding trout. But a drastic shift of methods merely because your creel is empty is only to surrender your position to an imaginary foe.

You will wish at such times that there were not so many ways to fish for trout. Well, you can eliminate some of the ways and simplify everything by leaving a lot of tackle home. If you take only drys you can fish only drys; if you take only wets and nymphs you are more or less stuck with them, and if you take only worms you can fish only worms and grasshoppers and live bait and hellgramites and small frogs and crawfish. Carrying a lot of tackle can be as ruinous to your character as to the shape, if any, of your jacket. If you haven't worms or hooks but must have them you can kick down the banks of the stream and cut the hair off a Mickey Finn. But such tactics are demoralizing, and the end hardly justifies the means.

I dislike such compromising though I have been guilty of it. We are too apt to go at our sport as if it were a business. In business, in making money out of markets, the part of wisdom is to relinquish an unsound position and take the opposite one. No lapse of dignity inheres in such shifting. For the end of the whole affair is profit and, within legitimate limits, there is no question of ethics, dignity, sportsmanship or any other of the vanities of men which should give a sport a higher moral rating than a business.

Trout fishing, we must admit, is a sport and therefore it proposes a different objective. The goal is not only trout in the creel but something sufficiently involved to satisfy the complex ideals we have erected for our sports. How we catch 'em is what counts. The methods are of higher importance than the spoils and that is why a man who will switch in an instant from the long to the short side of the market will maintain his wet-fly position through a day of failure rather than take a trout or two by a shift to worms. The fact that we could kill trout with dynamite but don't is all the evidence we need of the importance of methods.

But perhaps there is too much fetish about methods. I know of no sport so ridden with taboos, so gangrenous with snobbery, so reeking with cant, as trout fishing. The purist is an aristocrat, the fly-fisherman a gentleman and the wormer a boor, according to the dicta of all that is false and cheap in this great diversion. If we must retain this system of caste we should at least be sensible about it. It is well to remember that there are wormers and wormers, and that some of them are as good sportsmen as any fly-fisherman. The sort of wormer we can object to is he who patrols a trout stream with a saltwater rod, pausing at each deep hole to plop in a lead sinker. Our objections, of course, can be little more than academic for this fellow does not catch many trout. Indeed he is a practical conservationist: his splashing sinkers and ponderous baits have put

down many a trout that would have been receptive to the next carefully placed fly.

Another kind of wormer who is a sportsman seems in the majority on eastern streams. I mean the chap who fishes worms with a fly rod, a fly reel, fly line and a big hook (so that undersized trout will not swallow it) and who fishes as taut a line as he can command. In not a few cases the fisherman who practices this sort of worming in April will be casting flies in May and June.

Wormers of this ilk are aware of the niceties of their craft, which are many, and deserve no contempt from the average of fly-fishermen. Indeed the truly expert wormer is as skillful as the mill run of flycasters in the mechanics of handling sensitive tackle. His upstream cast can be a quite delicate maneuver. It calls for nice rod work on any water, but on the small brooks which are the wormer's natural range it demands a high degree of skill. In worm fishing a downstream procedure is usual and, in slow water, effective. Fast water, however, will straighten out line and keep the worm on the surface. Since the idea is to keep the worm down, this type of water presents its problems. Wormers get around it by the splitshot or the upstream cast. A worm thrown upstream from a point below and to one side will sink and drift down toward the angler at optimum depth. The cast itself is difficult enough if the banks are overgrown or if some feature of the terrain or foliage makes a long cast necessary. But consider the sequel to the cast. What happens after the bait hits the stream is apt to be a trying business in which a *sporting* success is dependent upon the impeccable handling of rod and line.

For in worm fishing slack line does not necessarily mean a lost fish. In fact a degree of slack just sufficient to let the worm drift naturally is desirable. More than this is desirable only to the fisherman who wants trout rather than sport. On a great deal of slack line the trout may calmly swallow the worm whole without being aware that a hook is attached. The fisherman feels no strike; indeed no strike may occur. He is aware after a moment that his line is not going with the current, hence he is either snagged or fast to a fish. He retrieves slowly, a trout comes back to him fighting as best it can with a hook in its throat or gills or stomach. The result, where small trout are numerous, is the taking of many undersized fish which cannot be returned alive to the water.

The conscientious wormer avoids this contingency. By keeping his line as taut as he can he gives himself the thrill of a well-felt strike and a fair fight with a lightly hooked trout. The upstream worm cast is a definitive job of skill. The angler purposely confronts himself with the makings of that situation he wants earnestly to avoid, an excess of slack line. He gets slack at once, the instant the worm touches the water and starts its rapid course downstream. As the worm approaches a point opposite, the slack increases unless it is taken up; as the worm goes below the angler the slack straightens, but now the worm comes nearer the surface and thus farther from the possibility of a strike. It is simple physics, and simple irony.

And the wormer's difficulties do not end there. His mode of attack and the nature of his usual battleground make imperative such qualities as quietness and stealth—factors that enter but academically into the fly-fisher's long-range campaigns. It is one thing to fire a barrage of flies fifty feet upstream, quite another to creep to the edge of a brier-grown bend of a meadow brook and maneuver a worm through the impenetrabilities of leafage and twiggage into the black water and then to let it out and down, the line drawing unimpeded through all the guides of the rod and down from the tip into that dusky little pool which is perhaps four feet wide, and then down-current, still free in this breathless moment, from any fouling. And if then the rod is dipped toward the water and convulsed with the amazing strike a ten-inch native gives on a short line it is clear why some anglers prefer worming in the small brooks. Strikes which are the rewards of fly-fishing have their spectacular excitement. But for sheer strength and ferocity I know of none comparable to the smash of the brook trout on a short line.

This opinion is, I think, uninfluenced by the sentimental preference I have always had for the native trout. Responsible for that are the associations of my first fishing, all of which was in the small worming streams, the pastoral quiet brooks that loitered through woodlots and fringes of farm fields not far from home. The native trout in those tributaries were wild, they had never known hatchery liver and their ancestors had graced the frying pans of the earliest Dutch. Their philosophy as to worms was unquestioning and their technique forthright. In retrospect it seems the best fishing I have known.

Because worming is small-boy fishing may be why some good fly men resort to it now and then. It takes you back as nothing else can; it can be as evocative of youth as certain rare odors. Sometime you may see a cork float idling on the middle of a broad slow pool at noonday. Surprisingly, to some fishermen whose tolerance of wormers is not what it might be, a tapered line is attached to the float and a four-ounce Leonard or Hardy is at the shore end of the line. A fly-fisherman is beside that resting rod, taking the lunch recess in a pleasant way. His conscientious fly-fishing from early morning to noon has been a strenuous stint. And the late afternoon will bring more of it. It is June and the dark falls late, and he will want to be thorough about the evening rise. But the slack hot hour of the day's middle is a time for ease. Let a worm go down this pool while the sandwiches are brought out. It won't hurt the rod: the rod rests on the bank, in a forked stick perhaps, and a little slack line is between the tip and the cork float. He need not even hold the rod. There will be plenty of strain later, the incessant wrist action, the complex problems of fishing in its refined forms. But just now, around noon, this chap can be a boy again with a worm and a #5 Sproat.

Nymph fishing is another method to complicate the game just a little more. The nymph is perhaps the most difficult of all artificial lures to fish correctly and its expert practitioners are a small and select company. The upstream cast presents challenges which only the elite can accept with assurance. The strike under water is almost always unseen; if a little slack is in the line the strike may not even be felt, and if too much is there the fish may well be lost. Various complications are involved: keeping the nymph down is imperative but in water even moderately fast this is not easy on a taut line. Consider the live nymph's rise to the surface or its underwater course in moving from place to place on the bottom. When it disengages itself from its stone and heads surfaceward to hatch into a fly it does not do so against a swift current. To simulate this action requires slack line. Drifting downstream on a taut line the artificial, unless weighted, will not sink except in still or slow water. In casting upstream, slack is presented at once. Most of it must be retrieved but if retrieved too rapidly the realism is lost. In still or slow water the crosscurrent cast can be employed but in fast water the drag can ruin your whole show. And the hazard of backcast hang-ups in any crosscurrent work is not a minor hazard at all. The successful nympher practices as ticklish a craft as there is in trout fishing.

And he is probably more cognizant of the feeding habits of trout than are the rank and file of dry-fly men. Many a rise of trout is a nymph rise, not a rise to any fly settling on the surface from the air. The observant nymph fisherman is on the lookout for this and he knows the sign which betokens it. Not all rising trout get what they're after. Here and there one rises too late, and just above its surface-break a fly—hatched in this instant from its nymph stage— is to be seen ascending. The keen-eyed nymph fisherman sees it and understands. The average dry-fly man, prone to the belief that any rising trout is surface-feeding, misses its significance. In this case the feeding is on the surface only incidentally, when the pursuing trout fails to catch its prey before the surface is reached. The real feeding is below; the surface-break and the sight of the just-hatched fly, escaping, only gives away what is going on underwater.

A more common sight is a nymphing trout feeding in shallow water and showing itself again and again as its dorsal fin or tail breaks the surface. Usually this occurs in a riffle or a small pocket off the main current. This, too, may be mistaken as a rise to a surface insect. A dry fly cast over such action may draw a rise but the chance is better if a nymph is cast above the area of the surface breaks and allowed to drift through.

The strike on a nymph is savage; at once the deceit is manifest and the attempted ejection made by the fish. A lightly hooked trout, able to do battle and to be returned unharmed to the water, is the gratifying sequence to the nymph cast.

Fishing with a fly spinner or a worm-baited spinner seems merely a way to advertise your worm or fly, and often you will draw an inquiry without making a sale. Both methods have always struck me as untroutish. If you should turn a bass fisherman loose on a trout stream and let him follow his natural impulses he undoubtedly would spin. On trout water spinning—or is it spinnering?—has somehow the look of an alien method. This gadget of bright metal which works on an automatic principle seems a concession to the machine in a sport essentially pastoral and quiet. Of course even the simple trout reel is a machine too, yet its use is almost subconscious; except in the occasional playing of a big fish one is scarcely aware of its presence.

The triple-hook or gang-hook spinner is certainly no sporting rig and might well be outlawed on trout waters. Yet I see no reason why the single-hook fly spinner, if used with a fly rod, should be objected to.

Possibly other spinners like mine have hooked many trout. Mine have not. I usually carry a couple and toward the end of a blank day with flies my thoughts will turn to these things. It is a pretty fair sign of defeat.

The spinner seems essentially an in-between, pinch-hitting gadget, and possibly there is no such thing as an exclusively spinner fisherman. Anglers for trout are fly men or bait men by choice, both using the spinner in certain waters or weathers or to satisfy a special mood. For no defensible reason the deep swift runs seem to me best suited to the spinner technique. April seems the month for it and the high discolored stream more appropriate than the low clear water of June. Yet I have seen trout taken on the spinner in the cystalline shallows in the late season—the sort of water that meant the dry fly or the nymph to me.

I find it a device to beguile those moments when all the circumstances of a day have contrived to defeat me, when changing flies has been frequent and futile and hangups have been many. In the tired twilights of such days I sometimes fling a spinner upon the flood. It is just another chance in a day full of chances that have gone wrong. But it is a different kind of chance. I see the thing twinkle into the deep green current, I feel its queer vibrant resistance as if a motor were running on the end of my line, and if I have any hope left at all this little injection will start it coursing in my arteries. Rarely does anything happen to relieve the creel's emptiness.

I have noticed, however, that a few trout I have hooked on these things have struck at the same point in the spinner's course. I like to cast it across stream, let it swing down with the current and back toward my side, describing roughly a quarter-circle arc. My strikes have usually occurred at the end of this journey while the spinner is revolving, stationary, in the water downstream. In fact I have seen trout follow the crosscurrent arc of the spinner, a foot or so behind it, and take it when the arc was completed. I offer this not as a how-to-do-it dictum but only as one observation in my scanty spinner experience.

The streamers and bucktails are competent lures, particularly in the shallows at dusk when the big ones emerge from their deep day-long hideouts to chase chub and minnows in shoal water. Streamers in action are good imitations of small fish especially when the stream is murky with rain or dark with the dusk. I like the Gray Ghost or the Muddler Minnow or a white marabou on fine evenings in the late season but only after the world is so dark that I can no longer see a large bivisible or fanwing floating at the end of a thirty-foot cast.

With whatever lure a man fishes, if he is a plugger he will plug and if he is a skipper he will skip. This matter of tempo is a matter of temperament.

Among fly men is the thoroughgoing and persistent soul who will count the number of dry-fly casts over any pool, nor stop until his quota is reached. He has not only a different temperament from mine but a different opinion of trout character. Of course it would be folly to assert that a trout who does not take a fly on the first cast will not take it on the twenty-first. The brookie and its cousins may be aggravated or coaxed into deeds so bizarre as to be distinctly out of character. But the nature of a feeding trout is to strike at once. If it is in that strangely hesitant and compromising mood which makes it "rise short" no amount of patience on the angler's part seems effective. Otherwise, if the trout does not strike at once I can at least surmise (1) it is not actively feeding, (2) it is not interested in my fly, (3) it has seen me, (4) it is not there.

In any of the four cases, why bother with it? I may kid a nonfeeding trout into thinking a hatch is under way by repeatedly tempting it with a fly. Such procedure is doubtless rewarding at times. Yet around the next bend may be a fish eager for my wares, one who will rush me at the first cast. I am not one to coax a trout overmuch. If it wishes to be sulky, that's its business.

The plugger thinks and acts otherwise. He will plug in spite of all. And maybe in the end his creel will be the heavier for his plugging. I fished years ago with a a dry-fly expert who was an archplugger if ever one lived. A counter of casts, he. A prolonged dallier at every pool. I would fish half a mile of stream while he covered a hundred yards. Consistently he would beat me, two or three to one. Trout mounded up in his creel by evening; in mine was much air. But my eyes were perhaps fuller of scenery, which is something.

Still longer ago a worming plugger used to go afield with me. A meadow brook, a coiling and leisurely watercourse, had a single largish pool, a plain extravagance for a brook of such modest ways. This pool was the bunk of my partner. I would leave him on its bank early in the afternoon, proceed far upstream and fish down, ending at length in the dusk at the big pool where my companion still sat. He would have four to six fat natives, approximately twice the number, and of twice the weight, of mine. He was going against trout nature (or so I thought), trying to coax them, waiting for them, beating them at last by the sheer formidability of his patience. I was going *with* trout nature, sneaking downstream, placing cautious and quiet worms in the little eddies, following the theory that a trout will strike at once if it is to strike at all. But my partner caught two to my one, time after time. The times I beat him seemed only the exceptions to prove the rule. Then, either my theory was untenable or my angling talents inferior. Either could well be the answer to this and to much else that has perplexed me about fishing.

And yet I am not a rash skipper. Aware of the dangers I try to resist the temptations. One of them is confronted again and again on familiar water. You are working downstream and just below you is a sweet pool or a deep run which has given up a good fish time after time. The temptation is to get on to it. You are almost certain that a trout is there and equally certain that no trout is in the lesser riffle where you stand at the moment or anywhere between you and the good water below. The urge to go immediately to that spot is powerful. I have succumbed to it more than once, deserting water of apparent mediocrity to get at water of great promise without delay. It is a bad plan. Often the highly touted pool yields nothing and as often the in-between rifts hold somewhere a good fish who will come to your fly.

Someone has said, "Fish all the water." It is good advice for the beginner on any stream and for the expert on an unknown one which happens to be high and discolored. But the experienced fisherman on familiar water knows the blank spots; when he passes them by he is not skipping but merely saving his time and wrist. These places occur in the best of streams. Putting a fly into them is as futile as putting a fly into your bathtub.

Water that has just yielded a fish should be given a second try, and a third. If you have had some surface play or other commotion with the first, the pool should of course be rested before your next cast. These are minutes to put a premium on your patience. A pipe smoked without hurry or the gathering of ferns for the creel gives the right amount of time. Do something like that, away from the stream, but watch the water for another rise. The trout you have just caught had a reason for being there. The place offered feeding advantages which another trout will soon accept.

And so you cast again. But nothing happens this time, nor the next. Another trout *should* be there but quite manifestly none is. This sort of actuality puts a blight on the most plausible fishing theory. . . . You glance downstream at the untried water—a long smooth run shaded under hemlocks and a steep rocky bank, black water with a fleet of bubbles on it. And you are on the move again. There is a restlessness generated by the stream itself, the urge to go with it. Only the most formidable plugger can resist.

Whatever your method, if you are catching trout it seems adequate. But when an hour or two hours or a morning goes by without a strike, then any other method seems superior to yours. Two hours of blankness on dry flies will make you dead certain that your partner, fishing wets, has a half dozen in his creel by now. At such times your position becomes shaky. But at such times—of all times —your position should be maintained. The day and the water have indicated dry flies to your best judgment and as yet you have no real proof that they are wrong. Barring a sudden and radical change of weather you should stay with them. The experience of changing to wets after a fishless hour or two with drys, and then meeting a man with a one-pounder just caught on a dry is worse than discouraging —it is apt to get a little of your self-respect.

Behind all the methods of trout fishing lurks the selfish motive. A man is credited with sportsmanship because he fishes a dry fly and takes two trout while another is thought to be of slack moral fiber because he fishes worms and catches a dozen. Yet each heeds his peculiar demon. The two are identical in motive, different only in that which cuddles the ego: the practice of a delicate craft or the catching of a mess of fish. The means are different, the ends are the same. Pride is pride, but the methods of pride are infinitely varied.

Places 5

Some trout streams are important for their trout, almost all for their beauty, a few for their associations and memories. In the last category are the secret streams of the past. The ancients who have been at their sport for fifty or sixty years can remember the whispered directions, the pledges of secrecy, the long and tortuous journeys to these segments of paradise hidden in the back country. Such prospecting and discovery once constituted the most glamorous aspect of trout fishing. But that is gone out of the world, now, except in the remote semiwilderness counties. Young anglers, casting over their first pools, miss this high adventure of finding a secret stream. The automobile has ended this unique excitement along with its general spoliation of the countryside. The motoring hordes have found all the streams there are. Some are still where they used to be but they are no longer secret. What was once the breathless private knowledge of two or three fishermen has become public information. The State has charted all the likely water, filled it with foreign trout and invited the public to come and get 'em.

And the public comes. Paths beaten by many booted feet line both banks of the once secret brook and its wild shy natives have disappeared, lost to pollution or the hostile company of rainbows and browns. Something essentially American has died with the native trout, a quality that was rural quietness and peace, unmachined enterprise and nature left to herself.

Most of the truly secret streams were small. The larger waters had names, a public sort of character, perhaps commercial importance. They were easy of access; if they held trout they were fished regularly throughout the open season. Unless restocked they became at last depleted of fish.

The little back-country feeder brooks were nameless, reached only by long tramping over the ridges and upland meadows which lay deep beyond the infrequent roads. In such remote rills, known only to ourselves and our most intimate partners, the brook trout swam and lurked and met its chilly destinies much as it had in the first days of the world. A few of these streams are still where they used to be. But man has proved that he can move a trout brook at will. In the name of progress he has built his dams and made deep lakes of the little valleys, bulldozed his networks of roads and erected his houses on the slopes where the deer came down to the stream to drink in the dusks of the past. Now in the summer nights the television blares a foreign tongue up hillsides which had known for ages the coon's cry and the booming of the barred owl. In the name of his deity of the dollar man has straightened other streams into ditches, dried up his springs by deforestation and let his sweet water run forever out of his lands.

The devastation is not quite complete. Some of the little brooks have escaped it; a few still whisper in passing to later generations of sweet fern, cowslip and witch hazel. But a change is upon even these. Their privacy has been violated. Paths trace their banks, bootprints dent their sandy shingles, discarded trash litters their once virgin glades.

All of this—we can dismiss it with a dark and deprecatory gesture —was bound to happen considering this nation's prior dedications since the current century began. Now that most of a once magnificent heritage is gone beyond redemption a handful of conservationists and ecologists contemplate the wasteland and wonder what can be saved out of the wreckage.

It is over, then, that private and tight-held knowledge of a remote and virgin stream. To me it was the essence of trout fishing. It could hardly be defined. But it was what I thought of when I handled trout tackle or heard the first peepers of March and breathed the ineffable air of another spring.

Meanwhile there is left to us survivors such water as has survived with us by the grace of a thousand circumstances.

A chapter headed *Places* may hold little of definite promise to the reader. Had I wanted, or been able, to make this book a technical one I might have called this chapter *Where to Find the Quarry*. But my ideas as to where to find the quarry are probably less thorough than your own. Further, the mere finding of the quarry has never seemed to me of first importance. Always I have liked better to find a pool which looks quarryish and then to test the pool for the quarry itself. Some of my angling friends are highly diligent in their searchings for certain natural phenomena which indicate that the trail of the quarry is hot, and scholarly in their application to the problems imposed thereby. They are rewarded in proportion to their valor. Once I too was passably studious in such curricula, but it was an effort because it ran counter to my temperament. I let it go along with much else that was arduous, trying, mathematical, scientific and generally a damned nuisance about a sport that challenged and rewarded me in other ways. To write of angling from the technical angles is all very pleasant, if you can. But for the actual play I had rather leave the exactitudes and precisions to chess, a sport able to accommodate these intrinsically beautiful qualities without interference by the elements.

Streams with reputations do not always live up to them and the obscurer brooks often hold a big trout or two. The tributaries of a famous river afford better fishing at some seasons than the river itself. Fishermen rather than the fish perpetuate and enhance the reputation of a stream. By story and legend, by the magic euphony of a name, the prestige of a river is won and held. *Beaverkill, Willowemoc, Neversink, Esopus, Brodhead*—such names owe their celebrity as much to the tongues and pens of fishermen as to the numbers and weight of the trout between their banks. Those who cast upon these historic rivers know them for what they are; the rest have their illusions. It is the old story of the prophet being not without honor, etc. An angler makes a two-hundred-mile pilgrimage to an illustrious river; the day he arrives a second angler—one of the local gentry who lives on the celebrated banks—gets into his Ford and drives away from the great stream for a little fishing on an obscure tributary over the next ridge. The odds are ten to one on whose creel will be the heavier at nightfall.

But I have no wish to disparage the great individuals among trout rivers. A reputation such as the Willowemoc's was not built on any flimsy base, and once the foundation was set there was no limit to the number of stories which could be erected thereon. Those among the nobility of trout water have a high order of virtue. But to fish them with consistent success demands the intimate knowledge of long and close association. Some, such as the Big Beaverkill and the Neversink, are long, deep, wide and of many moods and tempers. I am a little uneasy in their presence as if my meager talents were not meet to cope with their vast implications. The Willowemoc and Brodhead are smaller, more tractable, better aligned to my humors. Now and then, however, I can enjoy to the full the luxury of easy casting over the ideal stretches the larger rivers afford. There could be few finer dry-fly waters than a certain run well up toward the fork of the Neversink. When I last fished it, all of thirty years ago, a deep channel caressed the west bank for a full three hundred yards of slowly curving river. The east shore was a wide beach of stones sloping at a gentle angle to the water. In the normal late-May stage the stream here was seventy-five to one hundred feet wide and you could wade halfway across without going above your knees. The current maintained the mood of quiet: no white water broke it, yet it was fast enough to give purpose and meaning to your dry fly's drift downstream and so uniform in its speed that the drag need not be given a thought. Behind you was the open desert of stones: your backcast was forgotten along with your other troubles. Before you was the smooth black progression of a noble river. From lower to upper end you could work it quite thoroughly in sixty minutes. But there was no need to clock yourself. If it took you all afternoon you wasted no time.

Such delectable pieces of water should not be come upon around every bend. Like the high moments of life or art, they should have the quality of rarity. They are the rewards of stream fishing, the compensating interludes of perfection between the long and arduous periods. In one way or another most trout water is stiff and challenging, some of it dangerous. Its problems are legion: problems of navigation, of the backcast and the drag, singly and in combination. It is a little wearying in a long day upstream or down. To the man who has fought the current and been patient with hang-ups for hours on end the emergence at last upon a restful pool comes as a direct reward from the gods.

And yet these mechanically perfect places may yield nothing but easy casting. I have overstayed the blissful repose of such water with never a rise, only to snag into a good fish immediately upon resuming the battle with the rocks and rapids upstream. I have flirted with the theory that the easier the water the less likelihood of a strike. It has winked back at me occasionally but about the time I think I'm in love with it, it does something to turn me cold. Once I was on the point of embracing it for good and all when, in a stretch of Sussex County (New Jersey) stream which for sheer ease of casting can hardly be surpassed I hooked and landed three browns and a rainbow, all of ample inchage, in the space of a hundred feet and half a hundred minutes.

There is no sense in my being dogmatic about anything in trout fishing except the proposition that I cannot catch a trout under a bridge. A whole bridge, that is. Broken-down bridges are different. In that remote and gentle time when life stood still in the clear air of the long afternoons, a collapsed structure, dating from an even deeper period of antiquity, spanned a brook deep in the woods near home. The road which had led to it had long since been healed by nature and the rattle of its occasional traffic buried deep under layers of time. It retained, still, a ghost of the form its architect had once drawn upon neat paper; its landward ends rested yet upon the dry earth but its middle was intimate with the water. In the complications of its broken and sodden planks a rectangular hole had been worn by the slow patience of the central current. A worm lowered delicately into this breach would immediately disappear in the unseen eddies beneath the remaining boards. Ensuing, then, was a moment of such ecstasy as only boys who have fished the little haunts of the wild natives can know and later recall. The underbody of that structure, the crazy hidden angularity of its mess of sunken timbers, was a favorite abode of the *fontinalis.* The strike would dip your rod fairly into the maze of boards and you would draw from the wreckage an eight-inch brookie. Such a convulsion in the small space would spook any other prospect who might have been lurking in the dark grottoes. I never struck more than one fish upon any single occasion. Attempts to do so would invariably lose a hook. That moribund architecture must literally have been festooned with the snells of Snecks, Sproats and Carlisles.

Such places are beloved of the native trout. It seems to prefer its water not clear and free but cluttered with roots, windfalls or the sunken wreckage of man's little enterprises. An old waterlogged boat, a tree trunk fallen to the stream bed, the ruin of a dyke or dam —any obstruction which creates its own extraordinary eddies and backwaters—is preeminently the place to look for the brookie.

All the rules can be broken, all the theories exploded. One, however, with a minimum of variation, is that the character of the stream determines the character of the trout. Big fish are found in big water *or in small streams accessible from big water.* The possibility of a large fish is present in a meadow brook three feet wide if it has depth, undercut banks, an occasional deep hole, and no dam or high fall in its course to the larger stream it feeds. In one of our early sorties my companion hooked and landed a sixteen-inch brown in a rill so small it could be stepped across almost anywhere in a half-mile course through an upland meadow. That brooklet, however, had all the qualifications cited above. Other big fish have been taken from it before and since, perhaps as surprising to their captors as the big brown was to us.

Some years after this early awakening our springtime custom was to fish another diminutive brook that wound slowly down a long pastureland. Its banks were high in grasses; a willow stood here and there giving shade at noonday to the Holsteins which promenaded those broad flats. Alders and witch hazel grew thickly in spots, arching over the trickle of stream. Under these tenements of the redwing blackbird you could with great difficulty maneuver a worm. But the native trout were there, waxing long and fat, and sometimes when your careful bait had ridden a few inches of water that were clear of vegetation you were rewarded with that paroxysm which is ever the strike of the brook trout on a short line. Eleven-inch, amply girthed beauties were not uncommon in that negligible rill.

On another kind of small stream, of wilder and more spectacular mien, you will never catch a large trout unless the government has recently been by, heaving in the contents of its cans. I mean those charging white-and-amber, rapids-and-pool-and-falls brooks that pitch down the sandstone and hemlock-bordered gorges of our eastern mountainsides. Even the governmental optimism—which can stock the Bronx River with trout—stops short of placing large fish in such water. Fishing here is all enshrined in the mountain beauty and the water beauty, the black pools with white suds slow-sailing and spent after the upper riot of the falls, and the redstone bottom brilliantly discerned here and there in the areas of sunlight. You fish only the pools between rapids and occasionally a spot where the fast water jams into a back eddy or stills a moment in the downstream lee of a boulder. It is a lively game of hazardous travel where the hobnailed cruiser is better gear than the wader, and of welcome rests at each little pool in the steep descent. But you must be content with the little ones, dark slender fish of seven or eight inches.

The reasons are simple. Trout born in one of these pools cannot ever get far above it. A pool may be ten feet across and half again as long. The range being tightly limited, so is the food. What drifts or drops into that brief pool and what grows on its bottom complete the available larder. The fish inhabiting these little places can get below at their peril; some do go down, win the lower and flatter stretches and grow big, but none goes far above. A high sheer fall is directly upstream, or at best a short run of navigable rapids, then another pool and another impassable fall. A second reason for the absence of large fish is extreme vulnerability to natural enemies. Many of these mountain pools are without the protection of deep water or the cover of overhanging ledges. Conceivably an industrious mink or watersnake can depopulate such a pool in short order. That anglers rapidly fish out this kind of water is debatable. It is hard to get at and hard to fish, and sometimes a mile from the nearest road. In the valley stretches where the surviving trout grow big on much food, ample range and plenty of cover against natural enemies man is most dangerous and fished-out water most common.

All of the trout water spoken of in this book is water you can reach without any great wrench from your accustomed routine. One finds a vicarious comfort, however, in imagining the wilderness rivers that still run their courses, not in northern Maine or southern Quebec but far beyond—up, way up, where the world has shaken off its last highway and its last piece of fabricated metal and is curving vastly into its northern peace.

Somewhere in that sweep of geography is a stream I have never seen and doubtless shall never see. But I can sense what it looks like: the length of its stride and the hunch of the shoulders of the trout country that cradles it. Galleries of shelving granite and low balsams watch the parade of its water. If a sound is not a sound without a human ear to record it then this stream is flowing forever in a silence. A few times in history it has broken into sound when a prowling Indian has emerged upon its shores, stood alone on a stone ledge and leaned to drink. Deer materialize upon its sand spits in the northern twilights like actors in pantomime, rehearsing the old gestures of those trite and hackneyed wilderness roles. In the high noon an otter slides again and again in the sun, a preposterous performance, a repetition of unabashed loud splashing and a flashing of wet fur, but no human eye or ear is there to catch it. Before all the bright world of a summer noontime the spectacle is enacted unseen. . . . The water itself has a greenness where the sun's rays plunge deep into the heart of a pool—some of that pigment, perhaps, which the sun synthesizes in ice. This water has been ice but recently and it soon will be ice again. In that brief liquid freedom it hurries, as if knowing the time to be short, toward Hudson Bay. Below the long white whip of a rapid is the spread of a pool, and deep in its green translucent chill are shadows side by side and end to end, uniformly pointed as iron filings to a magnet. Deep under the little surface waves a hundred of these shadows come and go, change places with each other, assume shape and design in a streak of sunlight and then fade and become one with the dark bottom.

You will see no such congregation of ghosts in the Willowemoc, Beaverkill, Esopus or any such. But you will see at least the water as it comes curving and crowding up to your waders, bearing its minute and variegated flotsam, its derelict insects and wingéd seeds. A million boots have plowed the gravel of this stream bed, a million flies have whipped its surface. It is old, old fishing landscape, scarred with its human contacts, familiar and friendly and kind to the frailties of anglers.

Despite the depredations of this century much of this water is still sweet to look upon and to cast over. And upon its lesser tributaries you may still fare beyond the sight of highways and the rasp of auto horns upwind. In these unfrequented glades fresh water is foaming along in the venerable tradition, washing stream-bed boulders as old as the earth. Here the seasons succeed each other according to ancient decree, celebrating themselves in the sanctioned rituals of color and sound. The blackbird nests in the misty alders; lush summer smothers the banks, quiets the slack water and the moulting birds; the red and brown fleets of October sail down the black autumnal pools; and a free trickle of open channel narrowly bisects the ice, mumuring a faint brave promise of spring.

Times and Weathers 6

Opening Day fell on April 1st when I was young enough to invest the date with a kind of religious exaltation and to make its observance a ritual of such import that the renewed pleasure of fishing was overlaid with a larger meaning. Looking back at these annual rebirths of ecstasy I am struck by the change that has been wrought in the keeping of this ancient festival. For, more than any other aspect of trout fishing as practiced today, this annual offensive illustrates its modern character.

More decades ago than I like to count, the first of April was only another first-of-the-month, another day for bills and commutation tickets and general settling of accounts. If it had any extracurricular significance it was that of April Fools' Day. As the opening of trout fishing it had been anticipated for weeks by a few zealots but these were not given to speaking of it to the lay public. Opening Day approached slowly from afar, inching her tortuous progress through the iron terrain of winter; for days at a time she would seem locked in the ice, unable to advance. But she would keep on in spite of all, waving her quiet banners to those few who watched her approach. And she would arrive finally, sometimes radiant with a bright and bird-filled morning but more often like a tattered refugee with winter still snapping at her skirts.

We would get up in the very early hours of April, long before daybreak, and go to our chosen stream. If we were going far we had a milk-train journey and a long walk at the end of it; if near, we had simply a long walk. We were too young to drive a car even had we possessed one; indeed only a few adult anglers were so equipped. I remember two old stagers who would drive eight or ten miles to their favorite water in a carriage. In the predawn silences of those far-gone April firsts which are the most remote in my memory—before my own first fishing—I would hear the *cloppety clop* of their horse coming down our street, passing and fading out northward in the dark.

Those were Opening Days worth enduring a winter for, Opening Days without disillusion. You went to your stream quietly while the rest of the world went to its work unaware of the great import of the day. And when you arrived it *was* your stream. You might meet two or three anglers in the course of the long day. But you didn't mind that; in fact you welcomed the exchange of trout talk. It was still *your* stream.

But that close and private ownership exists no longer. It has been split 100 for 1, and stocked dividends declared. On the annual orgy of the opening the stream once yours is the joint property of a hundred other licensed fishermen. Long before daylight their cars are parked at every bridge and every footpath; in the predawn hour their gear is assembled and with the first dilution of the darkness they are off, taking their stands at twenty-foot intervals and heaving their lures and baits. It is friendly enough and, withal, not noisy, a typically American piece of camaraderie. But it is not trout fishing. I don't know what it is. A kind of convention, perhaps, the Annual Conclave of the Northeastern Fly, Bait and Surf-Rod Wielders Association, and its Lead-Slingers Auxiliary.

My custom for many years has been to pass it up, to go quietly about other business as if nothing of earth-shaking consequence were astir. That old glamor of the lonely dawn, the unheralded arrival of another trout season, has passed into limbo.

But this early élan of the shock troops is not of a hardy and durable fiber. In these ranks are bass men and saltwater men and nonanglers with borrowed gear who think they might like trout fishing. Their enthusiasm is that of the alien for the native thing: it is spurious and thin, the mere appeal of novelty. Time has a way of dissolving it. By late April and May the traffic is appreciably attenuated and by the shank of the dry-fly season all of those early kibitzers and camp followers are gone back to their rightful trades. Trout water is the property of trout fishermen again.

The first of May ushers in the second act and shares the dramatic values of the official opening. April is a gray-green, half-winter month, a month of high water which is part melted snow and ice and brown with the washed bare earth. Any of its unpredictable days is capable of brandishing a blizzard. May puts all that behind, turns the corner to summer. The hum of life is again on the land and the green of the woods begins to look as if it meant to stay. Birdsong has lost its hesitant, winter-reminiscent shyness. If the early days of May are stormy and cold the name has still its magic. Merely to remind yourself that May is with you is a warming stimulant. You need no longer take a snow flurry seriously and a thermometer in the forties is only stunting for the moment. The normal will return, and soon. April may do anything but May will not let you down.

In these first summer-pointed dusks the wood thrush affirms its belief in another year, and over the quieter trout waters the first honest hatches of flies are astir. It is the victory at last.

From now on you and nature coast through the season. Fly-fishing improves with the maturing May, reaches its peak around the second week of June, and then—sometimes with a suddenness that is startling—the crest has passed. There will come an evening in late June or early July when you will know that the best of your fishing is over for another year. The stream is low and so relentlessly clear that only the deep pools afford coolness and cover for the trout. Along the banks the vegetation stands lush and oppressive in this final triumph of the summer, this ultimate product of nature's chemistry. The stillness is electric and hot, holding the close drone of mosquitoes and the far mutter of thunder. The stream is dark and slow under the trees, subsided and tired. No perceptible hatch is on the water and no trout is rising anywhere. You are thorough about your casting until the dark falls at last, but you do not raise a fish. . . . Another year. As you drag your waders up the bank you reflect a little sadly on the evanescence of a trout season.

But it is not definitely the end; trout fishing cannot be thus neatly bracketed. From now on to the legal closing there will be intervals when those alert to catch them may know a vicarious return to May and June. A cool day with rain or some less obvious weather change that might pass unnoticed may give back for a moment the old excitement of freely rising fish.

September trout fishing, unheard of in my early years, seems a kind of State-granted bonus to those who would prolong their sport beyond its appropriate time. From the standpoint of creel contents, on stocked streams, September may be as good a month as any. It is just prior to the spawning of the chars, of which the brookie is one. The relation of the open season to spawning is here ignored. If a stream is cleaned of gravid fish in September it will be heavily stocked again before next April. Spawning or no, it will always be in trout. There is something a little sad in a contemplation of this artificiality, this almost synthetic contrivance.

The fishing itself, in September, has something of the same irrationality. To the traditionalist it doesn't belong. Fallen leaves litter the surface and sink beneath it, presenting to the flycaster a hazard he should not have to face. The backdrop—the high mature goldenrod, ragweed, asters and gentians and autumnal tree foliage—is hardly that of trout fishing. The still and frosty mornings of late September are meet for the sound of a shotgun and the smell of smokeless powder, not for the Junetime sounds of a trout reel and a wood thrush. September fishing is an evocation of ghosts, a second childhood of the trout season, more like a haunting recollection than a living experience. It is a ghoulish disinterring of something better left buried.

Sometimes July can run amuck and out-April April, surprising you with a cold and prolonged rain that puts the streams back to early-season levels. In such sodden fishing weather Mill and Arch and I were camped on a northern river.

That week was a series of chill dark pouring days, some of July's early children, brats of whom the warm lavish mother seemed ashamed for she would not come out and be seen while her wayward offspring were showing off. The woods were overloaded with water; under the drenched trees it fell in the same volume as in the open. The river rose hour by hour like an incoming tide. Its little beaches gradually disappeared under the flood. Wading in midstream, knee-deep and easy in the normal July, now became impossible in a waist-deep brown torrent.

Fishing should hold at least the prospect of a fish, but this kind of fishing seems flatly to deny even the prospect. I tried it anyway and found after a while that it has certain sedative properties which no psychiatrist should ignore. It has, perhaps, something in common with night fishing. A sameness and totality of environment is peculiar to each, whether the element is water or darkness. The normal clear-cut differences in one's physical surroundings lose their definition in the ceaseless wash of rain. One's eyesight is fogged; his reflexes, untested for hours by a strike or any sign of a trout, become similarly dulled. He sloshes along close inshore, finds his infrequent casting spots, gives his sodden line to the flood and himself to a pointless routine.

In this comatose condition I was headed downstream. Below me the river surface was broad and streaked with gray, stippled with the myriad pimples of the falling rain, merging with the color of the sodden world as if the downpour were stirring into the river the leaden pigments of the sky. The river vanished around a bend in the rain mist far downstream. Close at my waders the water was brownish, full of its own cloudy weather. The banks dripped into the stream; each tiny inlet poured a triple volume to the mother current. A few familiar landmarks were awash. Downstream was a long grassy island with two straight tall hemlocks, spaced on the island like the masts of a battleship. The island boasted a beach, a handy place for cleaning a trout or washing a creel. Ordinarily a sandpiper would be teetering along that pebbly strand. But now the strand had disappeared under the extraordinary tide; so much of the island was under water that its very shape seemed strange. No life stirred upon it now. A day might come, I thought, when the sandpiper would be there again teetering on the recovered beach, glad as a schoolboy at the reemergence of the sun.

But this was a day for sane men to be indoors, drying lines before the warmth of a log fire and listening to the rain on a tight roof. For fools or bitter-enders it was a day for worming or spinnering or wet-flying, in that order of their dismal promise. I was following the last method with a Coachman as tail, Cahill and Montreal as droppers. In the slow rhythm of casting, the rod swished dully in the rain-filled air, shooting from all its guides its own cross-angled spray which immediately was absorbed in the vertical downpour. The inside of my creel must have had its own rain, a drip, I thought, sufficient to keep a trout fresh without ferns or grass, but as yet no trout was there to test so mad a theory.

The afternoon wore along in its dim unchanging light. I waded through it, inured at length to the saturation of everything. There was no clear reason why that rainbow should have struck when it did. The cast was just another cast—the 487th, perhaps—and it landed upon water of no distinction in all the murky monotony of the river.

My reflexes were misted over, keyed to the dull pitch of the day. I struck back finally, a sluggish automatic response, and was surprised to feel the resistance of a heavy fish. The Coachman had it, as I saw after I recovered my senses. Gorged with all the food of the torrent it broke water halfheartedly once or twice and between times fought with the customary ardor of a catfish. I netted it at length, and trudged and sloshed back to camp where Mill and Arch were taking their siestas under the good brown canvas.

That rainbow should not have have elated me. It had hooked itself in an off moment, fat and lazy after a debauchery of feasting. My delayed strike would likely have missed clean any lean hard rainbow in the bright, low-water, surface-feeding weather. . . . And yet, to come back with a good fish won from that flood while your partners snoozed on their cots. . . .

Arch turned over and cracked his eyelids as I opened the tent flap and dripped in. "Anything?" he yawned. "One rainbow—about fourteen inches," I answered casually, thinking that would bring him bolt upright. But he only murmured, "The punishment fits the crime," and went back to sleep. I think I know what he meant. I think it was the sort of riposte men can utter in that hinterland between sleep and wakefulness, where genius seems to visit us all.

A year later we were on that stream again and we had, this time, such weather and water as are typical of July. The sun arched through an incandescent sky; under it the land was breathless and still, as if waiting for a cataclysm. Heat pulsated over the fields and woods. It was a time of still and moulting birds, a time of quiet cows slow-chewing in the noon oak shade. There had been no rain for two weeks; there was no sign of rain now. Nature was forgetting about rain; she had mislaid the rain card in her follow-up file. Meanwhile the white days succeeded each other. The west wind blew them by in the afternoons, but the mornings stood motionless and silent in a shimmer of heat. The river was shrinking day by day. It whispered over its crystal shallows, complaining of the drought, and its current slowed almost to a halt as if trying to conserve what little was left.

Fishing that water was an exercise of stealth and extreme care with 6X tippets and tiny flies. The still morning hours were almost barren of a rise. The afternoon wind would bring some slight improvement, ruffling the surface and seeming to impart to the trout a surface-feeding urge.

The afternoon wind would die at dusk, the evenings come on breathlessly still under the motionless red violence of the west. These were such evenings as in May and June would bring on the mayflies but now in this dusty shank of July no large insects were over the water. Gnats and midges were close over the surface, such as I have seen many times without the accompaniment of rising trout. Yet the fishing in the twilights of that run of days was among the best in our experience. The Black Gnat, Adams, and Iron Blue Dun, on #16 hooks, were consistent takers. It was "fine and far-off" fishing if I have ever known any.

Before the daylight completely died the rise would be over; from then on excitement could be had with the streamer or large wet fly as the big brown trout moved into the shallows.

Thus one July and the next.

Dawn is a troutful and a beautiful time to fish, especially in the late season. It is the dampest hour of the day and you will do some of your wading before you reach the stream. Night takes a while to dissolve out of the woods and water: on still mornings the transition seems labored, remnants of the night remaining for some time over the stream. These wraiths and eddies of mist glisten in the growing daylight, seeming to condense on the guides of your rod and along your line, glittering in a million tiny points so that your fishing, for the moment, is in a jeweled setting. Precisely this interval, before

the realistic charge of daylight comes like a stern parent to end this playful nonsense of dawn, is a time to draw a rise. A hush is over the world and no one is in sight upstream or down. Bird notes on every hand are only a part of the stillness and the moisture: the wood thrush's iteration drips into the dawn like drops of dew shaken from the high leaves.

Now is a time to be keen, apprehensive and alert to every sign of a rise, for the best fishing of your season may be at hand. A rising trout in the dawn hour is a trout in your creel if you are diligent. This fellow means business, he is definitely on the feed. I have known fewer short-rising trout, fewer merely playful fish at daybreak than at any time of day. The rise may not be so prolific or prolonged as in the evening but it is apt to be more businesslike. Its individual participants manifest a directness of purpose which may leave them before the setting sun. The ideal fishing you have looked forward to for months can be just ahead of you now. In half an hour you may be in the thick of it, but of course you will not recognize it then for the high point it is. Such recognition is always tardy: later you will reflect that this furious dawn hour was the hour you had dreamed about in the long days when the snow was melting.

And if you are after dawns as well as trout, June will give you the better moments. Those of the early season contain scarcely enough drama to warrant attendance at their showings. An April sunup on a cold and windy morning is so gradual a metamorphosis as to be scarcely perceptible and without benefit of music worthy the name. It holds little sense of the rising curtain, little of the promise of the burst of day over the June waters. It is a realistic, almost cynical show, like some of the painted and written art of this era. Dawns are properly times of great sentimental import and they merit a fitting accompaniment, a fanfare and flourish, the ecstasy of birds, the dew-jeweled meadows and the sun. Nature is capable of pomp, of ritual and regalia, and of genuine drama. You witness the unveiling of all creation when a June sunrise is forward over the trout waters.

In the bright weather of the fly-fishing season noonday commonly brings a lull to your streamside activities. Nature herself sets you the example. The trout are down in the shadiest depths, the birds quiet at the height of the sun. If there is a wind it seems to ease a little and the stream itself appears to slow its pace in this hushed interlude.

On the west bank of a Delaware River tributary is a spot so ideally situated for taking the noonday lull that we contrive always to meet there for lunch. Under an ancient oak on the high bank you can see the stream for a hundred yards above and below, and all of this water is potential of fish. To eat and watch is better than merely to eat, and your postprandial smoke can be quietly adventurous with that stretch of water. In this slack hour almost any overture of nature is unexpected, full of a spontaneous and artless appeal. Things that might pass unnoticed when you are intent on your fishing materialize along stream in this stillness of the day's peak. You smoke drowsily after lunch, resting your eyes on the eternal current. As you focus upon an eddy that swirls white around a boulder close to shore you realize suddenly that you are looking at something other than this static and familiar setting. A mink is there, on the inshore side of that boulder where a little strand of wet gravel separates the rock from the bank. Or a statue of a mink perhaps. The thing is a perfection of stillness there in the bright sun, a breathless and taut suspension of the quickest, intensest life in all the woods. The sun gleams upon its sleek immobility and in that charged second of time you feel that you are seeing something you are not supposed to see, one of the inner secrets of God. A lightning turn and a dart shoreward, and the black sharp motion merges with the dusk under the high bank. The stream curls whitely around the boulder, as before. "Hey," you say to your partner, "I saw a mink then." And you wonder if you really did.

Or you may see a rise, even at this unlikely time of day. A bulge far up, almost at the turn, and the widening ripples. (Always eat lunch where you can watch the stream. There will be plenty to talk about and talk is supposed to aid digestion.) What was that fellow coming up to? Is there a little hatch on or was it just a derelict miller floating by? Well, if it's a hatch you'll see some other rises. Maybe you go and cast over it. Maybe not.

We usually do not fish any lunchtime rises. We sit and speculate upon the likelihood of a recurrence later. It is a moment for rumination, not for fishing. Dashing a hundred yards upstream to fish a single rise, leaving behind a half-consumed lunch, is akin to rushing out of church to follow a passing fire engine, abandoning a half-said prayer, perhaps, or a half-sung hymn.

On some noons no movement of beast, bird or fish is visible upstream or down. But there is always the motion and the voice of the stream, and this hour is a good time to watch the water and to listen to what it has always been trying to tell you. In our haste to cast over a rising fish or to get around the next bend we are apt to be heedless of the water's ancient teachings. Now, at noon, listen to it a while: it may simplify trout fishing for you. It may simplify living for you, indeed. It is a direct and unequivocal force, at once as naïve as a child and as wise as the ages. It follows the simple and sure course of its truth, downstream to the sea, an easy habit it has had since the first day of the world. Such candor, such directness of career, will not adjust itself to the changing complexities of the twentieth century, that moment in a life extending over countless centuries. The twentieth, indeed! Among these complexities are your fanwing Royal and the Boulder Dam, and each is adjusted to the eternal physics of the flowing water, not the water to it. A hint of a lesson is here—something about the durability of the simple and the true and the transience of all that masquerades as such. The water is so forthright, the attempts of man to wrest a dubious prize from it so involved! The water will always be master of any fishing situation, master of the angler and his gear and of the trout itself. You can wonder, then, about all our involvements with the mechanics and morals of fishing.

The water continues by in the high noon. It is not cajoling or pleading or urging. It is only stating gently its old wisdom, the simple things men are afraid of. But I must turn away from it. A little of such pure and elemental teaching is too much for the stored clutter of my mind. I seek refuge in the familiar comforts of all my artificiality. The car waiting at the roadside, the miscellany of tackle in my pockets are better-known friends than the stream. The water goes on. But I can't look it in the eye anymore and I find its spoken wisdom intolerable.

DOWNSTREAM AFTER DARK

Fly-fishing at night seems to be practiced mostly by men who have trout streams running through their farm fields or backyards. This business puts a premium on an intimate knowledge not only of the stream but of its adjacent terrain for you must find your way back in the dark unless you fish until dawn, and that is not the usual custom.

With the upstate rural gentry the hours are nine to one (and the odds against the stranger sticking it that long are the same), and the conventional motive is big trout. Moonlight nights afford easier progress but the dark of the moon is held better for fishing. The theory: trout find less prey in the total dark and hence are more eager for your wares.

Night fishing has a charming informality, its practitioners seemingly unfussy as to fly patterns. Almost any streamer, bucktail or large wet fly will do. An honored dogma holds that all flies must look like silhouettes to the trout, seen against whatever pale light distinguishes the night sky from the night water. But if the fly is down, the trout must see it not against the sky but against the dark of the water or the bottom. Further, in any light at all the angler can see a white marabou better than a Muddler Minnow, and this is a point to reckon with.

The bait fishermen offer minnows, night crawlers, hellgramites, small frogs. Crawfish and mice also have their champions among the night prowlers.

But for all its casualness as to technique and freedom from some of the exactions imposed by daylight, night fishing is a perversion, a going against nature. Man is a diurnal animal, no more adapted to fish at night than is an owl to hunt at midday. You have only to try it to feel the strength of the taboo.

My first fishing venture after dark was along the middle reaches of the Willowemoc many years ago. Mill and I were encamped above DeBruce in the calm and simple era when that hamlet, even in the trout season, was still staunchly agricultural and native. The post office was a focal point of offhand trout talk; it was there that Mill and I, observing the casual goings and comings—and the enviable creels—of a few natives who roamed abroad at night, decided that we might as well have a share of this fat fishing.

In the long twilight we snugged down camp and set out. We would give it an hour or so as a fair test; then, whatever happened, we would return. Looking back on it I recall that an unspoken apprehension was in the air as if there could be some doubt of our getting back at all. A slide along one of those slippery mid-channel boulders in the darkness. . . . We arranged that Mill would go a hundred yards downstream before getting to work, that I would start approximately opposite camp, and that we would try to maintain this relative position throughout. The reason for this strategic placing of the two principals was simple. Obviously we must separate, the stream in these reaches being not large enough to accommodate two rods on the same water. I, being much the lighter, would be less able to stand firm in the current and thus Mill would be in position to snare my carcass as it came floating by. Of course, should he fail to see the derelict or his cast fail to hook into the seat of the derelict's waders—or, if *he* should be the one to founder . . . but these contingencies were beyond our simple resources.

There would be a late moon, well past the full; until then we had only the stars and the pale guidance of the stream. As I remember, I had a #4 White Miller on the tail of a shortish leader and no dropper, thinking thus to reduce the nocturnal hazard of hang-ups.

Knee-deep in midstream I felt my physical way along the slippery unstable floor and my mental way toward something approximating confidence. It was not impossible, as I had supposed it might be. It was difficult, yes, with a hundred complexities unknown in daylight, a hundred obstacles which the sense of sight—now operating at 2 percent of capacity—could circumvent. But in time I acquired a kind of sixth sense that seemed a reliable pilot. My feet became surer, learning when to brace and when they could afford to slide a little. The mere wading became almost a subconscious affair, allowing some of my attention to focus on the cast. Here only the sense of touch gave some dim cognizance of the lay of the line, for even the big White Miller could rarely be seen.

But my first half hour of casting was a blind and groping thing. Lengthening line overmuch was plainly disastrous, resulting in a bad hang-up of my backcast in the first few minutes of play. Holding myself to a routine of twenty-five-foot casts I did better. Miraculously the White Miller stayed with me. Occasionally I could see it go by as I flicked it back and forth, a small winged ghost in the smother of the dark. Fishing the central water I could judge the fly's whereabouts, the pull of the current giving the clue. Elsewhere the sense of touch was too indelicate to avail: back eddies close inshore, still pockets on the downstream side of boulders, broad shallows of a slow deliberate drift. In such places I relied on luck alone.

Night fishing with bait doubtless holds some of the thrills which fly fishermen persistently deny themselves. To swing a field mouse or a mole or an eight-inch chub downstream is to acknowledge the possibility of an enormous trout taking hold. But there are other nocturnal dramas to which even the fly fisherman has entrée. Who has witnessed or heard the charge of a great trout through the shallows in pursuit of chub, while the surface erupts with the fleeing prey, will not soon forget it. At night all of nature is hunting or hunted. The night sounds record the activities of the little people, the muskrat, fox, raccoon and owl, the alarm of an awakened bird in the streamside alders, the far high question of a heron swinging over the woods way aloft. While the world of man draws into itself and is muted, the world of nature is active and unquiet. This is the daytime of half the wild community, the business hours of the night hunters. You are close to the heart of nature at night, nearer the secret shy truths that come into the open after dark.

The ghostly river murmured ahead of me and I followed it under the stars. The dark water and dark air became as a single element. The night welded the two; I could not see where one left off and the other began and I seemed a part of this anonymity of all creation.

I came out of that semihypnosis with a start, realizing all at once that I was connected with some active part of the darkness. No whim of the current, however freakish, could have effected that quality of tension which had seized in this moment upon my line and rod. The strike of a big brown trout in the dark, as I learned that night, has no counterpart in stream fishing. It is a slow and stealthy and ominous pull, a quiet warning, calm as the air before a storm. I had underrated the power behind this almost hesitant connection for now the initial rush downstream amazed me with its force. The vibrant weight convulsed rod and line with a strain that seemed insupportable. The moment of that rush was charged with the desperate hope that I could turn it before it reached a pitch of fast water immediately below. The moment dragged out in the darkness with the complaining reel giving up yard after yard, and I knew that additional pressure would be needed. I applied it, expecting a break. But everything held. The fish came up short and now, reluctantly, it yielded to the reel.

Beyond that point there is need to cite only the factor of luck which alone was decisive. Making no second major effort downstream the fish was fought in a broad slow run where no sunken snag facilitated its escape and where the footing, even in the dark, was not insecure. Fearful of the water below I worked the trout gently upstream, let it run a little, reeled back what it took, let it run again, keeping it always within limits and still fearing a final break of the leader. But it came to me after a while, slowly through the black water. A surface surge of the exhausted body, close up, was audible above the undertone of the river. The net lifted it clear at last, its head and upper body almost out of the frame. By the flashlight's beam I killed it with a stone, then held it silhouetted against the night sky.

If this were a technical book this chapter could be called *When to Find the Quarry,* a nice sequel to the previous one explaining where to find same. The approved textbooks have it, if they touch on such elementary knowledge at all, that April is a good time for the wormer, June for the dry-fly man. I am no longer a wormer, often a dry-fly man, but I am no beginner (in point of time served) and I give it as a mature opinion that very likely the best of all trout-fishing times are March, which is before the season opens, October, after the season has closed, and the times in season when you are not on the stream.

In March it all lies ahead of you: the good times and bad, the full creels and the empty, the moments of ecstasy and of aching disappointment, the look of water and woods and meadows and skies, the renewed companionships of camp, the June evenings when the hatch gathers and the air is electric with the possibility of a three-pounder, the joy in a good rod's performance and the misery of hang-ups, all the delight and labor and pain of another fishing year. All before you, now in March. The curtain lifts.

Or in October, when it is gone again, when another winter must forge its iron and another spring melt it down. Now the departed season abides with you as a composite memory of a temperate and restful color, studded here and there with bright unforgettable gleamings. A sense of relief rather than regret attends the season's passing; a responsibility is lifted and a strain eased. You can visit your stream in the deep autumn and know a peace in viewing it now without the inner thrusts of its angling problems. You can look at its sun and shadow and feel its wind for what they are, not as strategic factors in your casting. It is pure ease and calm in October, unfretted by the urgencies of June. Leaves fall into a pool like the faded memories of the summer; the water is black and cold and slow, waiting for the ice.

But the ideal time for sheer perfection of fishing is ever the time when circumstance keeps you away from the stream. Every trout season has its peak, its climax of a few successive days when all the elements combine to achieve the ultimate ideal. You may study the almanacs, consult your records of past years, time your affairs to let you free when the time is *right*. But still you will miss it. You will not miss, however, the honored greeting of guides, hotelkeepers and the native gentry who meet you at the end of your northward migration. It is ever the same: "You should have been here last week." This simple dictum is elaborated, then, by a recital of the rain or cold spell which has spoiled the prime of the water, and by the recounting of sundry fabulous catches made in the peak days just gone. . . . And if you are not greeted thus, beware. Three or four days after your return home a wire will reach you. "Come up again. They're hitting." (When you cannot possibly comply.) Or a penciled and labored letter: "You ought to be here now," with the usual embellishments.

If you want your trout stream to be perfect, keep away from it.

Luck vs. Skill 7

The trout angler probably assays a slighter content of superstition than the deep-sea fisherman or even the caster and troller for bass and pickerel. Possibly these various degrees of addiction to the occult are in direct ratio to the extent and depth of each fisherman's water.

The ocean has ever been man's favorite repository of mystery and dark legend. Strange and fearsome creatures come up to the surface of the sea in the drawn nets. These are visible evidence of that unapprehended life of the submarine grottoes, an otherworld of such forms as are foreign to the land and the shallow land-bound waters. Some of this dusky inscrutable character of the sea may well have been instilled into those who for generations have dropped their lines and nets into its depths. One whose seine brings up such oddities as giant rays and ocean sunfish may be a bit more vulnerable to superstitions and offside beliefs.

The bass fisherman has a semblance of sanity as he sits in the stern sheets of a rowboat heaving his plug at the edge of the lily pads. Yet he too may harbor a nice assortment of bats under the crown of his Stetson. No such fathomless pits of the unknown lie beneath his skiff as those under the deep-sea man's trawler, yet he is fishing over a bottom he can neither see nor fully understand.

The trouter is closer to the known and familiar elements of the land. Much of his fishing water has a bottom he not only can see but can feel with the soles of his waders, and at low water becomes dry land, frankly open to his minute inspection. His mystery has definite limitations: nowhere is he directly connected by water with the crypts of Hades. Yet even in him are traces of those murky fancies which fishing seems to synthesize in its victims.

Certain common superstitions are to be met with everywhere in the trout country. Probably others less common could be unearthed but only by an efficient snooper for likely these are more jealously guarded. A belief in charms and amulets and hoodoos is not usually advertised by the victim. He is a little ashamed of it; while not doubting his own sanity he fears that others may do so if he reveals any sign of intercourse with demons. Those loud proclaimers of a belief in this or that sorcery are mere pretenders, affecting an identification with witchcraft which they do not have at all.

To a couple of trout anglers of my acquaintance the worst and most frequently committed faux pas of all those with which fishermen are commonly affronted by the lay public is the wishing of luck. The layman simply does not know the amenities (and Emily Post is so far silent). When he says, with a cheerful wave of his hand, "Wish you luck," or "Good luck to you," his curse is uttered in good faith. Perhaps he even believes his wish will be fulfilled and certainly he has no idea that he is ruining a day with his supposedly innocuous words. If he should say "Tight lines," or "Leave a few for seed," he would not be offensive at all. But nine times in ten the word "luck" is prominent in his felicitations, bringing the blight immediately upon a fishing day.

I know one who will go to any length to avoid the mention of a proposed fishing trip for fear that someone will wish him luck. Driving to a trout stream he will make no stop anywhere en route. A stop means a chance engagement in talk with a gas pump attendant or the man in the corner cigar store who will almost certainly utter the fatal words. Hence his gasoline tank and his tobacco pouch are full when he leaves home. If his trip is so long that a stop must be made on the way he will wear his street clothes and pack his fishing gear out of sight. Disguised thus as a traveling salesman or mere tourist he runs little chance that any misguided well-wisher will fasten the hoodoo upon him.

Keeping records and various tabulated data on the number and size of trout caught, flies used, weather and whatnot is a business pursued by those practical souls who do not suffer from—or enjoy —superstitions.

Following a run of fairly prosperous sessions astream, one of my angling friends fell to musing upon his totals. I cautioned him not to think of them but the warning might as well have been left unsaid. His statistical venture, at first generalized and harmless, grew specific and deeply involved. Presently he was committing many things to paper. Ruled lines drew themselves out, column after column of figures and notes got themselves down in black and white. His interest in the job quickened to excitement. It saddened me no little to see this birth of another bookkeeping angler, another statistician to menace the trout waters, for this chap had seemed above this petty addiction. But despite his burgeoning enthusiasm I could feel a sinister and dark influence growing in that room, almost as if the lights were dimming. I knew what it was: the scowl of one of the Imps, of course. Something else was being put down in one of *its* books, and filed for future reference.

And not far in the future, either. Two days after that fateful evening we were on the stream again. The day was ideal for the dry fly, cloudy and cool and still, with a northeasterly prescience of rain. All afternoon flies were over the water and no hour was without a few authentic rises. In the deep dusk, after six hours of the sort of fishing I enjoy only a few times a season, I walked back to the car. My partner was there ahead of me, dejectedly folding up his gear. He shook his head as I approached.

"Just the day I thought it would be good, too," he said. "You get anything?"

I opened my creel and put it under a headlamp for his inspection. He drew out a couple of the better ones and looked at them in silence. He is unaccustomed to this sort of ratio of my creel to his.

He was less than usually talkative on the drive home. I guessed that he was brooding upon his records, trying to reconcile today's blank with his newfound delight in statistics. How, he was thinking, would this goose egg appear in his neat columns headed "fish taken," "fish released," "fish killed"?

The weather held and the next afternoon we were at it again. I did not fare so well as the day before but I brought back three fair trout to the car when the darkness closed down. This time my partner was not there ahead of me; indeed half an hour elapsed before I heard his waders clump-clumping up the path from the stream. From their sound I could guess the story. When you have fished with a man for years on end you can almost measure his luck by the tempo of his homeward gait.

I gave him the rhetorical question and he raised his creel lid under the headlamps as I had done the night before. "This is our deluxe model, madam," he began, drawing forth a one-pound rainbow. A ten-inch brown emerged next. "A type sample for the trade —a popular number for those who must consider price."

There were six all told—deluxes, type samples, and in-betweens. His normal ascendancy was reestablished. The two to one ratio proved that all again was well with the world, recovery had set in, business was definitely on the upgrade, he could go home to his wife and children and look them in the face.

"It will look good in the record book," I ventured.

"No," he said, after a pause. "It won't. The record book was burned last night."

Other fishermen's fortunes are allergic to different species of pollen. Grass in the creel when starting out will put a pox on many an angler's day. Grass or ferns or moss—anything that anticipates a caught trout. That is a gesture of bravado or overconfidence, hence it incurs the disfavor of the gods who expect and appreciate humility in their subjects. Tackle in the creel until the first trout is killed, and then the ritual of transferring tackle to pockets and gathering damp vegetation for the bedding-down of the trout is much better. Such humble procedure will take you right into the hearts of the Crimson Imps who determine your sporting destinies. Indeed there are disciples so abject that they almost fear to go astream with a creel, whether grassed or not. The mere creel could insult the presiding deities, put you on record as taking for granted the capture of trout. But surely such salaaming and kowtowing could go too far. It might produce a devotee so groveling that he would not carry even a rod.

Other strange notions are not concerned with humility before the gods, and these victimize not only the timid souls of fishing but the most virile and aggressive practitioners. A trout hooked and netted on the first cast of the day is a widely accepted token of failure to follow. Hours destitute of a strike are sure to ensue, or a good trout hooked and lost. This special superstition, one of the best liked of any, has its kin in other fields. An occasional ballplayer is secretly or openly sad when his team wins its first game of the season, and some poker players will throw down three kings rather than open the first pot.

The idea that a trout cannot be caught under a bridge is a rather ordinary, first-reader superstition, shared by hundreds of mere beginners in witchcraft, including myself. I am a little ashamed that so popular a bugaboo has claimed me. Yet I find myself observing it in the majority of cases. If going up and over a bridge is easier than wading and casting through, I am inclined to go up and over no matter how troutish the dark water underneath. I simply do not catch trout under bridges.

Rarer perversions are to be unearthed only by acute and persistent observation; probably those few which have been surprised are but a minute fraction of the swarms hatched in the secret dusks of the minds of fishermen. Not all are darkly precautionary against evil. Some are buoyant and positive, concerned with good luck only. The opportunity to exercise them is a rare piece of fortune while the lack is not inimical to good luck but merely neutral.

A fisherman once confided to me, while we ventured upon the edges of this hazardous terrain, that his sole and complete talisman was the finding of a trillium. This charm was so potent that his faith in it afforded him full release from the lesser taboos such as being wished luck, the carrying of a grassed creel and all similar folderol to which he had deferred in the days of his novitiate. It had to be an unexpected find. Looking for a trillium, even wandering near a spot where he thought they grew, had no efficacy at all. He had once stumbled upon a white one, so long ago that it would have died out of his memory except for the sequel. He had been approaching a favorite pool—a piece of water which had given up many a good trout but so far in that season had yielded him nothing. This time, however, he hooked and landed a two-pound brown, the biggest fish of his career. The fact of the trillium had escaped his notice then; indeed it was only the strange habit of his mind to associate apparent trifles with matters of large import that recalled the incident, perfectly dovetailed, the next time his eye caught the gleam of one of these blooms, tropically brilliant in the northern underbrush. That was years later (the trillium was not a common flower in the area of his fishing) but his mind flashed him the bygone hookup with the two-pounder, still tops in his records. In the lip of a long pool just below—with the flower still visible from his casting spot—he snagged into another heavy fish. In minutes he had it in the net, in an hour on a butcher-store scales. Two pounds, again. This time the trillium had been a purple one; that proved the color not a mitigating factor.

And that was not all. His voice became solemn and hushed. It had worked a third time, this very morning. This time the bloom had been white but the trout had been of the usual trillium-begotten proportions. See? He opened his overlarge creel and drew out the fish. He needed no butcher store this time. From a pocket he produced a scales, hung the fish on it and held it up for me to witness the fulfillment of his miracle. Two pounds.

"Where is the trillium?" I asked, tastelessly.

"Oh, I never pick them," he said. "I look at them once, then look away. I try even to forget where I saw them. . . . Say, you won't mention this to a soul?"

And it is only in the pure spirit of research that I give it to you here. This chap was no seeker of favors; he was humbly appreciative of the largess bestowed, without asking for more. Of course he never went back to one of his potent blooms to see if it would work a second time. That would be asking too much and conceivably could lose him his high apostolic privilege.

Practical men can see a kingfisher pick a chub out of the shallows and think only that they have witnessed an interesting act of wild life. Others, properly steeped in the lore of sorcery, appreciate the great fortune implicit in this spectacle. Having witnessed the kingfisher's kill they will go forth, armed with something of the bird's professionalism, and catch themselves a few trout. This division of the lore, like most of the others, has its by-products, its meanderings from the central principle. A lone traveler over one of these most shadowy bypaths of the black arts is one of whom I have dark rumor. This one will go to some pains to spy upon a heron catching frogs. If there is a heron-haunted pond or backwater near his stream he will give it a look, before fishing, just in case. This has caused no small amount of eyebrow-lifting among the more smug and respectable disciples of orthodox magic. He has been warned that trout fishermen should have no truck with frogs but he has a pat reply that neither should they traffic with chub and dace, the natural prey of kingfishers.

It is hard to define where orthodoxy leaves off and heterodoxy begins. How do you place the notion that the likelihood of heavy creels is enhanced by wearing a blue bow necktie with white polka dots, season after season, upon *all* of one's appearances astream? Or that parking your car on the left side of the road will bring about the same result? Or that fishing with a woman in the party, or indeed with a woman anywhere on the stream, is fatal to your chances? Are those notions accepted as sound, and if not, why?

But you must never question. The truly expert demonologists will tell you that you must never analyze or attempt to find reasons, or be intolerant of the other fellow's taboos and fetishes.

It is easy to remember what is pleasant to remember, easy to believe what one wants to believe, and to these human frailties most of the legends of luck owe their vitality. The successes, the times when the charm worked, are remembered but the times when it failed are forgotten. Fortune-tellers owe such credence as they enjoy to the same human quirk, the capacity to remember one prediction that came true and to forget ten that didn't. Conceivably much fishing success ascribed to luck is more properly attributed to skill. Skill gets to be an old habit with some anglers. These grow so accustomed to their proficiency they are unconscious of it; they wear it as they wear their fishing jackets with never a thought that they've got it on, so easy is its fit. With such men outstanding success is often credited to luck in one form or another. But the unobtrusive skill was there all the time, functioning, making hard spots look easy, dealing smoothly with each situation as it arose. Take away that high talent and what is termed good luck might vanish as well.

Of course there *is* much pure luck, good or bad, in trout fishing. Happenings beyond human control can result in a good fish caught or lost. A fine field lies open here to sophistical meandering. The pasture bars are down but there is no need to go far inside. . . . If half of your fly's hook breaks off midway in the battle with a big one you will lose that trout in a trice. It can be reasoned that you should have detected the hook's weakness beforehand and discarded it, but this may be asking too much. A fisherman frequently examines his leader and line but he takes the steel of his hook for granted. If he looks at it now and then to make sure it is barbed and sharp he is giving to prudence all it deserves. The loss of that fish is, I think, luck of the worst kind. So is it luck when a sudden thunderstorm puts down a fine rise of trout in the only hour you could give to fishing.

On unknown water I have the feeling that luck—good or bad, depending on my success—is with me. On familiar streams where I am dealing with known terrain and fairly well conjectured probabilities of trout, this feeling is minimized. Yet it is always present, in greater or less degree. It assumes importance in inverse proportion to the contents of my creel. A run of fishless days will have me believing I am hexed, that almost every move I make has some unlucky significance. But in a spell of successful days I am inclined to forget the factor of luck. Success begets confidence and confidence begets success, and that fine upward spiral is the best restorative of streamside sanity. It will scatter all the gremlins beyond the reach of your farthest cast.

Fish Sense 8

On a June evening years ago I was walking along a streamside path on my way back to my car. My rod was disjointed, my gear stowed; I was through for the day. It had been an almost scoreless session: two small brown trout lay on the moss in my creel. The day had been, for me, one of those duds which can occur in the best of the fly season. No definite evening rise had occurred though a fair hatch of insects had been on the water.

The path took a straight course along the edge of a wide field. Immediately on the right was the stream, a slow and curveless stretch of it bordering the field, separated from the field only by a low margin of growth. Three fishermen, all strange to me, were a little ahead on the same path, apparently headed home as I was. The rods of two of the party were down; that of the third member, in the rear of the little procession, was still assembled.

As they trudged along, a hundred yards ahead of me, the rear guard hesitated occasionally to glance at the water. Five or six brief inspections seemed to convey nothing of moment to him but on the next one he stopped, stepped down to the stream, waded out a little way and commenced casting. The two men just ahead of him looked around, noticed his defection from the ranks but went on.

From my point on the path at that moment I could see every foot of the water under his brief scrutiny. No sign of a rise had been anywhere upon it.

What, then, had so intrigued his attention? Probably, I thought, he had raised a fish there earlier in the day and was now trying it a second time, or he had had other past experience to draw him to this place. Later investigation disproved both hypotheses.

Letting the question hang in the air I went ahead to watch him. His first cast, a short throw of twenty-five feet up the east bank, drew no response. His second, six feet beyond the first, brought immediately a spectacular leaping rise and in a few minutes a one-pound rainbow was in his net. The brief struggle was dexterously handled, all of it being confined to the west side of the stream well away from the point of the rise. The angler looked up, saw me and smiled but said nothing while he waded quietly ashore, killed the trout and put it in his creel. As he raised the creel lid to receive this latest entry I caught a glimpse of the contents.

"Offhand," I said, "it looks about ten fish and about six pounds."

"Pretty close," he said. "Nine counting this one. I think it will be ten in a moment. Another one's in there—at least one. . . . Want to try him?"

I declined with thanks and a gesture of my disjointed rod. "I'm folded up. Besides, you marked him down, somehow. Damned if I know how. I'd have passed that water—and I noticed your two partners passed it."

"It looked trouty," he said. He lit a cigarette and squatted on the bank. "All that commotion may have put the other one down."

Further than the fact that "it looked trouty" no explanation was forthcoming as to why he had stopped here so abruptly to fish just these few feet of water among several hundred similar feet upstream and down. I reflected that almost all water can at times look trouty to me, and that this flat drift looked probably as untrouty, according to my obviously fallible standards, as any water I had seen today. I reflected also upon his pronouncement that another trout was there. He had not said *perhaps* or *maybe*. He had said "Another one's in there—at least one." There was something impressive about his quiet assurance upon matters which to me have always been essentially speculative. It was impressive because of the weight of supporting evidence in his creel and because it had no taint of the smugness often implicit in the statements of opinionated nobodies. It was offhand and casual but convincing as truth.

In its strange presence I could not ask the questions I wanted to ask. Sit still and watch, his taciturn figure seemed to say. Never mind reasons.

So I sat, as he finished his cigarette there in the deepening dusk, and tried to appraise him. So far as appearances could be informative he was undistinguished. A slight and graying man, he looked as if he had been banged around a good deal by life, but had survived it all by a kind of passive but tough durability, that armor by which the meek intend to inherit the earth. His rod and general ensemble of gear were mediocre, his clothes had seen long service at an office desk and in the commuting trains before they had been pensioned off to take their declining years astream. . . . Never mind that either, I reminded myself. The trout in this fellow's creel and his uncanny precision in spotting that last one had the ascendancy over all else.

He went easily into the stream again. The casting commenced, the false casts, the lengthening of line, and while it was executed with a fair skill it was short of the genuine artistry which that creelful would seem to presuppose. These contradictions annoyed me a little. Here was an apparently ordinary fisherman getting extraordinary results.

The first cast and the second and the third evoked nothing. I began to wonder about that conviction of his but if any doubt were on his features I could not perceive it. He went ahead in his methodical style, throwing his dry fly into the gloom upstream. His fourth cast floated back to him, and his fifth. But on the sixth the eruption of a savage rise was white in the twilight. A big rainbow danced across half the width of the stream, sounded for a moment, leaped again, ran the gamut of the usual rainbow repertoire and came at last to net. The man waded ashore and added this new and largest item to his collection.

"That's all for tonight," he said, and started to take down his rod.

Again I wanted to fire questions at him and again I was unable to. I said, "A great show," or something like that, and went on up the path.

Another car had been parked near mine; leaning against it were the two companions of the deadly one, waiting for him. As I approached I wondered if they knew how deadly he was, or if perhaps they too had the same talent. I stopped, deciding that I would ask some questions here and if possible decode certain secrets which manifestly had been eluding me these many years.

"Your friend took two good rainbows in the last fifteen minutes," I began. "As many fish as I've taken all day—and much better."

They evinced no surprise.

"One more than I've taken all day," confessed one.

"And from the unlikeliest water of the whole creek," the other added, "if he got 'em both where we just left him."

"That's where," I said. These replies were reassuring, indicating at once that I was in the company of average men, not of magicians. I could talk to these two on their level, question them as man to man, not as a small boy to his father.

"Is it the usual thing with him?"

"I suppose so. You saw his creel, didn't you? We don't fish with him often, in fact he doesn't fish much himself. Can't get away from his job except now and then."

"But he must have fished a great deal in the past. The way he went at it, just now—"

"I know—the certainty, the absence of any doubt. I guess he has fished a good bit—as a boy, perhaps. . . . The way you saw him take those two is the way he's been doing it all day—ambling up and down, looking at the water here and there and suddenly deciding to try some place, like as not a place I wouldn't waste a minute on. And every spot of water I've seen him try today held a trout, except one. That one proved him human, I guess." He laughed a short grunt of a laugh, as if at the futility of his own efforts, and lit his pipe. "*I* don't know how he does it."

Well, apparently I was getting nowhere. The heart of the mystery was impenetrable as ever.

The first speaker spoke again slowly, as if he had studied his words in advance. "Neither he nor his methods yield to any sort of analysis. They are spontaneous and impulsive—at least they seem to be —yet invariably right. . . . I have fished for trout a good many years and frankly I don't consider myself a dub at this business. On a couple of days this season I took the limit from this stream. But today it beat me."

"Same," I said.

"Well, you see what *he* has done with it—the same day you and I had to work with. Would you call it a dry-fly day?"

"I was sure they'd work."

"Me too, though I did experiment with wets a little, out of sheer desperation, late this afternoon and caught my only fish of the day on one of 'em. He, however, could see plenty of reason for wets. He told me he'd been fishing them all day, until nearly dark, and in fact took all his trout, except the two you saw, on wet flies. He changed to drys just before you met him—just after I caught my one trout and about the time I was thinking wet flies might redeem my day after all. Apparently the wrongest moment of the day to have such a hunch."

"You didn't switch to wets when you saw his success with them?"

"I didn't see it until tonight. I was way downstream, out of his sight all day, even at lunch. Besides, I probably wouldn't have switched—I am stubborn enough, crazy enough, to try to pit my system against his. . . . John, my partner here, switched early. But don't ask John how *he* made out." His laugh was a kind of appraisal of both their failures.

He continued: "I have been thorough with nearly a mile of water today. My wrists and legs are shot. But the wrist of our friend has been conserved and what exercise his legs have had has been mostly on dry land, promenading the banks on his sentry go. And even that exercise has been light. Walk fifty yards, stop, sit down and watch the water a while. If it 'looks trouty' go in and cast and catch a trout. If it doesn't, move on fifty yards and sit down again. He spends half of his fishing days on his fanny—an ideal I had considered unattainable in fly-fishing. And while he's sitting he *thinks* like a trout."

The talk was still getting me nowhere. I had stopped to learn something from these consorts of genius, not to be further mystified. But now the genius himself was coming up the path and our discussion of his rare talents must cease. There was a gentle austerity about him, an unapproachability that kept you ten feet away. It protected him as the guardrail protects a priceless museum piece.

The man who had been talking sighed softly into the darkness that was now deep and firefly-studded. "I have heard or read of a rare thing called 'fish sense,' " he said. "If it exists, this guy has it."

Call it "fish sense" or what you will, it is the gift of perhaps one trout fisherman in every ten thousand. In the course of a lifetime you may meet one such wizard, or two or three. If you never meet one at all you will be fortunate, for nothing is quite so dispiriting to your estimate of your own ability as to measure it against his.

Reasons for this phenomenon are simply not discernible. It is not dependent upon a technical virtuosity with tackle or a profound knowledge of insects. Those in the very top echelons of angling have not necessarily been singed by that rare bright flame which is fish sense.

Its possessor seems a transcendentalist in his fishing. He will be orthodox today and get his creelful; tomorrow he will flout all the theories and get his creelful again. He will take trout in the shallows when every expert on the stream is fishing the pools. He will kill the limit on nymphs or wet flies when the accumulated wisdom of your fishing life tells you dry flies hold a greater promise. Possibly at times even he is skunked. But he seems to know where a trout lies at any given moment and what will take it, and that is the simple but great sum of his genius. *How* he knows is something else. Probably a couple of planets were in rare and favorable conjunction at his birth.

Over many seasons I have met only one other fisherman who seemed possessed of that exceptional faculty. His exploits are not to be recorded at length here: they had the monotony of perfection. I mention him to emphasize the extreme infrequency of his kind, and because his character and the events attending that meeting are worthy of mention.

At the time I encountered him he was operating over a northern stream in the late season. The weather of that week was such as to try the patience of a saint and to upset the calculations of practically all the fly-fishing sinners who lived through it. In the evening of the first day a sudden and violent thunderstorm put down a brief but promising rise of trout. The evening of the second day was a duplicate of the first, that of the third a triplicate. Three times in succession the defeated and dripping fishermen—myself among them— dragged back from the stream with empty creels, after two hours of intimacy with a downpour and lightning.

Not, however, he of the uncanny insight who happened to be at the same camp. The camp had a tight roof and this fellow was not prone to forego its advantages in such weather unless there were trout to compensate him for his soaking. Clearly he discounted such compensation for he remained dryly and comfortably within while the others were concurrently drenched and whitewashed.

During the hot mornings and afternoons of this week he would take a little easy and casual fishing. One of us who accompanied him for a morning reported: "He takes 'em all along, almost everywhere he casts. And regardless of size he releases every other one. Said it was one of his rules." Yet his creel consistently averaged twice the numerical and avoirdupois content of any other in the party.

He was quiet about it, however. Some characters could have been thoroughly objectionable in his position. The I-told-you-so type would have made easy capital of that third evening when those on the stream retired, sodden and empty-handed, to the stronghold he had refused to abandon. He voiced a few words of polite chagrin at the failure of the others, as if he knew that effusiveness could be misinterpreted by the tired nerves and strained tempers of his campmates. His position was delicate indeed but he held its precarious balance intact.

The fourth evening threatened to be like the others. We could see it coming on, and the disgusted majority who had braved the other three were unanimous in their veto of any further attempt.

I stood with the modest and proficient one, looking at the ominous black pile-up in the western sky.

"Tonight," he said, quietly, "I think the rain will be different— short showers with spaces between and maybe some active feeding in the intervals. Nymphing, possibly."

"You're going to try it?"

"I'm tempted to. Want to go?"

I looked at him a moment, wondering. Maybe he didn't believe what he said about the rain but thought he was *obliged* to go, this once, merely to share the discomfort the others had endured.

"No," I said, finally. I had had in truth enough of that sort of fishing, even if he were right that the rain would be "different." But there might have been another reason: some shadowy omen of my failure against his success. I would repeat my blank of the previous evenings, but he would score as he always did. Maybe I shied from a final contrast of his ability and mine, though in such a comparison I had no reason or need to be proud.

He went out, alone, as the first salvo of thunder reverberated over the darkening heavens. We watched him from the porch of the cabin as he receded down the slope toward the water. We stood there in silence as he disappeared upstream. In the past few days he had attained an extraordinary stature among us. Our feeling was unacknowledged but each of us knew it was shared by the others.

The storm banged through the hills for two hours. The rain fell as he had predicted, in violent brief spasms with intervals between, but the lightning was almost incessant. A calm darkness came at length but he did not return. Sometime after dark one of us spoke of the possibility of a fall, a broken leg perhaps. You could never tell —it had been known to happen. Someone produced a flashlight and as if at a word of command we went out and upstream. And we found him after a while, or what was left of him, under a lightning-riven hemlock at the foot of a long pool.

Not until later, while arranging such of his effects as had been spared by the unpredictable technique of the lightning, did we discover the tiny nymph on his tippet and the six trout in his creel.

Big Ones 9

In that moment when his first big fish comes to net, a trout angler is awarded a kind of diploma. From now on he has a changed feeling for fishing, a heightened respect for his quarry and for the stream that yielded the big one. And though he doesn't admit it, he has also an additional cubit of dignity. The challenge has been met; that ultimate encounter, long anticipated with a mixture of confidence and doubt, has been joined at last and won. This prize in his net is the grail of many pilgrimages, the reward of long and patient pain.

"Big fish" may seem an elastic term but on the trout waters of the Northeast the designation is fairly exact. It means a dimension well beyond the usual run—a trout of eighteen inches to five pounds or more, though the latter are the rare giants of the northeastern streams and seldom taken on light fly-fishing tackle. On these waters the majority of trout caught are seven to twelve inches in length. The thirteen-, fourteen- and fifteen-inchers are distinguished enough to be much desired. But they are not *big*. Trout of sixteen or seventeen inches are rare, so rare in most water as to be worthy of photographs, postcards to friends and the eventual ministrations of a taxidermist.

But these, too, are not *big*. The non-trout-fishing layman, seeing one of this ilk, might remark "nice fish" and think no more of it during the rest of his nonfishing life. Perhaps the sure way to get an accurate pronouncement upon whether or not a trout is *big* is to show it to a man who has never had a trout rod in his hand or a trout thought in his head. Then record his first spontaneous reaction, if any. If not any, your fish is not *big*. Such a man is used to seeing bluefish and shad on counters in fish stores. His forbears for generations have seen bluefish and shad on counters in fish stores. It is useless to explain to him that the trout, though a superior game fish, seldom attains the length of even the common run of bluefish and shad. To him a fish is something with scales and fins, about two feet long and four pounds heavy. If he has thought about it at all he knows that a trout is a fish, hence a trout should be two feet long and four pounds heavy. All right, you show him that sixteen-inch rainbow who slammed your fan-wing Royal in the dusk and carried it from the smooth lip of the pool to the riffle at the head so fast that you fed it line with a prayer—that fish who jumped two clear feet in the air and danced on its tail over half the pool's surface before it gave in at last and was brought, expiring, to net. You show him that sixteen-inch, one-and-a-quarter-pound beauty, and all the fish-store shad and bluefish will come into his mind. He will grunt, "Um-m, nice trout," and go back to his calculations upon the probability of a bull movement in Steel.

That sixteen-incher is not *big* either. But a twenty- to twenty-four-inch trout will draw some snort of amazement even from the shoppers for shad. From those who fish for trout as you do—they who know the extreme rarity of anything that long with spots—your twenty- to twenty-four-incher will evoke something more profound than mere amazement. A gleam of something approaching religious wonder will kindle in the eyes of such beholders. Your two-foot trout is no mere big fish to them. It is the elusive stuff of dreams crystallized into solid matter before their eyes. It is achieved ambition, pure success in a form that can be touched and hefted, the ultimate secret of dark water revealed. Those who have landed a comparable fish know your experience; those who have not will imagine that experience as it never was. For it does not, after all, hold quite the content of dynamite and drama with which imagination can invest it. The feel of a one-pounder hung on a light rod and 4X leader leads to exaggerated ideas about the feel of the giants of three pounds and up. The ratio of violence is perhaps less than three to one.

The average angler will run into a big one sooner or later, either by purposeful design or pure accident. If the former he is prepared with tackle that will hold the giant and is apt to be less impressed with such prowess as is displayed. But if, as rarely happens, he connects with one of these torpedoes while casually throwing a #14 dry fly over smallish water in the hope of raising a ten-incher, he will likely be shocked into an estimate far exceeding the actuality. This surprise trout may well get away before the fisherman gets a good look at it, and go down in history as "at least twenty inches and three pounds." But likely it was not more than sixteen inches and a pound and a half. A fish that size can feel tremendously heavy on light gear and is big enough to carry away a fine leader if not adroitly handled.

Probably most large trout that get away are those hooked in small water or in big water while angling for small fish. The shock of surprise is inimical to skillful handling. Streams holding big trout rarely yield one to a fly in the daylight hours, hence most daytime fly-fishing is for the average sizes. The surprise big one, if landed, is a more worthy capture than the big one deliberately sought. Taken on a small fly and light leader it is free to do battle against minimum odds.

But the purposeful conspiring for big trout has at least the thrill of anticipation and, if successful, the satisfaction of any job consummated according to design. On the prowl for a three-pounder you become a specialist; you have renounced the easier rewards of small ones for the rare chance of a whopper. The thing has the gambling appeal of any long shot. Swinging a big streamer into the twilight shallows is one of the headier adventures of trout fishing. It is a grand way to end a day of finicky maneuvers with dry flies. It caps a day of precision with an hour of gusto and sends you home with your balance restored.

And maybe you will go home with something more tangible wrought from this hour of dusk in the long pebbly shallows. Look and listen and you may see and hear a big brown move into the shoals from his day-long hideout. In the June twilights I have seen fish of twenty inches and upwards chasing chub a rod's length away, a great surge like a bow wave marking the course.

Cast your streamer across stream, let it go down with the current and retrieve it slowly. Jiggle it as it comes back to you and let it rest and sink a little now and again. In the darkening water it is a fine counterfeit of a live minnow lost from his school in the enemy country and disabled or tired. Wade slowly and quietly down and let the current have your streamer again and again. Keep the contingency of a strike in the forefront of your mind without excluding all else. There are other things: the night sounds along shore, the caress of the night peace along the flanks of the country, the sudden coinage of fireflies in the dark air. Let these pleasant concerns command you a little.

For the strike of a big brown in the dusk or the dark is not explosive; it will not wrench you too violently out of any reverie. It will grow on you as you realize that something besides the current has engaged your streamer. But if the trout's strike is unspectacular your own response must be immediate and strong.

Now it starts. Now that reverie has left you and you are caught up full in the ecstasy of high strife. There is a moment now when your reel gives out a sound you have never heard it make. Yard after yard of precious line is leaving your guides, entering the water in this mad charge upstream or down.

Let it go for an instant. Then check, not abruptly but slowly, feeling his weight. You know how much line you have, including your backing; you know the approximate length of line when the strike occurred. The difference is your margin of safety—or part of it. The rest is hidden in the bed of the stream: rocks and roots and snags, a run of rough water below, and if he gets into any of these he is lost.

Then keep him away. Keep him in open water if you can and say a prayer for your tackle as you prepare to turn him. For you've got to turn him now. You can't let him get snagged or reach the end of your line at full speed.

Now apply the pressure. Something less than the breaking point usually suffices to turn any but the largest fish.

Does he come around? If he doesn't, hold him where he is with an even pressure or let him go a little farther if you dare. If he is

downstream, wade down with him, keeping a taut line. But don't try to horse him back; a lost fish will be the almost certain result.

If he does come around, half the battle is already yours. This point in the struggle with a big one holds, I think, the essence of victory as truly as the final moment of the net. You are calm at the end. You have known for some minutes that, barring an unlucky break, you will land your fish. But this central heat of strife is all uncertainty; it is your power against the trout's with no assurance as yet that yours will prevail. And then, at the point of greatest strain, it does. This is the moment that gives the feeling of command, the confidence that you and your gear are up to the emergency.

But it is not yet over. The rest is charged with many dangers and one of them is slack line. As he comes back to you strip in for all you're worth, and as he goes away again get your reel into play. Feed him line slowly with your left hand (which must grasp the rod too), and with your right reel in the slack between the reel and first guide. This is highly important: a mess of loose line here has lost many a big one. In the excitement of battle you can step on it, trip on it, foul it on a snag. Get that line stowed where it belongs, on the reel. From now on play the fish from the reel if you can. It is easy as he goes away but as he comes toward you you'll have to strip again, for the single-action trout spool is a slow retriever.

Wear him down. Relentless but gentle pressure does it. If he is truly big this may take a long while—twenty minutes or more. Be sure he is thoroughly tired before you yield to that growing temptation to finger the net. He will not get away now; if you have played him twenty minutes you may be sure he is well hooked. Give him a minute more to make certain; then draw him in easily, watching for that final surge which can lose him right here. Don't jab with the net. If possible, hold the net down-current from the fish and let the current ease the fish into the meshes. Then scoop.

If it is your first you may be excused anything at this moment: a shout into the quiet night, a dance all by yourself on the bank. But if it is your tenth your prospects of salvation may be much improved if with wetted hands you remove the streamer and turn the trout gently back to its element.

Some anglers release no large fish, knowing them to be predators upon smaller trout. Others, letting the balance of nature take care of itself, know a quiet and secret satisfaction in returning a big trout to the water.

But when you lose a big one midway in the battle the shock of loss seems insupportable. The ensuing emotion is comparable to nothing else in the psychological gamut. For an interval not measurable in time your whole being has been dedicated to that throbbing resistance on the end of your line. The pull of the fish against your wrist and against all your hopes and prayers is, so long as it holds, a perfect emotional satisfaction and a solvent of all your mundane cares. Its natural consummation, the capture, is the good aftermath of ecstasy, but the thwarting of that end is frustration in its most bitter form. He is a philosopher, indeed, who can smile as his pressure is suddenly unrequited, that tautness suddenly slack.

Probably every trout stream of fair size holds a few giant and well-nigh uncatchable fish about whose shadowy presences the legends have clustered. Never a season goes by without their being seen and heard, hooked and lost, and occasionally caught.

Years ago I fished a Delaware River tributary which long had had the reputation of harboring trout whose size and intelligence were alike remarkable. This stream was moderately stocked in the early season with browns and rainbows of ordinary stature. The rainbows eventually migrated downstream to larger water, possibly to the Delaware itself. The browns stayed. Good creels were customary through April and the first half of May. After that they became scarce; by the last week of June empty creels were the common lot. Those not familiar with this stream's reputation concluded that it was "fished out" of its early-season stockees. This theory held a percentage of the truth—maybe 10 percent, according to the old guard who had knowledge of the stream's legendary colossi. These maintained that the big fish had accounted for far more of the early-season stockees than had all the April and May anglers combined. This contention was not without its factual as well as imaginative appeal, as any close observer of that water in late June or early July would agree.

By then all evidence of small and medium trout had disappeared; the fine summer evenings wore on with almost no sign of a rising fish though the over-stream air was active with insects. I say "almost no sign" because there was occasionally a rise that would give you gooseflesh on the warmest evening. If one such occurred behind you, you looked around and saw the subsidence of the eruption and the wave rings spreading away, as if a ten-pound stone had been dropped in at that point. That, however, was a trout. In the course of the same evening you would see one come up. You would see the twenty-four-inch flanks roll on the surface or perhaps break clear, and the great fan of a tail follow the flanks down. Of course you would cast over it and if you were lucky at hundred-to-one shots you would draw a strike. Those were about the prevailing odds.

Those big trout were consistently and studiously sought but very few were taken. They constituted a kind of perennial population of that water, as against the unfortunate transients introduced every April, and they seemed wise in the ways of men. On a long-gone summer afternoon a brown trout we estimated at five pounds rose repeatedly, over a stretch of three hot bright hours, in the largest pool of the stream, a spread of water two hundred feet long and more than half as wide. Four anglers beside myself attended this matinee and a couple of them angled diligently for the star. He paid not the slightest attention to any item in the most varied assortment of flies and baits I have ever seen heaved at a single fish. But he continued to take his encores, rising to nothing that was visible on the surface, sometimes in midpool, sometimes inshore where we could marvel at his great spotted proportions, often within a foot of a nicely floating dry fly or other lure. We decided at length that he was not feeding but thumbing his nose at us, devoting the calm afternoon to the indulgence of his sardonic sense of humor. . . . He was stalked again that evening and far into the night by three or four rods with another great miscellany of baits attached. "He *must* feed sometime," you would hear, with more hope than faith in the speaker's tones. "A body that big needs a lot of food to sustain it." But that fish had his private and secure dining habits and they were not concerned with anything impaled upon or decorating a hook. He was not taken that night. I have no record of his subsequent history but I doubt that it ended at the hands of a fisherman.

I wished him well. I should have liked to take him, yet the presence of such omniscient giants as he, sentient in the deeps of a great pool, gave glamor to that stream and to all the fishing upon it. His capture at last would slay that inscrutable dark spirit. Brought to land and killed and folded into your creel or mine and carried home, he would be no more than five pounds of trout meat. I hoped always that when he died he would die the natural death of such trout as can evade all their violent enemies, and that his body would drift to sea in the closed season, unseen by any man.

Off the Main Current 10

Fishing the smallish out-of-the-way waters can be a welcome relief from the sturdier obligations of the big rivers. One long accustomed to the broad perspectives of the Beaverkill, East Branch, Esopus, et al., has his tried techniques for fishing each pool and riffle. He has campaigned too long on these rivers to need a plan of strategy in advance.

But the small waters, particularly if unfamiliar, present a host of problems. This fishing is tight and confined. Casting space is at a premium and must often be consciously sought out beforehand. The need for concealment in this short-range action is ever-present. If it is not "fine and far-off" fishing, assuredly it is fine.

Finicky too, and ticklish, and stealthy. On the big Junction Pool of the Beaverkill a false move—a slip of a wader or a single sloppy cast or retrieve—may have no ill effect at all, but on a pool six yards wide it will put down the fish you are stalking.

The little waters provide their rewards, often unexpected and bizarre—the close look at a feeding fish, the surprise strike of a big one in a small pool, the taking of a trout through alertness to some minute natural advantage. Though such fishing is difficult it has a sauce and piquancy one can relish now and then after the heavier fare of the big rivers.

In one of my more inept performances a rainbow of about an even pound came to my net on a smallish stream. This water, later heavily fished, was in that year seldom disturbed by anglers. It was a stream full of "likely-looking" places, richer in its variety of water than in the trout which should have inhabited it. One of the best of its covers was a deep fast run virtually unfishable with a fly from any angle. Both banks were overhung by the crowding forest and dropped steeply into four or five feet of water. No accommodation for the backcast was to be had on either side. At the upper and lower ends were wadable shallows but at each a right-angle bend presented a most formidable challenge to a cast. The deep and trouty run in between could be fished by drifting a wet fly or nymph down-current from the upper end, and that was the only way. Many times I passed that water with a fond and envious look and a sure conviction that all the trout in the stream were there.

But upon a day in the off-season a great wind blew a giant syca-more squarely across the stream at the center of the run. And lo, the following year a man could fish that water, standing or crouch-ing on the windfall and casting up or downstream as he liked.

Despite this new vantage point the casting was still difficult. The log was three or four feet above the stream and the depth of water beneath was such that you could conceivably drown if you fell off. The dense growth on either bank necessitated casting straight up or down the middle of the stream, here about eight feet wide. Otherwise your backcast would foul at once.

You could essay all this, if you were a dare-devil type, by walking out on the log and making a stand-up cast. Or, as I preferred for reasons of safety and partial concealment, you could straddle or side-saddle the log.

Adopting the latter, I sat on the log facing upstream and cast a dry fly up the center of the leaf-free alley over the deep and swift water below. One needed a fast retrieve of slack here and a smooth pickup of line and leader preparatory to his next cast. One could ask himself a question out there, too: If a strike, then what? Just what will you do if you hook a fish? Play it from the log and try to net it from the log, with the water three feet below? Or try to retreat to the bank with it? And suppose it runs under the log?

The answer was to proceed to the far end of the log where it was a little lower and where a well-concealed but stout limb gave you a foothold just under the surface. From this vantage point you could cast and play your fish.

But I didn't know the answer on this, my first attempt. Sitting there facing upstream, I was asking myself the usual questions of all who first hazard this dizzy casting platform when the strike occurred. Not, however, where it should have occurred, upstream, but behind me. That rainbow had taken a badly executed backcast in the instant the fly had flicked the water. The unlooked-for strike and splash behind me, the abrupt stoppage of my forward cast before it had even begun, and the feel of a fish far heavier than any I had expected, gave me another question. And this one seemed at the moment beyond my strained resources. I tried to turn, to face this untoward development downstream. I tried to lift one wadered leg over the log. But the log was slippery with recent rains. . . .

I suppose a fisherman's instinct is to hold his rod high when he goes overboard. I may have done so—that part was confused and blurry with the uprush of stream water. But my rod was still whole and the rainbow still hooked as I caught some foothold on bottom and emerged. I fought it out with that fish in water up to my chest, netted it at last in a shoreward pocket and climbed the steep bank.

The smaller waters offer, too, certain likely little holes and pockets easily unnoticed and passed by. If I fish them I think there may be a slight chance of a fish, but what chiefly involves me is the odd allure of ferreting out such obscure little eddies.

A stream of my acquaintance, in its casual meandering through a timbered bottomland, has a habit of dividing itself here and there, diverging into little rills that break abruptly from the parent water as if tired of the routine of the main current, to explore a while for themselves. Always they return to the mother channel before getting very far, like rebellious children who run away and become homesick at nightfall. Some of these rills are tiny indeed: when the summer foliage is prime they can be passed unnoticed by a man wading the central current. But they will bear investigation. The first time I put a fly into one of them—a purling pocket of water the size of a washtub—I was amazed by the quick strike of a ten-inch native. The commotion was like a tidal wave in the diminutive pool. A twenty-foot shark in a millpond would have borne the same proportional relationship to its habitat. Since that astounding catch I have never passed by this miniature basin in my forays up and down that stream. No further trout has come to my creel therefrom. Doubtless the one was all the reward I had any right to expect.

On completely strange water you will have more of such casual adventure. When you do not know what is around the next bend you have the essential makings of drama. A trout stream can play you no end of pranks. Sometimes you have warning of a sudden change of character: you can hear a steep falls ahead, or a long whip of white water, before you come to it. But often no advance word informs you of some abrupt departure upon a revolutionary tangent.

Small streams have been known to disappear underground, emerging many yards away and leaving you bereft of trout water until you have found the exit. One with such molelike proclivities was the Hell Diver Brook, a backcountry watercourse occasionally visited by us in earlier years. In that era the worm was the chief lure in our employ. On Hell Diver that was just as well, for the attempted manipulation of a fly would have evoked certain oaths of which, in those tender years, we had no graceful command.

The Hell Diver raced merrily down a laurel-dark ravine. Following it a little way and not knowing its name (one we gave it privately for it had no recognition on respected maps) you would have been impressed with the purity and innocence of its character. In April that character held pretty well; it was a fair-running brook all down the ravine. But come June and low water, disillusionment was in store for you—the sort you experience when an innocent child thumbs his nose at you. Some malicious influence got hold of that guileless youngster among brooks and turned him into a brat of the first water ere he had run a half mile of his career. For suddenly and without warning he plunged out of sight at your feet, leaving you, as it were, marooned on dry land, stranded far from home with all your trout gear and no place to use it.

Up to this point where the Hell Diver earned its name you would have picked up perhaps two trout, perhaps none. At any rate, here at the apparent dead end of a blind alley, was your place to become inspired. Dropping a worm into the mouth of that little tunnel was

like lighting the fuse of a firecracker. The explosion would occur in two or three seconds, and the eight-inch brookie who had assaulted your worm felt like a one-pounder as you coaxed it out to the light of day. Usually you could repeat this performance if you were patient enough to rest the water. After that the action subsided and you had nothing to do but move on. But where to, since the brook had left you?

Following the stream bed down the ravine you would find the tunnel's outlet in seventy-five yards. But if you were particularly observant you would find something else before you had gone half that distance. An opening a yard or so wide—a casual breach in the rocks of the stream bed—led into the approximate middle of the hidden passage. At moderate water levels it was easily seen and sometimes audible with the rush of water inside. But when the ground growth of late June was thickly matted the opening was as hard to find as a woodcock on her nest, and the subsided water made almost no sound.

Having taken a trout or two from the upper opening of the tunnel you might repeat, with the same tactics, at this middle orifice. It was a fishing hole such as I have never seen before or since. A few yards away no stream was in sight anywhere, indeed you had to be directly above that hole to catch the glint of sunlight in the water passing below. Any stranger to the brook, watching you from a little distance, would have wondered at the remarkable spectacle of an eight-inch brook trout taken out of dry ground!

Below the outlet, as far as we ever fished, the water was no more rewarding than above. For reasons unknown to me the trout seemed to prefer the darkness of their little grotto. The underground water temperature was perhaps less variable from month to month. If some special food not common to the open stream was there our examinations of trout stomachs did not reveal it. All of the fish of that brook—in or out of the tunnel—were darkly beautiful, as if wrought of deep shade. Other factors, such as certain minerals in the soil, may have influenced this pigmentation. I have fished deep-amber streams in hill country where iron has been mined and found trout of the same tenebrous shade, the red spots gleaming like rubies in their dark setting.

Other streams, far from having the self-effacing character of the Hell Diver, exhibit the opposite traits. There comes to mind a stream deep in the Poconos, once fished by Church and me, which at a certain point proceeded to multiply itself four times before our very eyes. The mother current did retain something of its identity for a little way. The offspring, meanwhile, meandered upon their separate and aimless paths. But within fifty yards they were all together again, the whole family, united in a great still body of water and apparently puzzled as to what they should do from here on. The active and purposeful career of the upper stream had lapsed, all at once, into a muddling lethargy. All signs of a central current had vanished; the slack water spread wide and deep among upright and fallen trees. This eerie lake was the abode of many species of the little people: watersnakes, frogs and turtles of all sizes, muskrats, wood ducks, various insects—and trout.

The reason for this sudden degeneration of a respectable trout stream was, of course, beavers. Later, having persevered through this fastness, we found the dam on the far side. Evidently the beavers had completed their job, found it up to their standards, and departed. They had their ideas of progress, as Chambers of Commerce had theirs. Here they had established a community for such reptiles, birds and insects as are by nature amphibian, and gone off at once to set up another one downstream.

The pond suggested Poe's "the dim lake of Auber, in the misty mid region of Weir." Its probable length, from the brook's entry to the dam, was two hundred yards, and its width about the same, but it seemed a mile when we crossed it. Its bottom was studded by boulders of all sizes completely or partly submerged; those jutting above the water formed islets preempted by watersnakes and by turtles asleep in the sun. Huge windfalls afforded treacherous bridges across tangled skeins of the wrecked forest. Some of them, already rotten when the water rose, gave no footing whatever to abet your passage. Many were covered with green moss and embellished with large squat frogs of the same color, muttering of their rum jugs and other guttural concerns with a slow iteration, or bulbously blowing out their throats in a meditative, blinking silence. The air was streaky with dragonflies. Our progress, once well into the swamp, became a series of tentative overtures at the oozy

119

bottom, one wader at a time, before consigning our full weight to the sludge of ancient detritus.

At the point of the stream's ingress the fishing was easy. Before the divided brooks coalesced in the pond each maintained its separate identity for a short distance. Each had more or less definite boundaries in the shape of what could be termed banks, for want of a better word, and we could keep some semblance of order and system in our casting.

There was something to work on, too, as we reached this point of the four-for-one split-up. Three trout rose, almost simultaneously, in three of the four branches. Church, armed with a small slate-wing Coachman, took on one of these fish while I engaged another with a light Hendrickson. The rights to the third rise were to accrue to him who first landed his fish. This privilege should have gone, by all the records and traditions of the past, to Church, and it did, though in this case something more than his commonly superior technique availed. The thing was a bit fluky, in fact, and I should have filed a protest.

I drew the first rise. But I missed it and was preparing to cast over it again when a heavy splash, on the far side of a stump across and downstream, caused me to change my plans at once. That, I thought, could be a two-pounder, and I would have no further traffic with small fry until it committed itself one way or the other. The splash drew an exclamation from Church, interrupted for a moment his little nursery sport with his nine-inch fish.

The cast was difficult: the fly should alight upstream from the stump, which was around a slight bend to the left, and float down to the fish. A two- or three-foot float was all I could give it without letting go too much slack. A vague jutting of oozy bank was between me and the point of the rise. By reaching far out to the right and employing a kind of side-wheeler I made it well enough, keeping the slack at a minimum and laying the leader fairly aligned with the fly's drift. The fly alighted softly and floated easily down, and I awaited the explosion. It did not come. I retrieved and cast again, not quite so well. And again.

Well, I would rest the fish for a space, change flies, maybe. But now I saw a slow stir in the water beyond the stump. Something appeared over its far edge, a thing like a man's hand. A head followed it, bigger than a fist, and presently the shell, and now all of the snapper was ensconced on the stump, immobile as the stump itself. I felt the thrust of a nasty suspicion. To confirm it I flicked my fly and hit the shell after a few false casts. The snapper took off from the stump and the splash was an echo of the one I had heard before.

This time the commotion drew no sign of recognition from Church. He was otherwise engaged. While I had angled for my hypothetical two-pounder he had worked over his fish in a business-like and orderly manner supposedly uncharacteristic of an artist. Presently his trout had hold of the Coachman and was being duly netted.

By then I was casting again over my original fish.

Church called across to me: "You give up the big one?"

"I'm resting him," I said. "The second time he rose he looked tired."

Church looked at me then as he had when he was painting my portrait—a searching and amused, squint-eyed expression that seems to be unearthing various embarrassing traits of your soul which you had thought were your private secrets.

"He was sluggish that second time," I said. "But he's heavy, and rising must be an effort."

"Two pounds, maybe?"

"Five pounds at least," I corrected, casting again.

"Huh?"

"Five pounds at a minimum." My fly was suddenly in the dead center of a swirl thirty feet downstream. This time I felt the good resistance of a well-hooked fish. "Whereas," I added, "This one will hardly weigh that many ounces. Nor will he drag himself out to sun his shell on a stump."

I glanced at Church again and saw the intent and hunting look relax, as it does when a difficult ear or cheekbone comes to life on his canvas.

"Thought that might be it," he said.

We fished on down to the merger of our various streams and beyond, into the indeterminate expanse of the swamp. The going was slow and the casting tricky. Probably the main stream kept a vaguely defined course through the flooded area and most of the trout stayed within it. But nowhere was a perceptible flow for a fisherman to follow. Finding the channel seemed a business of taking soundings. If you were up to your thighs or waist you were not in the channel; if you were up to your neck or over your head, you were.

A few authentic trout rises were seen at intervals but most of the splashes were made by startled frogs jumping off logs. Once two big watersnakes, swimming along together, made a great surface swirl just ahead of me, and again a muskrat steamed past on a straight course, as if sure of its compass points. I did, however, cull three bona fide trout from all this extravaganza of zoology. They were deep-fighting natives, not large, but strong and active as the wild brookie should be. I lost two others among the interlaced ruins of sunken trees, and a leader and three flies to the same hazards.

We became widely separated but kept in touch by shouting now and then like a couple of tramp steamers blowing their foghorns at each other. I beat Church to the dam by a half hour. He wasn't lost, physically. But he had been waylaid at times, between trout, by certain ghostly highwaymen who camp on his trail, follow him down trout streams and ambush him when he leasts expects it. He is never quite free from these bandits. There is a good trout rising just ahead, but beyond the fish, or maybe in the very rise, is something else. Some quality of color or line, light or shadow, some slant of perspective: one of the holdup men again, and he must be dealt with. A veritable gang of these desperadoes lurked in that swamp and they kept Church overtime. He attained the dam at last with a cargo of ideas for various pieces of canvas, watercolor paper, copper plates.

"How about the trout?" I asked.

"Oh, I picked up five," he said, dreamily, opening his creel to check. "No, six—I forgot the one that rose between the two birch trees—"

Sportsmanship 11

The major virtues of mankind are ill-defined and difficult of eluci-
dation. The virtue of sportsmanship is no exception; indeed it is the
vaguest of the lot, the least amenable to definition and analysis.
What is sporting to one man is gross to another. What I call sportsmanship you may call simple lust, or you may call it self-denial or
asceticism.

Much has been written about sportsmanship in trout fishing;
largely it has been concerned with stream ethics as a part of the
ordinary code of politeness among gentlemen who happen to be for
the moment on a trout stream instead of somewhere else. To
weight with even more words the subjects of stream manners and
consideration for the fish is only an exercise in redundancy. We all
know enough to keep away from the other fellow's water, to kill
quickly any trout we keep and to wet our hands before touching a
trout we intend to release.

Sportsmanship implies something beyond these common attributes of decent men, and something beyond what is known as the
amateur spirit. Rather it is a tenderness of heart, a sense of gladness
in the happiness of a life other than one's own, including the trout's,
and a sense of sorrow in all that detracts from this ideal. There are
skillful amateur fly-fishermen who are brutes, professional seine-
haulers who are kindly and great of soul.

Sportsmanship is not a static or permanent system of morals but rather a flexible code capable of growth, capable of advancing as men become more civilized in other ways. It has advanced a long way, if ever so slowly, since the first dinosaur was pot-shotted from above with a boulder rolled off a ledge. This progress, then, must be leading to a definite consummation. Since refinements of gear and methods tend to make the kill more and more difficult it may be demonstrated quite logically that the consummation is no fishing at all.

Sporting ethics as conceived today tolerate the killing of fish and game—in fact the kill is the core of the matter—but do not tolerate methods of killing which are inhumane or easy of accomplishment. Mere killing is not honored; skillful killing is. So in order to kill a trout or a grouse skillfully one must devise a difficult method of killing. A snap shot at a grouse in full flight, made in a split second as the bird dissolves in the November woods, is an extremely difficult way to kill that grouse. The difficulty challenges skill of a high order; the acquisition and exercise of that art are the essence of the sporting appeal of that particular kill. A big brown trout may be easy to hook with a live minnow at night but almost impossible to take with a small dry fly in broad daylight. Hence, according to the code, the latter achievement is worth ten of the former.

It is still true that men must kill, but this blunt truth is so repellent to civilized men that, though they will not give it up, they will make it difficult. To make it difficult is to make it sporting, and to make it sporting is to make it excusable. While the concept of sportsmanship embraces the act of killing it draws farther and farther away from mere slaughter. Then, in following that course, it may be argued that the true if unconfessed objective is no fishing at all. But if we do away with fishing we do away with the necessity for sportsmanship. Sportsmanship, then, must presuppose some form of the chase with capture and kill the ultimate end. As sporting ethics become more refined the actual kill must be made more difficult. As if pretending that the goal were the complete elimination of the kill we must approach that goal but never reach it. For once reached, the whole show and its reason for being evaporate into thin air.

It is a fine summer evening, and conceivably he appreciates, as we do, the goodness of life at such a time. The water is warm and that outer world above the water is teeming with the choicest harvest of his year. A fly hatch is alive above the surface and he takes the clean and foreign air for its juiciest morsels. His sorties above water are made in the same spirit of physical zest as a human diver's plunges below. The man knows he will return to his world of air in time; the trout as certainly knows he will fall back into his element. It is the beckoning of adventure, the appeal of the briefly hazardous act, for each braves an element he cannot endure for long.

This fellow is a big one in the goodly prime of his career, clean and hard from a life of breasting the eternal current. But the June evenings are his restful and his playful times, that zenith of his year when food and fun are easily had. He is perhaps a little off guard as he comes up to this one, perhaps a little drunk with the rich and easy living of June. There are parallels in the lives of men: ease and luxury may breed a fatal lapse of vigilance. . . . That fat fan-wing is the choicest fare of the year. He is not ravenous for it; he rolls up lazily to take it —as a well-fed man takes another tidbit that is passed to him —because it's there for the taking.

Only then, in that lazy and unsuspecting instant of taking the fly, does the shock of the deceit strike into his heart. He has felt the white pang of a set hook before; perhaps in the storage of memory the experience lives as a dormant nightmare. Now it is awakened again in this desperate panic and ends at last in an exhaustion of body, a swooning of senses and a suffocation of air as he is drawn out. If he is returned to the water he recovers slowly in some deep hole of the stream. Otherwise his life is snapped out at once or allowed to leave him in slow gasps over a stretch of an hour—depending upon his captor.

That, of course, is not an isolated fancy. It happens approximately in that detail, if my imagination is anywhere near the mark, each time you take a trout. . . . Your day astream has been a good one. You look back upon its aspects of woods, water, sky, the performance of your rod, and in your creel the evidence of your success. Some men have considered all that, and beyond, and given up fishing for the rest of their lives. An idea has caught hold of them, an irrevocable revulsion at taking a life in many respects superior to their own. An ultimatum, answerable in only one way, has been issued. These men are perhaps sentimentalists, perhaps not. They have seen a certain light, an individual truth, and for them it shines brightly and suffices.

A hundred practical arguments support the opposite view. . . . If I don't take a trout someone else will. The entire scheme of nature is of the hunter and the hunted, essentially a scheme of violence. The trout I refuse is the victim of the next predator, human or other. . . .

Possibly such rationalizations have dimmed that light to my eyes. Having thought as deeply as I can into the question I can still conclude that, to me, the fair killing of trout for sport is a worthy thing.

There is no absolute answer: it is relative to the individual, and it lies deep in that subsoil of character whose many components include all experience. We can make our decisions only on such indications as we find near the surface. Conscience is the final guide. If nothing in you is deeply offended by the hooking, playing and killing of a trout you surely have a moral right, by the only precepts measurable by man, to take that fish. If the procedure is offensive you will of course drop it.

And as certainly you will renounce the whole of trout fishing when you renounce the taking of the fish. For this is the heart, and the heart cannot be cut out if the body is to live. The camera alternative—ever a popular cry to the hunters who kill with fire-arms—is no good, even were it practical. The sweet scenery of a trout stream, the soft orchestrations of the riffles and the wood thrushes at dusk, the utter peace of the world of the trout waters—these are but embellishments upon the central theme. Without them the sport would be a mockery. But without the heart the appendages will stiffen and die. To deny that ultimate aim of trout fishing—the catching of trout—is to deny the meaning of all that surrounds it.

Big Stony

"LANK"

March Brown Genesis 1

In the early spring of a long-gone year Professor Kent and Tom Garrison and I first saw what is now our length of the Big Stony. It was an idea of Tom's to go up there in March. Tom wanted a preview of a trout season, pleading that March was too slow in passing, that edging his trout tools for the coming season and practice-casting in his backyard were no longer even vicarious thrills, and that unless he saw trout water with his own eyes, immediately, he would go mad.

So the Professor and I went, a couple of singularly glum and unheroic martyrs to the dubious cause of saving Tom's sanity. The objections we shied at Tom did not move him at all, being concerned only with certain shadowy ideas we entertained about previews of trout seasons—or previews of anything, for that matter. We told Tom that looking over trout water in March was a snooping and premature kind of thing, akin to opening Christmas presents before Christmas or setting off firecrackers on the third of July. There was such a thing, we suggested, as the appropriate season and the fit environment. March, we held, is no more the time for exploring trout water than July is the time to be searching out grouse coverts.

All of which had upon Tom the approximate effect of Ping-Pong balls volleyed at a rhinoceros. "Mere carping," he said. "Come on."

Had the day been of the sort not infrequent in the Northeast in March this expedition would have resolved itself into a quick and easy victory for the Professor and me. In a blizzard we would not have gone at all or, going, would have given Tom one look at the first suggestion of trout water met with in our journey, gagged and blindfolded him and driven him home.

But the day was up to some preview of its own. Tom said it could be a preview of June. The Professor remarked the spurious quality of the imitation but admitted that the day had its points. The air temperature was in the upper sixties and the warmth ate downward into the old crusts. The earth's winter coat, already threadbare in the early morning, was in tatters by noon. Great areas of the old brown and gray-green body were exposed again, drowsy and stiff, stretching and yawning in the warm and wakeful air.

We drove steadily north and west but the rout of winter continued all the way. The road was a succession of wet and dry areas from the melting and evaporating frost. Old drifts of granular snow ran off the slopes, filling the roadside gullies and racing downhill. The little valley brooks ran full with the sudden flood and each swamp and pond was vibrant with the peeper chorus as we drove by. Redwing blackbirds were everywhere over the fields, crows were raucous with the onset of their vernal lusts, and once, high up, a line of Canada geese marched steadily into the north. In the little towns the houses took in the spring through their open doors and windows. Grown men, hatless and in shirt sleeves, stood on the sidewalks discussing this resurrection of the life; boys played marbles in the wet streets, and on a soggy lawn we saw a game of one o' cat in progress. Summer stood over the land like a cresting wave, about to break.

In this spell of redemption Tom was nursing an inordinate and utopian vision. His original premise—the mere sight of trout water —had been, it seemed now, only a decoy to coax us into his car. Once headed north, with the spring unfolding on all sides, his ideas became expansive. Nearby trout waters would not satisfy his acute and special craving. Before noon we had crossed two familiar streams and paralleled a third for several miles. They were high and brown but they were full of memories and should have been, then, full of hopes. But Tom gave them only a glance from the wheel, never slackening his sixty-mile stride as we sped by.

"We'll go up, way up," he said dreamily, as if talking to himself, as if affirming in speech some great ambition that raged in his heart.

"They'll all look the same," said the Professor. "Big or small, they all have the color of March."

"Let your imagination change it, then," Tom replied. "You're supposed to have imagination—you two. I'm not. But I can see 'em in March and love 'em for what they'll be in May and June. You see 'em in March and hate 'em for what they are now. But I'll show you something—"

"As a manifestation of God's gentle hand," said the Professor, rising to Tom's challenge of eloquence, "they thrill me. But as trout water they leave me cold—about thirty-five degrees by my stream thermometer."

"Listen, I'll show you something before this day's sun has set. Did either of you ever hear of the Big Stony?"

"Is *that* where we're going?" the Professor asked, pointing his question to no one in particular, his eyes slanted across the brown and seeping landscape. "It'll remind you of the Mississippi just before the levees break. . . . A hundred miles farther on—and we've gone a good hundred now."

"Two hours," Tom said, "to the loveliest trout water this side of Hudson Bay."

"And all posted," the Professor added.

"Sure. By an old feller named Wintermute—where we're going."

"Know him?" the Professor asked, giving me at the same time a curious sideways glance as if some suspicion had dawned in his mind.

"Nope. But I want to," Tom said.

Ahead a long stretch of unpeopled road climbed between the fields to a far wooded ridge. Tom pressed up to sixty-five. "An hour and three-quarters," he muttered and lapsed into silence. The farm fields gave way to the edging encroachment of timber. We took the summit of the ridge, saw the far forested world heave and dip away into the haze of the north.

At one thirty we turned off the concrete upon a winding strip of macadam. Tall woods on either hand, rhododendrons green-black on the slopes and under them the lingering snow. At a quarter of two we came down a long hill, emerged into a little clearing of cutover land and saw immediately on our left, like a stage set when the curtain goes up, a brown torrent of a river thirty yards wide. Tom drew to the side of the road and stopped.

"I've never seen it right here," he said, getting out of the car.

We followed. A stout wire fence ran between road and stream. On a fence post, as the Professor had prophesied, was a poster. To his credit he didn't say "I told you so." Perhaps he didn't even see the sign. He was focused on the water.

There is no mistaking it, even in this untoward time of year. We stood leaning on the fence, looking at the Big Stony's sweep down the long straightaway above us, studying the potentialities of features still above the surface and trying to see its June water three feet below this level, transparent and sun-shot or shadowed green.

"God," Tom breathed, after a while, and the single word sufficed for the sum of our collective thought.

We turned to the sign then. It was a good sign of heavy linen, as well made as the fence. It carried the usual warning against trespass, hunting, fishing, and the usual announcement of the penalty therefor. Its author was one Christopher Wintermute, as Tom had foretold.

"A forbidding name," the Professor suggested, looking around as if he expected to see the ogre coming at us. "A get-the-hell-out-of-there and a charge-of-rock-salt name. Maybe we have no right even to stand here and look."

"A good name. A fine, upstanding, country name," Tom said, bristling with some curious loyalty to this man who wouldn't let us fish his water.

"It looks unfished," he added. "Let's follow it up a little way, in the car, and see what happens to it."

The road wound up the valley, playing tag with the Big Stony. It would curve away from the stream, separated by meadow or woods, then slant back to it again. Twice it brought us up close to the water. Each time we stopped for another inspection, and each successive vista seemed better than the last. Our imaginations played on the unseen stretches between and conjured visions which scarcely could have exceeded the actuality we came to know later. Even in the March flood the river bore the hallmark. It offered trout cover in endless diversity, casting stretches to chal-

lenge even the Professor's sleight-of-hand magic, others luxuriously open.

The wire fence and the neat wooden-backed signs persisted as we went upstream. No house or building of any kind came into view. The road angled to the right, away from the stream, and brought us to a crossing. We took the left turn to get back to the river and followed it a half mile to a bridge where we climbed out again for inspection number four.

A straight run of water was visible for two hundred feet downstream. On this side the Wintermute signs were again in evidence but the fence had disappeared. Upstream, a little above the bridge, was a fork in the river. The northerly branch, the larger of the two, was called the Little Stony on our topographic map. The other was nameless. Here fence and signs were absent but a distinct fisherman's path threaded the north bank of the Little Stony. Clearly we stood now at the top of Wintermute's water.

We leaned over the rail, looking upstream.

"Well," I said to Tom, "you can fish it up there next month—if someone doesn't post it in the meantime."

"Don't want to," he said. "Down there's where I want to fish it. Let's look at it some more."

We crossed the road to the downstream side and studied it again from this angle as if to perceive some minute feature which might have eluded us before.

"Does it look all right to you?" Tom asked, after a minute.

The Professor and I pronounced it—so far as discernible from appearances to date and so far as its June behavior could be foreseen in its present unruly demeanor—perfect. "But why?" the Professor asked.

"Okay. Then let's go see Wintermute."

"Eh?"

"Think he'll have fresh eggs to sell?"

"Listen, you skeptics. Did I drive two hundred miles to torture myself with a careful inspection of the finest unfishable trout stream in the world? I have enough nightmares when I'm asleep."

"He's being coy," the Professor said in an aside to me.

"Know where he lives?" I asked.

"Of course," Tom was deadpan, and the Professor looked at me curiously again. "I'd better tell you before we see him. I have it on good authority that he wants to lease the fishing rights here—to a responsible party. . . . Do you feel responsible, at all—?"

"What authority?"

"Chap named Andrew Hatch, with whom I have a fair acquaintance. One of the top surgeons of the world. Ever hear of him?"

We both admitted to knowing the name but not the man.

"Well, you will," said Tom. "He's abroad some of the time and carving up people all the time. But when he gets a minute to himself he'll come up here to fish and be an active member of our club—"

"Club?"

"Club."

"But how—"

"Easy. Doc Hatch never fished for a trout in his life but he wants to learn. He knows old Wintermute somehow or other—spent a summer on his farm some years ago. He's agreed to put up for this thing if I—and you two experts, whom I mentioned to him—think the water's any good after giving it a going over. He'll issue stock, purchasable by a limited membership in such amounts as each member can afford. Character and not wealth to be the desideratum. Have you any character, either of you? . . . He doesn't care a damn whether the stock is fully subscribed or not. He'll hold the bag until, if and when it is subscribed. . . ."

He was going on, but the Professor and I didn't half hear him in our state of semishock. . . . "Now, are you proud to know the man Doctor Hatch appointed as his emissary in this epic enterprise? Or have you still some objections, you conscientious objectors, you antipreviewers, you sophists—?"

In fifteen minutes we were closeted in Christopher Wintermute's little office adjoining his sitting room; in an hour the details were arranged subject only to further and closer inspection of his waters.

Not until on the way home did anyone voice the question so important after an act of creation.

"What'll we name it?" the Professor asked.

"Name what?"

"The club, of course. What else is on your mind?"

"Oh, the something-or-other Fly-Fishing Club. We can't allow worming—except to poachers."

Tom looked out at the dun landscape of the late afternoon. Maybe its color, and the color of the Big Stony as we had seen it today, gave him the obvious lead.

"The March Brown Fly-Fishing Club," he said. "All those in favor —"

The Angel and the Ghost 2

Among those who have fished up and down our length of the Big
Stony, two—one a member, the other neither member nor guest—
have been outstanding in March Brown annals.

Apart from the fact that he is the founder of our club, Doctor
Andrew Hatch deserves prior mention. He is distinguished in more
ways than one, but one is his debt to me. For the Doctor is one of
the few souls on this earth to whom I have imparted a fraction of
that jot of trout-fishing lore which I own, somehow, in fee simple.
I have shown Doctor Hatch how, according to my lights, to put a
dry fly over a rising fish. I have liberated his line from the rhododendrons that flank the Big Stony, and unsnagged his flies and tied
barrel knots and Turle knots for him, on his first heroic day astream.
And some day, if and when he masters the advanced curricula
according to the doctrines of Professor Kent or Tom Garrison or
Bob Harlow or Win Stokes—all of whom long ago washed their
hands of me—the Doctor may remember, with a fondness tinc-
tured with pity, him who guided his first stumbling steps among the
Random Rocks.

But let that distinction pass; beside his others it is nothing. I speak
of him here because he has been the major spirit, the central focus,
the dominant uproar of our fishing days on the Big Stony and because through his eyes the others may best be seen. The Doctor
knows everyone up and down the river—March Brown members,

guests, employees, landlord and poachers, fishermen and nonfisher-men, male and female, storekeepers in Stony Forks, school kids and farmers. To be with the Doctor is to experience laughter, usually the comfortable chuckling sort which rises easily from the top of the lungs but occasionally the belly-churning kind to which, hitherto, you had been a little ashamed to give vent. And yet the Doctor's genius is certainly not slapstick. He has a wistful innocence and a shy wisdom, and his fishing seems to contrive a curious juxtaposition of the two.

His arrivals at the club are hailed, his departures are mourned. In the brief intervals of his occupancy the days crackle with drama. The Doctor has adventures astream or in the village and brings them back with him in the evening, in lieu of a creelful of trout. And after supper, when the fire is blazing in the big room and one or two diehards are still on the dark water slinging bucktails and dodging bats, the Doctor will get out his trout gear and his day's batch of news and overhaul each with loving care. At one and the same time this eminent surgeon can grease a length of tapered line and a bit of gossip picked up from Dave Strouthers, station agent at Stony Forks.

From the Doctor's store of raw material I have fabricated most of the stuff of the following pages. Not all. Professor Kent's story of Sam Fario was given to me before Doctor Hatch matriculated at our finishing school for fly-fishermen. It is related here almost word for word as the Professor gave it. But the recording of Lank Star-buck's last night on the Big Stony was made possible by Doctor Hatch's deductions from his intimate village-gleaned knowledge, unshared by us, of certain domestic circumstances contributory to the tragedy. The Doctor pieced that thing together like a jigsaw puzzle and made a full and convincing picture in the end. Viewed objectively it was a triumph of amateur sleuthing. Knowing the Doctor as we did, however, it was something else. A labor of love, a crusade whose grail was the simple vindication of the venerable myth of the March Browns.

For Lank Starbuck, our ancient and honorable poacher, had oc-cupied a unique niche in our hearts. His character had grown leg-endary despite the acute reality of his nocturnal raids on our waters and his recurrent depletion of our never-too-abundant supply of trout. Reports that his loot from our preserve often graced the meager boards of a few needy families in Forks Township were too well authenticated to be ignored, and added more than a little luster to his curious halo.

Starbuck was not only a fisherman of great prowess; he had some mystic affinity with the water itself. Operating always in the dark he could negotiate certain stretches of the Big Stony which were trout hangouts but so treacherous and difficult to fish that we never engaged them even in daylight. He would leave, sometimes, a bluntly penciled note, gloating and defiant, impaled on a snag in some furious run of water: "A 3-pounder here last night. Thanks." Or "Night crawler fetched him here, 11:30 PM, June 10. 4 lbs. 2 oz. Much obliged." We deliberated upon the legality of having a warrant issued for his arrest, on the evidence of the notes. The legal grounds appeared sound if we could prove the unsigned notes to be his. But we took no action, and after a while we realized we were ashamed to. Against so gallant an enemy such tactics would be sniveling indeed. I think each of us came to that conclusion separately and held it for some time before any of us gave it voice. Its first mention, made tentatively as if unsure of its reception, revealed at once the unanimity of the thought.

We went after him in other ways. We tried to catch him in the act. We posted ourselves upon the stream on nights we deemed auspicious for his enterprise. We instructed Foster Prentiss, our guard, to be always alert for this supermarauder. It came to nothing, nothing at all. We never saw or heard a sign of old Starbuck. But his depredations continued. On a night when all of us were planted at supposedly strategic spots upstream and down he took a three-pound brown from the Club Pool itself and left his note on the steps of the clubhouse, held down by a stone!

That mortifying instance and, I should add, most of Starbuck's plunderings occurred before the Doctor's arrival as an active member. The Doctor, with his village acquaintance and entree to village gossip, might have been able to apprehend the night prowler. I doubt it, however, for Starbuck not only had the loyalty of the township folk but was too gifted in his own right to be mastered by even the Doctor's high talents. But such speculation is futile; the Doctor would not have lent himself to that cause.

For after a while, as the legend grew, none of us wanted to end it by taking him. Our custom is to hold a winter meeting, along in mid-January. Future plans are discussed, the treasurer's report is read and an appropriation for the coming season is voted. We come away from that session believing that another trout time is ahead of us—something we had previously doubted, what with the snow a foot deep and the thermometer at eight above—and that instillation of faith is perhaps the real purpose of our winter caucus. In a meeting years ago Win Stokes moved that we call off all further attempt to capture Lank Starbuck. Win made an eloquent appeal based upon the ascendancy of a beautiful legend over our gross satisfaction in the extra trout we might take if Starbuck were removed. Win ended his oration by reminding us that "even now, as I say this, Starbuck is likely taking a three-pounder through the ice of the Club Pool."

His proposition was voted down, however, after due acknowledgment of its nobility of motive. Professor Kent, in a devastating rebuttal, pleaded that the withdrawal of defensive measures would spoil the fun for Starbuck and indeed would vitiate the legend, since a poacher who operates at will against undefended positions is sure to go soft in time and to be, henceforth, a poacher unworthy of the glorious tradition in which he, and we, had been reared. The Professor added that the same objection stood in the way of an honorary membership for Starbuck—a solution the Professor now admitted had crossed his mind. But Starbuck would never accept it; he was too proud to be thus cajoled by attempted appeasement. And should he accept, the Professor said, it would end Starbuck for himself and for us. It would be abject surrender on both sides.

So we kept our guards up against old Lank. At least we did in theory, having committed ourselves to the prosecution of the war. Just what any of us would have done had he met the old ghost face-to-face on the stream cannot be known, for none of us ever met him there. Sometimes one claimed to have heard him but there was never verification, never actual sight of him operating on his beat. We were like children who hear Santa Claus in the chimney on Christmas Eve. There are times in a man's life when any casual sound is thrice weighted with import. We saw him occasionally by day, around his farm or in the village, and on such routine path-crossings we greeted him as we would greet Chris Wintermute, our landlord and streamlord, or Caleb Wilson who kept the general store in Stony Forks, or any other neighbor. In our exchange of glances or salutations there never was hostility, never an implication by look or word of the undercurrent of our ancient feud. Only after dark, downstream from the Forks bridge, was Lank Starbuck our worthy enemy.

There came the time of his mysterious hegira from Stony Forks to the city, and his five years' absence, and the day of his return (shortly after our watchman, Foster Prentiss, had moved away and his successor had been appointed) and the night of that day.

Tom Garrison, fishing early, found him the next morning. His gaunt old frame was draped like driftage around an inshore boulder at the head of the Monolith Glide. No mark of violence was upon him. The current through the Glide is gentle; Starbuck's body had eased into it from above, snubbed against the rock and held. A five-pound brown trout, one of the biggest fish ever taken from our water, protruded from the back pocket of his denim jacket. His hand clutched his many-jointed rod, broken off above the second ferrule.

Examining Starbuck's remains the Doctor said at once that he had died of drowning. The coroner, summoned, echoed this conclusion and opined that Starbuck had been dead seven or eight hours.

None of us fished that day, or the next. A strange solemnity shrouded the clubhouse of the March Browns. We wandered in and out, looked at the stream which for once held no objective whatever, and busied ourselves with trivial concerns, or with desultory talk, or with silence. Surface-feeding trout erupted for a while and subsided beneath the deserted waters. Late in the afternoon of the second day Win Stokes, walking the banks above the Elbow, found the upper half of Starbuck's rod and brought it back to the house. (The two pieces remain there still, suspended from their guides on the wall of our living room.)

Doctor Hatch drove to Stony Forks and returned after dark, looking thoughtful as I recalled it later, but in the general state of our preoccupation it wasn't noticed. The morning of the third day we attended Lank's funeral at his house in Stony Forks. The finality of that ritual or perhaps the mere passage of time edged us back, by late afternoon, to the normal pulse of fishing. Win and Tom essayed various parts of the river with such flies as they had faith in, and the Professor and I prepared to do the same.

Doctor Hatch had been curiously silent since our return from the cemetery. Going outside to put on our waders the Professor and I found him on the porch overlooking the Club Pool, nursing a drink in a sort of glum meditation uncommon to him. He looked up at us. "I've got it," he said.

Somehow we knew at once the implication of the pronoun.

"Sit down," he said. "Both of you. Have a drink and bear with me a minute. . . . Listen—" and the story he gave us then I pass along to you in "Old Poacher's Return."

(Here I confess our error in having hired the guard who succeeded Foster Prentiss. Happily he has gone from our employ and from Stony Forks.)

Out of the Doctor's township-wide acquaintance and store of local knowledge I gleaned certain homely details of the Wintermutes, senior and junior, essential to the writing of "When All the World Is Young." And to his faculty of being on the spot where things are happening (the Doctor could have been a great newspaper reporter) I am indebted for the material of "Challenge at the Elbow." As for "The Compleat Tangler," he is the Doctor himself as we saw and knew him in his first week on our river.

The River 3

Messrs. Rand and McNally may not know of the Big Stony and possibly their files do not list it under "Rivers—B." But I have felt its gray cloudy power in the April spates, and in the long twilights of June I've seen trout rising in its subsided riffles and pools. I have slipped on its smooth stones and taken its cold shock as it spilled into the top of my waders. I have traced its career back to its origin and found its circumstances and surroundings traditional to the birth of most rivers. With its childhood I have little more than hearsay, with its teens a passing acquaintance, and in the contemplation of its old age a sad residual emotion. But with its prime, its middle life, I have what I think is an understanding.

In the course of a river there is a fine analogy to the life of a man. The Big Stony is a personality to all of us, a sort of honorary member of the March Brown Fly-Fishing Club. It has a certain authority enjoyed by no one else in our organization. Its moods are our law; indeed they are the recipient of a kind of pagan worship. For its smile or frown can make or break a day's fishing, and in its sustained benevolence a whole season can be prosperous. To propitiate it we have done everything but offer a living human sacrifice, and Doctor Hatch once darkly intimated his intention to do that.

The wooded ridges spread out from a high plateau like fingers from the palm of a hand. Somewhere in that remote upland, some-where lost in a damp close gloom of rhododendrons and hemlocks is a little cavity in the leaf mold of the forest floor. Looming up beside that minute basin, shadowing it totally from the shredded sunlight, is a ton of granite, mossy and encrusted and deeply wedged into the continent. Water seeps from under that stone, fills the little hollow slowly, overflows it and trickles away, feeling the gravitational pull, into the residue of the wilderness centuries. The ancient detritus and the black earth and the fern roots appear to blot up that thread of water, for in the space of five yards from its spring it has disappeared. But it hasn't been blotted up; it hasn't been stopped. It has found merely an easier passage underground: some rift between the tangled roots and the veined granite, some threadlike channel more receptive to its progress than is the littered surface terrain. Being of the essential quick of nature it is following nature's immemorial line, that of least resistance. It will return to open air in a little while and flow on the surface in the normal way of streams. Meanwhile it is moving and gathering strength as it moves, and already, in its tiny form, it is resistless. For a dark and tremendous force is above and beneath it; the stored seepage of every storm and the subterranean upsurge of a mountain. The little basin fills, quickly after a rain or slowly in a drought, obeying that secret upthrust of the earth, fills and overflows and trickles away, for it holds a destiny too great to be confined: the life of a river that has just been born.

Fifty yards on, it is up again to the surface, sparkling and clean from the gritty scouring of the earth. And now it is perceptibly larger, having found nourishment in the dark passage. But it sprawls and gropes like an infant, creeping over the little stones and around the big ones, dividing and merging and dividing again. It picks up another trickle, and another and another: new influences from the outside world, attracted to it and adding to its stature.

The plateau dips; the palm of the hand divides itself into the spread fingers and between two of them the rill finds its groove. It is gathering speed now and seeming to add substance from the exercise, and channeling at last the individual course of its childhood. It is rill-size, a step across its miniature stream bed. Where a deer leans to lap its surface in the forest dusk it attains dignity as a waterway.

The ridges rise higher and recede from its little banks, acknowl-

146

edging its status, now, as a valley stream, and from their wooded slopes smaller rills merge their courses with its superior power. And now a shape never before seen flashes in its own body, a tiny dark form with brilliant spots. In a little pool under a waterfall is another, larger, and in a back eddy farther along, a third.

A brook now, and into the haunts of men, and the ridges on either side have backed farther away and their longer slopes send down the fattening rills. A name at last, identification on the maps of men as the Little Stony. Still little, but a name, a ranking, and in the very name the promise of growth. Depth here—depth enough to shadow deeply the bottoms of the pools, and in the still gloom and the sun-shot fast water more and more of the dark forms with the bright spots, larger now. And in the restful stretches other forms materialize—slower bottom-dwelling forms that roll sideways and coin bright silver on the deep sand.

Past a house or two, a barn, deeper into the land of men; past men poised motionless on the bank or brushing men's legs where they stand in midstream. Big enough now to flow over all but the largest boulders, and gathering size and force every yard of the way. A spring trickle comes in here, a brook farther on, committing their little aims to the ultimate destiny, the union at last with the sea.

A breakneck romp over a sharp slope of stones and the ability to roar as the pitching bank-hemmed waters hit the downgrade, and the ease of the slow-coiling pool below, with bubbles from the air-charged tail of the rapids stippled on the black surface. The oblique pouring union with the south branch, a body scarcely smaller than Little Stony itself, the intimate commingling of the two, the marriage of the waters at the Forks. And there is the end of the youth of this river. The banks are wide apart now, and a grown-up stream marches between them. The Big Stony. Action is adult action henceforth, purposeful and strong; ease is mature ease, meditative and profound. The frolicsome life of a river is done with its brookhood.

The first stride of the Big Stony into the March Brown preserve is a man-sized stride. Under the Forks bridge it walks with dignity and a long pace into our posted precincts as if scorning the no-trespass signs—a restrained riffle in an easy downgrade march, two hundred feet straight as sight to a sheet of glass that curls downward and splinters iridescent in the sun. Viewed from the Forks bridge seventy yards upstream the Big Stony appears at this point to lose itself in a bright mist of diamonds. There is a turn immediately below, a pileup of water against the left bank and a running charge that subsides in the forest-gloomed Top Pool of the March Browns. From here on for a few thousand yards the river achieves fame among mortals. It is celebrated and lionized; certain sentimental utterances of men get hung upon it like labels for its diverse moods. The natural phases of its career, its driving actions and spells of introspection, are neatly pigeonholed and tagged, titled like the successive works of an author. Below the Top Pool there are, in downstream order, the Poacher's Pocket, the Deeps, the Pasture Pool, the Monolith Glide, the Club Pool, the Elbow, the Random Rocks, and the Outpost.

Below the Outpost the river leaves us as it came, gently and without haste. Under a cable with a sign on it the Big Stony goes out of our lives, whispering into a long riffle and disappearing to the right under the green-black shadows of the leaning hemlocks.

Fifty miles below, the road skirts a small industrial city and, just beyond, comes again beside the river. Here you realize that a great change has been wrought, that the better part of a lifetime has slipped into the past. Meeting the Big Stony here is like meeting a man you had known long ago in the clean hard prime of his powers, and finding him now aged and soft and bloated with some poisonous dissipation. At the Outpost you had stood on a left bank of hemlocks and rocks and rhododendrons, and the amber water had been deeply impregnated with sun and the blurred pattern of shadows. Here, after those fifty miles, the left bank is a dyke of ashes and rubbish and dusty weeds. The river is slow and tired and resigned. An unnameable thick color clouds it, a blue that is not the mirrored sky in the Pasture Pool but a blue of chemical distillations, a pigment that would be evident in a tumblerful scooped from the stream. Gray scum ridges the waterline of the marginal rocks, and a flood mark from last winter is like a leprosy on the banks.

That is the end—or almost the end—of the Big Stony. It has a short span of life below the town, a slow coiling through the flat country of its old age. The town recedes; certain shadowy properties and feeble gestures of nature move up close to the river again.

Through a stretch of sparse woodland it seems to recover some measure of the purity and vigor of its youth. But its malignancy is terminal now; as it loses its identity forever in its confluence with a mighty seabound estuary the old willows lean from its banks as if administering extreme unction to the dying river.

Sam Fario 4

"It's a strange thing," I was saying to the Professor, "how women who fish seem to have the killer instinct to a much greater degree than men."

The oak chunks, still a little green, had caught on at last. My waders and heavy socks were drying slowly, draped over the fire screen. The Professor had arrived late that afternoon, too tired after a day's drive to essay the evening rise. I had been out there until dark, throwing a dry fly over the Club Pool and a shallow riffle downstream. But chiefly I had been watching something else—the fastest and most violent piece of trout-fishing action I've ever seen. Thinking about it afterward it seemed to confirm certain old ideas about women who fish.

"I haven't noticed it particularly," the Professor said.

"Have you fished with women much—or watched them fish?"

"With one, a good deal. With others rarely. The one I fish with has so little of the killer instinct that I wonder, sometimes, why she fishes at all."

The Professor is older and wiser than I and a much better fisherman. Sometimes when talking to him I feel like a small boy talking a little over his head on an exciting subject newly and imperfectly learned. He wouldn't want me to feel that way, but I do. But what I had witnessed on the stream tonight was a cold irrefutable fact to plank down in front of the Professor's erudition.

"Maybe it's the way nature evens up against maternal tenderness," I suggested. "Some women who don't fish have it too. Businesswomen and women who go in for competitive sports. Just watch a woman tennis champ polish off a third-rate opponent. They do it differently from men. They're merciless."

"How does this thing show itself in trout fishing?"

"Get him to the net and get him there quickly. Did you ever see a woman give a nine-inch trout its head for two minutes? Or a nineteen-inch trout, for that matter, any longer than she had to? Or put a good fish back after she caught it?"

"They're rhetorical questions and I'm supposed to say no. But the answer is yes—for the one I've fished with."

"She must be the exception to prove the rule. The woman I watched tonight was typical of the rule. She could cast and wade like a man and she used imagination and brains in her fishing. But she was a killer. She was ruthless, like all of 'em."

The Professor looked at me curiously for a moment, as if about to ask a pointed question. But that sharp interrogation softened in a meditative look of amusement, a kind of inward smile. He got up to poke the charcoal off the oak chunks and was rewarded with a nice purring blaze. "Tell me about her," he said.

I took advantage of the Professor's renewed fire to turn my waders inside out and drape them again over the end of the screen.

"I passed her upstream early this evening on my way down to try the Club Pool. She was not fishing then, just sitting on a big rock smoking a cigarette. I stopped and asked her what luck and she unwound an eighteen-inch brown from her creel. I noticed her rod and gear in the minute or two I was with her. The rod was a nine-footer and looked powerful. A #12 Quill Gordon took him, she said, up in the Poacher's Pocket. She seemed to know her place names along this stream but I've never seen her up here before.

"I went on down. I dabbled over the Club Pool a while, picked up a couple of panfish and went below to try the shallows above the Elbow. I found a fourteen-incher there after some time. It was getting a little dark by then and I decided to go back.

"As I got up to the Club Pool again she was in the broad reach just above its lip, working slowly upstream with a dry fly. I stopped well below her, to watch. I sat down and lit my pipe because I didn't want to appear to be snooping if she should turn around and see me. I felt a little sneaky—but I couldn't help looking at her casting.

"It had a quality of smoothness beyond any words that come to me offhand. It had grace and accuracy, but they looked ancient— if you know what I mean. They had always been there—she seemed so used to them she could take care of them subconsciously, like breathing. There was no apparent effort to achieve any effect or any result. It was all easy and rhythmic and a little drowsy, maybe, like the wind blowing in the trees. No great length of line except at one place—I'll tell you about it—where she suddenly amazed me by shooting a good sixty-five feet. The rest were thirty, thirty-five, forty. The floats were short but lifelike; the drag never bothered her though it would have played hob with a long inexpert cast and a long float in some of the places she worked over. The retrieve was mostly with the rod, and the false casts were few and slow, seeming to carry the rhythm. It was about the least fussy casting I've ever looked at.

"Where she shot the long one, and the way she did it, showed her killer instinct. And what happened directly afterward proved it beyond doubt. . . ."

The water of the Big Stony charges narrow and deep into the head of the Club Pool, then widens and slows downstream. The main current hugs the far bank but some character of the bottom creates a secondary drift there, a flow at right angles to the real channel, and that secondary current sweeps in toward shore on the Club side. It's shallow here for perhaps fifteen feet out from shore where it drops off sharply. It's a spot I've seen passed up again and again by fishermen who were too intent on the main channel along the far shore. It should be fished before the channel gets any attention at all, and fished from as far down-current as possible because a trout in that shallow can see a long way.

I didn't say all that to the Professor. He needed no description of the Club Pool, knowing it and how to fish it better than any man in the world. I told him merely that this woman was approaching that stretch as I watched her.

". . . casting easily with her short throws and short floats. A little hatch of the blue quill was on the water but nothing was coming up. In a few minutes she was in range of that shallow water off the

head of the pool. I was curious to see how she'd fish it—whether she'd wade through it while fishing the main channel or start casting over it from where she stood.

"At this point she reeled in—I figured to change flies. And just then a fish rose far up, where that right-angle drift breaks away from the head of the pool. A good bulgy rise, one of those up-curving lifts of the surface that a good trout makes.

"She seemed very deliberate in getting her fly changed. Her back being toward me, I couldn't see whether she was taking all this time to decide on her fly or perhaps having trouble with her leader. Maybe it just seemed a long time because I had seen the rise and was keyed up to it. If she gave no sign of having seen it I was going to tell her.

"Or maybe she was studying the layout, trying to decide on a tactic. That thought occurred to me too, for there were more ways than one to fish that rise.

"But I don't think so, now. I think she had her mind made up all the time—the way she went after that fish when at last she got her fly changed. No reconnoitering but an immediate frontal attack. Up to that moment not a cast had been over forty feet. But now, with the target a good sixty-five feet upstream, she aimed at it. In about four false casts, still easy, she had it all out in the air but eight feet or so, and on the next she shot that much and let it all come down. If a handkerchief had been floating over the precise point of the rise her fly would have settled on it.

"He had it the instant it touched, as if he'd been waiting for it. The same lazy upsurge, no splash, just a swelling of the surface and the wave rings, and he was down with it. She stripped in a few feet easily as he came toward her, then held him against pressure with her rod high while she reeled in the slack below her first guide. Very pretty, so far. But I perceived in a minute that the line she had gained by stripping she considered velvet or net profit or something, and she was going to keep it. It looked as if no one had ever told her about giving back what you borrow from a big fish before you win it for keeps. When I saw that trout's size, the first time he rolled up, I knew she'd lose him, the way she was giving him hell. No light tippet was going to stand that sort of stuff. If he wasn't two feet long the difference wasn't worth arguing.

154

"He came downstream and went by her. She turned to face him as he went below and gave him the butt as if she had a surf rod in her hands. I couldn't stand it anymore. I shook myself loose and went up to her, feeling guilty about my snooping even in all the excitement. But I knew she needed me or anyone who had ever had a big trout on and knew what it could do to light tackle. For the moment I forgot that she had another big fish in her creel. If I had remembered it I'd have concluded that someone had given it to her.

"I said something to her, excusing myself for offering advice, about the need to give him line. She looked at me then—and listen, she is beautiful—with a kind of disdain. Her mouth was closed tight —she was gritting her teeth on that battle—and it didn't open a millimeter to smile or to answer me. In fact, as if by way of reply, she started stripping in line again.

"Well, I knew he was gone, and I was going to be kind of glad of it. But he wasn't. She brought him in, so help me, over her net— as lively then as when he'd taken the fly. By all the laws of every- thing she should have lost him there. But she scooped him out, thrashing like a shark, and took him ashore in the net. The whole thing had taken less than five minutes and she hadn't moved a yard. With me it would have taken half an hour and I'd have gone down the whole length of the Club Pool, babying that fish and praying every step of the way."

The Professor got up to nurse his fire again. "Too bad she had to put back that one," he said. "Maybe we ought to waive our rule of only one big fish a day—where women are concerned. Yet it's hard to break with a tradition that old."

"Well, you've come to my point yourself," I said. "She didn't put it back."

"She didn't?"

"No. When I saw her last she was heading toward the kitchen with both fish. I tell you they're emotionally incapable of releasing a big one, rule or no rule—and all our club traditions can go to hell."

The Professor turned from his business with the fire and looked at me sharply, intent as a pointer rounding up to a bunch of quail.

"Did you see her kill the second fish?" he asked.

"No, come to think of it, I didn't. She carried him away in the net without stopping to take down her gear. But remember, it was almost dark. She could have killed him in the kitchen, or had the cook kill him, where there was some light on the subject."

The Professor knocked his pipe out against the side of the fireplace, refilled it carefully, lit it and blew a couple of puffs that curled over the fire screen, caught the draft and rushed up the chimney. He settled back in his chair and was silent a moment. I knew he was about to talk, about to launch upon some narrative, probably in rebuttal to mine. That's the way he begins a story: gets his words organized into platoons and squads, some sort of practical marching order, before giving the command.

In this space of silence I looked across the smoke and the lamp-light at him and thought about him, thought of how empty and pointless trout fishing could be without him after you'd known it with him.

In the past four or five seasons his attendance upon our water had been infrequent and uncertain. There had been two tragedies in his recent past, and the second had profoundly affected his fishing. I don't mean that it had touched his fishing skill: that had always been in a class by itself so far as our club membership was concerned. But something had happened to his keenness for fishing. It hadn't been killed or even blighted. Maybe it was only mellowed, like an apple after a couple of frosts. But it was different.

The stark facts were that his wife had died in childbirth eleven years ago; and the child, a boy, had been struck and killed by an automobile six years later. Since the death of his son the Professor had made only a few brief trips to the club water and had missed a couple of our January meetings. I had heard that he had married again but I didn't know the details. Up to this evening I had not seen him in two years.

"I'd have given you this sooner or later anyway," he began. "But after your experience tonight it's appropriate that I tell you, now, of something that happened to me when I was last on this water, two seasons ago.

"There are *two* women in this thing. The elder was the Aunt, important here only because her actions helped to reveal the character of the younger who was, of course, the Niece. The Aunt could be your Exhibit A, beautifully illustrating not only on the stream but in the confines of this club the womanly fishing characteristic you speak of. The Niece would not have conformed.

"The Aunt was a large and formidable and freckled fisherwoman, militantly physical, emanating a kind of hearty outdoor robustness all over the place. She was up very early in the mornings, stamping about, wallowing in her cold bath like a walrus—her room adjoined mine and you know these partitions are not strictly soundproof— and devouring great platters of ham and eggs for breakfast. Then to the stream which she would flail unmercifully with a stout ten-foot rod and wet flies three sizes too large.

"All of this might have been mildly amusing had the decent qualities which should go along with so resounding a character been evident. Strangely they were not. She tried to bully the Niece with her mere seniority. She would post the Niece upon a stretch of water and announce her imperious decrees for the day, as to lures and procedure. From what I learned of her precepts and from the amount of air in her creel each evening I judged of the Aunt's talents as angler and teacher, and mentally I conceded a mark of about C-minus in each. She did, however, take a few fish, most of them horsed out in the dusk on bucktails and her large wet flies. The Niece had taken none up to the third day, much to the Aunt's articulate disgust and, I was sure, unspoken delight. The Niece bore her defeat like a lady however, despite the Aunt's frequent innuen-does, pointed at her own superiority to her pupil, which she let drop at strategic moments.

"The bully, however, had picked the wrong kind of prey. The Niece—I judged her to be in her middle twenties—was a girl of spirit. The signs were unmistakable despite the nicely tailored cloak of her reserve. The tradition of respect to her elders, on which the Aunt had tried to capitalize, was strong in her but the integrity of her own character was stronger, and it was going to be served. I could see a rebellion smoldering and I determined to apply the bellows. I would teach her to fish if for no other reason than that she must, before I left camp, trim the Aunt as the Aunt deserved to be trimmed.

"On the fourth day I asked her to fish with me and she accepted.

"She proved to be an apt pupil. Her gear was mostly good—a really fine rod and the right weight of line for it—and that gave me a head start in teaching her to cast. Her leaders were wrong and she never had heard of tippets. I rigged her up, there, with my own stuff. Plainly she had been reading about trout fishing; she had a typical book education without the practice. A skeleton knowledge, as all such lore is—the bones of theory without the good meat of experience. But she was otherwise equipped in a good way. She had an easy athletic grace, reflexes rare in a woman and totally lacking in the Aunt. It was a good basis to work on. We took it easy, and by evening she was laying out forty feet with some accuracy and handling her false casts and retrieves well.

"By that time I had taken five fair fish and released all but one. She had had a few rises and had actually taken a ten-inch brown which she had brought to net at the Pasture Pool very nicely indeed. I could see she was disappointed—she had wanted something more to show to the old vixen. I was a little uneasy myself, the five-to-one ratio seeming a bit top-heavy. A fair hatch was on and trout were coming up to it, and I knew I could take several more if I kept on. So I declared myself through for the day.

"It was a little awkward. I didn't want her to quit and she didn't want to either. Though she had accepted like a dutiful student all I had tried to teach her she had a fine aloofness, a way of keeping to her own water, well away from mine. I respected that in her, yet I didn't quite know how to show it. Letting her go on alone was suddenly a displeasing prospect, yet I felt that to tag along, just watching her, would be embarrassing to both of us. So I told her to carry on while I sat on a rock and had a smoke. That was at the Monolith Glide. I had heard that a tremendous fish had been seen there but I hadn't given it much credence.

"She started upstream to fish the riffle above the Glide. But at that moment there was a brute of a rise directly opposite us.

" 'See what you can do with *that*,' I said.

" 'I'll toss you for him.'

" 'No. I'm down and I'm staying down. Now go ahead, and I'll keep out of it.'

The Professor got up and knocked out his pipe again on the side of the fireplace.

"It was semidusk by then and maybe I was imagining a lot that I couldn't see. But I thought she looked at me then with an expression I had never seen on anyone's face before. It was a compound of emotions, packed tight and close. It had a trace of everything: nervousness, a little fear, a shy and terrific will to get that fish, and over it all, like a kind of veil, a soft wash of surrender to me. . . . All right, I know you're thinking I couldn't possibly see all that in one woman's face in a single instant, and you're probably damn right. The answer is only that I knew something, in that moment, which gives conviction to any crazy tangent of one's imagination. I knew I was in love with her.

"What happened in the next two or three minutes was so swift and so furious that it got beyond my full comprehension. I am still trying to take it all in in retrospect, still wondering how big a fish he really was. Her cast was one she could be proud of in the tension of the moment. The fly settled lightly down, two or three feet above the point of that first boil. He rose with a great deliberate dignity. He may have hooked himself—I don't know—anyway he was on and immediately going away from there, upstream. I remember her saying quietly: 'No advice please. You gave me this—now let me handle it.'

"He didn't stop. He didn't even slow down. He took her casting line off her reel as straight as if he were measuring the length of the Glide. She had to turn him somewhere, and she had backing line —I'd made sure of that. I was about to yell something about trying to turn him with easy pressure but not too much. But I didn't. I had told her I'd keep out of it.

"I don't know what she did to brake him, and she couldn't remember afterward. Doubtless she applied too much pressure but fortunately she didn't hold her rod high. Anyway, he was suddenly gone. All at once the whole business was deadly slack. It was like silence after some great racket that's been banging in your ears for a long time. . . . I've lost many a fish but none of 'em ever affected me as this one did—maybe because I wanted this one more than I ever wanted any of my own.

"She looked around at me, shook her head and reeled in. That was all. I don't know what I said—if anything, it was futile and banal. Her fly and tippet were gone. I had to go to her to tie on another tippet because she didn't know how to tie a barrel knot. I realized, without asking, that she wasn't through yet. When I stood next to her she was shaking a little and, by God, I had difficulties with that barrel knot and I knew she saw it.

"She went ahead, upstream, while I sat down on my rock and resumed my smoke. She drew away from me, casting and wading easily, and the dusk was getting a little thicker. Trout were coming up here and there—not many, but those that rose looked as if they meant it. Mostly they were out of her range.

"I took my eyes away from her briefly to watch the nearby water. If another rise occurred here I was going to call her back. When I looked at her again she was into something and in a moment I saw that he was big. He rolled once on the surface and I saw his flanks. I judged him to be about a nineteen-inch fish and heavy for his length.

"I started toward her but she waved me back. 'Let *me,* let *me,*' she said.

"He came downstream and she came with him, and I backed away. He swerved and bored over to the far side toward a nasty mess of roots. But she turned him and he was still on, heading upstream now like all possessed, and she followed him again, holding the pressure. He came up again and showed himself. I started to yell something but held it in. She was doing all right and I saw, after a while, that her fish was well hooked. He won slack a couple of times, coming toward her, but he stayed on, and as he went away she'd give him what must have been the right amount of pressure. All of this was on her own, mark you, and maybe she had profited by the loss of the other one.

"I knew she had him, after fifteen minutes or so, and I think she knew it too. Her whole lovely figure—if you'll excuse me again— was expressive of victory, and only she and maybe I knew how dear that victory was.

"I didn't go near but I called out to her to give him a whole minute more. I couldn't help that bit of advice. I've seen too many fish lost that way—some of my own included—and I was damned if I'd see this one. Aside from that piece of counsel she did it all herself, devising her own technique as she went along. I had my watch on her and called to her when the minute was up. She brought him in, eased him over the net and lifted him out."

The Professor's pipe had gone out. He lit it again and tossed the match over the fire screen.

"Listen, I was imagining a lot of things again, perhaps, but I tell you I saw then an abstract quality personified in the flesh. I saw the emotion of triumph—which cannot, supposedly, be rendered without shouts or gestures—manifest itself in that girl who still was silent and who still made no sign. An inexpressible elation and relief, as she took her fish ashore. And she was considerably upstream from me, maybe two hundred feet. As I walked up toward her I saw her light a match and bend over the fish for a moment. Then I saw her go back into the water with the fish still in the net and her rod still under her arm. I saw her dip both hands in the stream, take the fly out of that trout's mouth and ease him in. I saw the big slow bow-wave he made as he swam away."

"But why—?"

The Professor looked across the lamplight at my astonishment. "Wait," he said. "There's something else you must know if all this is to make sense."

"The summer before my son died—that was five years ago—he was up here with me. He was just six that summer, a little young for fly-fishing. But I had bought a six-foot three-ounce rod for him —not an absurd extravagance because I used it myself at times— and I coached him along. He was putting out twenty feet of line and leader within a week. Occasionally he would have a strike but several days went by before he landed a fish. Of course I did the actual landing but the boy kept him hooked and brought him in to my net. It was a brown trout of twelve inches—a beautiful wild fish with haloed spots—and it must have felt like a tuna to that little kid. Then something funny happened. He had been tremendously keen about fishing up to that point, full of questions and ideas of his own. He thought about fishing all day, dreamed fishing at night, talked about currents and backcasts and the drag. Then, when he had at last brought a trout safely in, some odd revulsion of feeling got hold of him. I was about to bend back the trout's head when he stopped me. There was to be no killing here. 'No, no. I want him for a pet, Dad.'

"Well, I carried that fish up to the hatchery rearing ponds. Luckily there was an unoccupied pool and I prevailed on old Bill Sykes to give it over to my son's fish. Bill, of course, is a wizard at trout culture. Bill and my boy took over the feeding of the new pet. 'We don't want to make him too fat, Bill,' my boy said. 'We want to keep him hard, like a wild trout.'

"The boy didn't fish again after that, but he would spend hours watching his trout in the hatchery pool. 'He likes it there,' he would tell me. 'He swims around fast some of the time and takes flies on the surface. It's good he's happy there—if he wasn't, Bill and I would have to put him back in the stream. And he'd be caught.

" 'We've named him, Dad,' he said one evening. 'Guess what.' I made a couple of tries, missing completely the answer that seemed so right when he told me. 'Sam Fario,' he said. 'I told Bill today that we ought to name him. Bill said, "the scientific name for a brown trout is *Salmo trutta* but some older-fashioned people say it's *Salmo fario.* How'd that do for an old-fashioned brown?" Well, the *fario* was all right but I never heard of *Salmo* for a first name. I tried to call him that for a while but it was hard to say, if you said it fast, and once when I tried to say it I said "Sam Fario" instead. But Bill said he liked "Sam Fario" all right so we decided to call him that.'

"When we went home we left instructions with Bill to keep us posted on the growth and state of health of Sam Fario. That was late July. In September the accident happened, one morning on his way to school.

"The next year I didn't get up here but I heard from Bill that Sam Fario was a much bigger fish. The year after that, after the season closed, I came up here for two days. Sam was still in the pool but getting too big for it. Bill was concerned about him. 'It's all right to keep him here forever,' he said, 'if you want him to get fat and slow. But your boy wanted him kept like a wild trout, remember?'

"There was only one thing to do—put him back in the stream. And that meant almost the certainty of his being caught. So I decided to appeal to something which could have been only the good will of men. Bill Sykes had a round flat tag made, with a sort of rivet device, to attach to Sam's dorsal fin. That fin was by now nearly three inches broad. Bill had the tag made one inch in diameter. On one side it read: 'I am Sam Fario, a boy's pet.' On the other: 'Please put me back.' It was a special printing job, guaranteed to be legible after a long while in the water—three or four years, Bill said. . . . I

162

didn't say a word to anyone and I swore Bill to secrecy. I was by no means certain of my ground—I mean in the moral sense. It was my private sentiment against the sporting rights of everyone on this water. I should have confessed it then and there but I decided only that I would confess it if Sam were caught and someone started asking questions. And of course Sam could have gone out of our water, up or down, and been taken. But I couldn't provide against that.

"Sam was over sixteen inches long when we tagged him and put him back in the stream, and he had nearly a year to grow a couple of inches more before the next season opened. Someone would probably land him after a long fight and then see that tag. Eh? You know how *you'd* feel."

"I see," I said. "At this point I can put two and two together and make four. When the Niece caught him the following year he must have been, as you say, close to nineteen inches."

The Professor got up and put more oak chunks on the fire. "To my knowledge Sam was never taken until that night," he said. "And when *she* took him she had no one to put two and two together to make four or any other sum. And when I saw her put him back it never dawned on me at all.

"After I got up to her she told me about reading the tag on his fin. Her words had a little catch in them—not entirely from disappointment. She was smiling a little, and laughter was just under the surface of her voice—as if somewhere, implicit in that tragic mess, she had recognized a neat little joke on herself. 'You fishermen are so funny,' she said, 'with your little rules and conceits. I couldn't think of breaking them.'

"But she didn't fool me. No one had ever wanted a good fish more than she had wanted one then—with that damned Aunt back at the club waiting to gloat over her when she came in. But when she got him at last she could release him, as soon as she saw who and what he was. She might have asked me to come and see the tag and if she should take it seriously. Equivocation is easy in a spot like that. And remember, my little sentiment was as foreign to her as the finer shadings of a Buddhist prayer. . . .

"I proposed to her that night, right there on the stream. I married her a month later."

With this announcement I gathered that the Professor's story should dovetail somehow with what I had witnessed on the stream an hour or two ago. But just how, I could not see. Things wouldn't fit as they should. The girl who had finished off a big trout as a tigress would a gazelle and who had kept him despite the presence in her creel of another big one, in defiance of a club rule—that girl would turn out to be the Professor's wife. But the apparent contradictions annoyed me, probably because I was too tired and comfortable just then to be enthusiastic about solving any mystery. And idly I was speculating on how big Sam Fario was by now if he still lived. Two years ago he was nearly nineteen inches—

Footsteps on the porch outside chased the ghost of an idea that was shaping in my mind. The girl herself entered the room. She had changed from her fishing clothes but I recognized her at once in the lamplight. When she had looked at me tonight on the stream I had known that I would not forget her.

"A stage entrance," said the Professor, greeting her and introducing me. "We were discussing you—and your sex—while you were in the wings."

"I waited for my cue to enter," she said, "without trying to eavesdrop. I caught something about these partitions being not strictly soundproof."

The Professor and I looked at each other.

She stood erect and tall before the fireplace, smiling at us like a child who has some mischievous secret.

"I didn't hear all," she said. "Part of the time I was wallowing in my bath like a walrus. But mine was hot."

We all sat down, she on the arm of the Professor's chair. "Any luck this evening?" he asked, with a fair show of innocence.

"Two big ones. One was Sam Fario." The announcement held a kind of mock casualness. But I could detect a tense eagerness under it, as if she knew her words had lit a fuse.

The Professor looked at her blankly without speaking. Then his face relaxed a little in an understanding not quite complete.

"The second one was Sam, eh?" he said.

"Right." She looked at me. "You know who Sam is?"

I nodded. "I do now. When I saw you take him I didn't."

"I know what you thought of the kind of tactics I used on Sam," she said. "It isn't my usual method. The *first* fish—the one I showed you upstream—really was taken on a #12 Quill Gordon and a 3X tip. But I *had* to get Sam, you see. I had terminal tackle, when Sam was on, that I hope I won't have to use again—a leader that would hold a horse. I carried it with me in case I should see him. Poor Sam."

I was still puzzled about one or two things, and so, I thought, was the Professor.

"He felt as if he were well hooked," she added. "But that part was just luck. If he hadn't been I'd have torn the fly out."

"What made you change in time to the heavy leader?" The Professor wanted to know.

"I saw Sam rise, my sweet. I saw the tag on his fin when he came up. It's about all that showed of him."

I sat there with things coming clearer to me, admiring the girl and despising myself, recalling how I had wondered whether she had seen the trout rise or not. She had seen not only the rise but the tag on Sam's fin as he rolled up. At sixty-five feet. And she had seemed to take a long time changing flies because she was changing her leader too. She had *had* to get Sam. And that was another question.

"Just to continue the inquisition," I said, "why did you have to get Sam?"

"Because I was sure he needed a new tag to protect him in his old age. And he did. No one could possibly read the old one. It's two years since the first time I caught him, and he'd been in the stream with his tag for a year then. . . . That's why I had to get him, why I put the heavy leader on when I saw him rise, why I gave him no more quarter than the rod could stand. Poor Sam. . . . Do I clear myself now?"

The Professor and I looked at each other again.

"He's much bigger," she said. "And he's lean and hard. You can see him tomorrow. Bill Sykes has him back in his old pool up there on the hill. And Bill will order Sam's new tag right away."

The Compleat Tangler 5

I forget who coined that apt if irreverent alias for Doctor Andrew Hatch. Tom or Bob, probably, for they were the superior wags of our camp. But it is no matter. His name and its reputation had preceded him to our club. Though its owner was still in his forties it was among the handful of names that would come into the minds of medical men, in New York and abroad, when confronted with a rare and desperate case. . . . There was, too, another reputation of the Doctor's, not quite respectable in the eyes of excessively prim folk, which had somehow drifted up to our club before he came to fish with us. This one was shadowy and not fully authenticated: Tom Garrison, who knew the Doctor before any of us did, had heard of it years ago, before the Doctor had become famous as a surgeon.

In the season that we first knew him and fished with him, in that year when he cluttered up our quarters with his multifarious gear, he was in process of germination as a trout angler. He was evolving. He admitted it himself. Later Tom shook his head over that. "It was not evolution as I have been taught the meaning of the word," he said. "It was revolution."

And it was. The labored course of the Doctor's fishing education was a series of coups de grace administered to the Doctor by nature and by certain sinister combinations of circumstance. But he had eventually and in a surprising way a unique satisfaction. It cannot be called revenge, for revenge upon nature is too large a prospect

166

for man's puny talents. But it was undeniably a vindication of sorts, a dramatic and telling stroke at something which may well have represented to him the collective heart of all adversity.

Doctor Hatch's complement of trouting gear—two trunks full, all new and shiny and expensive—was the most amazing array ever unloaded upon the porch of our modest club. It was complete several times over; Bob Harlow later called it "overkill." The Doctor arrived with it, in an equally new station wagon which was doubtless another piece of his fishing equipment, one evening in May.

"I know it looks vulgar," he said to Win and me, who were there at the time. "But if you don't know how to select the right stuff—and haven't time to find out—you have to take everything, eh? I came away in a hell of a hurry. Name's Hatch."

We shook hands, liking him at once. If we had half suspected him of ostentation when he arrived with his two trunks of gear we were disarmed by this frank admission of his novitiate. . . . We were to become inured to the Doctor's peppering of epithets in his most casual talk and his sustained epics of blasphemy when circumstances were particularly maleficent.

"Let's empty the damned stuff on the floor," he suggested when at last the trunks were ensconced in his room. "Then, as you tell me what's worth using and what isn't, I'll put the good in one trunk and the bad in the other, shut up the bad one and forget it."

Bob Harlow came in at that moment, as the trunk lids were raised and the treasure revealed. We introduced Bob.

"Where's your party?" Bob asked with seeming innocence, gazing spellbound at the extravaganza of trout gear. But the Doctor smiled suddenly and knowingly at all of us. He was perspiring a little from his struggle with the locks. "It *is* a bit redundant," he said. "But do I have to explain all that again?"

"Don't notice him, Doctor," said Win, "unless you want to put him in one of your fly boxes. When you've trafficked with bugs as long as Bob has you become either an entomologist—or an insect. The Pale Evening Harlow."

The Doctor had been a systematic and neat packer: one of his trunks held his fishing clothes, the other his tackle. He essayed the

clothes trunk first, emptying it item by item which he handed out
for our inspection and verdict.

There were, to begin with, four fishing jackets, two heavy and
two light. It was the Doctor's idea that perhaps these were no more
than were needed by a man who couldn't predict the weather two
weeks in advance. Two of each, he explained, so that he'd have a
dry one in reserve in case he fell in the stream or was caught in an
unexpected shower. For expected showers there was a rainproof
cape with hood attached.

"Stow all of 'em except the light green one," ordered Bob. "It's
going to be dry and warm for a week. And," he added as an after-
thought, "you'd better lock up your trunk when you put the others
back. Win is about your size."

"They don't tempt me at all, Doc," Win said. "I'm trying to look
like a poacher so that maybe I can fish like one."

Critical comment and endless debate attended the hauling forth
of Doctor Hatch's wardrobe: his three pairs of wading pants and
shoes and two pairs of boots, his collection of socks, breeches, shirts,
a cork-lined hat and two plain hats, his bandannas, windbreakers,
sweaters, gloves, his lounging robe for evenings before the fire, his
adjustable kapok collar for saving his life if he went down in a piece
of heavy water, his two head nets. . . .

"No kepi against the bats?" Bob asked solemnly. "It's too bad,
Doc, but you'll have to keep off the Club Pool at dusk."

"Bats? Hell, bats never occurred to me. I brought snake-bite
remedies—"

"Bats are infinitely more dangerous than snakes. I'd sooner fish
without a rod than without a kepi."

"Don't let him scare you, Doc," said Win. "He's terrified of bats
—afraid he'll evolve from the nymph stage one of these evenings,
out there on the Club Pool."

The Doctor dug into the other trunk where his tackle was. Six
rods were handed out and examined, Leonards and Hardys and
Paynes ranging from a two-piece six-footer to a ten-foot job that
looked and felt as if it could throw a dry fly a quarter mile. There
were as many reels, with lines of appropriate sizes, and two or three
extra coils, just in case, the Doctor said, and no less than three line
dryers. There were two pigskin leader pouches full of leaders and

another full of tippets, and three aluminum leader boxes to carry astream. There were literally hundreds of flies, dry and wet and nymph, and a great galaxy of streamers and bucktails.

"No spinners, thank God," Win said, "or bait boxes or hooks. How'd you know?"

"Self-defense," the Doctor said. "Somebody told me you guys had a sycamore tree with a stout limb where you hang people caught using spinners or worms."

"Damn," Bob said. "I bought a new rope today from Caleb Wilson. But now I guess we won't need it."

The Doctor explained that he got four dozen of each fly pattern rated as a killer by the tackle-store people. There were plenty of boxes to hold them, a big stock box and a nice smattering of pocket-sizes. . . . The Doctor was warming to his work, pulling out items of tackle like prizes from a grab bag. There were line dressing and amadou, a couple of dry-fly oil bottles harnessed for attachment to a jacket, a spring scales, a hunting knife, a stream thermometer, two landing nets and two creels.

At this point Tom came in from the stream. He stood in the door looking past us, wide-eyed, at the extensive properties of the Doctor. He drew me aside.

"I thought these precincts were zoned against commercial enterprises," he said. "What *is* that—all that in there? A Hardy agency setting up in this place?"

"Better than that," I said. "It's a preview of next winter's Sportsman's Show."

A few more items were still to come. Two pairs of surgeon's scissors, affixed to chains, came up from the trunk bottom. "I wanted *something* in this damned outfit to be homespun," the Doctor elucidated, "so I swiped these from my hospital. What better function than to snip leader ends, eh? They're nice because I didn't buy 'em." He was puffing a little by now. "In a sense they save the whole lousy collection from exhibitionism, what?"

We agreed that the scissors had a practical virtue and represented a proper sentiment.

"This is another beauty I didn't buy." The Doctor was in his trunk again. "Mixed it in our lab." He came up with a large bottle labeled

NITRIC ACID—POISON. "Take a whiff of the fumes," he said, handing the bottle to Bob.

Bob hesitated, regarding the label. "You'll like it," the Doctor said. "It'll remind you of the open road in lilac time."

Bob uncorked it and sniffed. "Gasoline," he said, "and probably paraffin. Doctor Hatch's dry-cleaner and floater for trout flies."

"You know it, eh? But of course I couldn't stump you experts. A damn good fisherman told me about it and I thought it was somewhat—esoteric, if that's the word."

"It is, slightly," said Win. "Slightly dangerous too. And some among the non-gas cult say it dissolves the stickum from the head of a fly."

"Well, I shall resign myself to becoming educated," the Doctor said. "There is one thing more." He was in the trunk again. "Then, by God, we shall have our reward." He came up with a small square box which emitted a ticking sound.

"Infernal machine?" Bob asked.

"We *might* tolerate worms when the water is high," Tom said. "But dynamite bombs—no."

"Ah, I have you licked at last, then." The Doctor opened the box and drew out an alarm clock.

"What the hell," Bob murmured. "We'll get you up, mornings."

"That is not its function, my friend. I, Andrew Hatch, am an early riser by nature. Its function"—he fingered its gadgets—"is to apprise me of the onset of the major and minor periods. . . . Are *they* esoteric to you?"

"They're *my* religion," said Win. "But I speak only for myself."

"Good. Now the minor period, let us say, is due at eleven A.M. I am fishing leisurely as hell, admiring the landscape and not too intent upon the probabilities of a rise. This clock is in the back pocket of my jacket. At eleven A.M."—he turned the hands carefully and a soft querulous whine issued from the clock. "Just loud enough to be heard above the sound of the rapids. And not unmusical, on the whole. . . . At five P.M. we have the major period of the day." He turned the hands again and the clock went "whang-g-g-g" in a tremendous voice.

"Jesus," said Bob. "Imagine that going off on your backside, just as you're casting over a ticklish spot."

171

"It would scare me to death," said Win, "in the calm of the afternoon. No, I do not surrender thus to technology."

"It does seem a little brash," the Doctor admitted. "And I can conceive of certain embarrassments which may ensue from its employment. However, to hell with that sort of carping. Gentlemen, I am going once more into the trunk."

He puffed up this time with a cylindrical package and a little leather case which could hold, in that moment, nothing but glasses. "Let me show this one on the porch."

We went out on the deck overlooking the Club Pool. The warm evening was full of spring: wood thrushes high in the near trees, the far lament of a mourning dove, the purr of the stream where it spills fast into the head of the pool. Two trout were rising out there in plain sight. "That one under the far bank is a good fish," someone said, in a routine way. The Doctor's Scotch and the porch chairs held a lazy comfort. We sat and looked at the stream and listened to a barred owl boom its notes down a long hill to the southwest.

"Have you fished this kind of water before?" one of us asked the Doctor after a while.

"Listen," he said. "Once I heaved-and-hauled for blues over at Plum Gut. A couple of times I piddled around the Sound, bottom-fishing for porgies and tautogs. Nothing to get any sense of handling tackle. What you gentlemen call *fishing*—no, I've never fished a trout stream in my life."

An odd specimen, I thought, looking at him across the gloom of the porch. A beginner at trout fishing, yet he had had sense enough to make intelligent inquiry. A man like that would do something well, other than his daily work. I thought of that other reputation of his, that shadowy lesser fame, and I began to believe in it. He was a little overweight with early middle age but I could guess that he had had, in a time not far gone, the build of a boxer. He had never been large but he had been well-knit in his day. His shoulders were broad but sloping rather than square; there was a narrowing from shoulders to hips and leanness was still the character of his legs. I might have been predisposed to that conclusion, having heard of that other and dusky renown. He had been, according to the legend, not only the financial backer for one Terence Mullally's gymnasium in New York (wherein overweight executives were hardened and drawn fine and taught something of the manly art) but a kind of alternate tutor who rather enjoyed pinch-hitting for Terence on Terence's nights out. He had in fact taught Mr. Mullally himself (if you believed the rumors) a few tricks of self-defense that might have caused the Marquis of Queensberry to spin once or twice in his grave. . . .

"But you're going to fish for trout, I should surmise, by the look of things," Bob was mumbling dreamily into his glass.

"The apprentice is going astream, yes. The masters can judge if it be fishing."

"You'll want a partner tomorrow," Win suggested. "Someone to introduce you to the stream, as it were."

"And to show me how to play gently with my new toys. I want a partner, yes, but I am kind of self-conscious about asking for one."

There were declarations by each as to his pleasure in convoying the Doctor up and down our pools and riffles.

"Let's go inside where we've light on the subject," the Doctor said. "You gentlemen can toss for the dubious privilege if you will. The sacrificial lamb gets a double potion on the next round."

Win had the only tail on the first throw and was eliminated, with appropriate expressions of regret. On the next toss Bob and Tom showed heads. My nickel's buffalo came up and that elected me.

"He'll do for tomorrow, Doc," Bob observed. "Elementary school the first day. When you're ready for the higher and subtler expressions of fly fishing I shall be glad to—" A wet wader sock, well aimed, cut him short.

The Doctor was up early, waiting for me, resplendent in his new regalia. We had a perfect morning, windless and full of birdsong. The sun was coming up unseen behind a big bank of lazy cloud, gray with peach and rose madder washed along its top like watercolors. "A high dawn," the Doctor called it. It was some saltwater phrase, I judged. . . . There would be a rise.

"Take some dry flies," I said.

I led the Doctor down to the Random Rocks, below camp, to start. We followed an old wagon-track road whose function was cordwood hauling; it wound along the edges of woodlots and dipped into breathless glades where hemlocks stood over us in a cathedral gloom. The smoke of the Doctor's cigar hung along blue in our wake. We came out at length on a little knoll above the sound of running water. A long flat of the stream, boulder-strewn, was below.

There *was* a rise, one of those businesslike early-morning affairs, not prolific but full of meaning and purpose. "God almighty, look at 'em!" the Doctor said.

I posted him halfway up this stretch with plenty of good water above him. "Try a gold-ribbed Hare's Ear," I said. "A little one."

"Pick it out, sir. I'll remember, next time."

He had an even dozen, on number twelves, in his box. The tackle-store people had kept the faith.

I stood with him a minute at his behest. "Show me where I'm wrong," he said.

He was wrong in plenty of spots. But the spirit of dilettantism was no part of his makeup. He made no tentative overtures or experimental probings at the great body of trout-fishing lore. He slam-banged in a frontal attack. Delicacy might have crowned his great offensive with some success but the Doctor knew no delicacy with trout tackle. He tried to get distance by sheer physical effort and his line whammed down off the end of his rod in a mess of kinks and coils. A good rise thirty feet upstream subsided in earnest. The Doctor looked around at me, puffing violently on his cigar.

"Show me once, Professor," he said. "Then you can go."

"First, let's get you straightened out. Reel in. Most of it will come all right until you get to the leader."

Another fish rose forty feet above us on the far side where the stream made a little riffle over a barely submerged boulder. The Doctor saw it. "Show me," he said again.

From this angle it was easy. The leader would stay out of it and the fly needed only a short float. I put out three or four false casts with perhaps an exaggerated ease and lack of haste. On the next I shot a few feet and let the fly come down. It was a trifle short but good enough. The fish took it, up close to the stone, a little sooner than I thought he would. But he was on. A fair rainbow, he slashed around for a minute, breaking two or three times before the Doctor's wide eyes and active cigar. I drew him to my net, an eleven-incher.

174

The Doctor seemed entranced. "By the Jehovah," he said, "I'm going to get the hang of that if I stay up here a month."

"It's simple when it's like that—a made-to-order situation." I was secretly delighted with this prompt success before my pupil. "But it *can* be difficult. In those spots you'll do better to watch Tom."

"You were damn neat about it—"

"You don't do this with your porgies," I said, bending back the rainbow's head. "But always do it with a trout, soon as you get him. Humane, and he keeps better."

"And if he's big?" he asked. "He won't be, but if he is—"

"A rock or a stout club, on the back of the head." A priest was somehow missing from the Doctor's collection. "I'll get some ferns for the creel and go on down. Your leader straight?"

"Yeah. It looked worse than it was. You go have a good time and get the dub off your conscience. I'll muddle along."

I knew he wouldn't. If he'd muddle he might get somewhere but he wouldn't muddle. He'd smash into it with the full weight of his fearsome ardor.

And then I began thinking of him not as a fisherman or as a lively presence around our camp but in his professional milieu. I tried to visualize him in his surgeon's garb in the hush of an operating room, in the light that focuses upon that table where hurt men are brought to lie for a while on the outer limits of life. There he would need the delicacy he wanted so badly here on the stream. In that place where the least miscalculation of the hand or mind would mean fearful failure he would need a rare cunning, a cold genius of fingers and nerves, the possession of which his every movement now seemed to belie.

But I knew he had it. Under his gusty surface was something icy and precise and calm. His fingertips, now so hopeless with a trout rod, could in their time and place quicken the ultimate dim pulse of life, caress the instruments they knew and make the miracle of resurrection.

But now he was escaping all that, adjusting the balance where a May morning was peaceful over the trout waters and the world was robust and clean and whole. He should have it while he could. He would be back soon enough to those antiseptic and whispering moments where death would leer over his shoulder and a life would wait on the genius of his fingers.

I went on downstream, beyond his sight. I ought not desert him for long, yet I believed he wanted to be alone for a space, working in his own way with his strange tools.

While the rise lasted I creeled a couple of brown trout whose combined weight was nearly two pounds. It was not remarkable but it was enough. I went back.

The Doctor had worked upstream to the foot of a steep grade of fast water that tails into the flat boulder-studded stretch we call the Random Rocks. He had waded over to the steep and shadowed far bank. Hemlocks lean over the water and rhododendrons fill the spaces between. It was no place for him to cast but he had been casting.

He was lamenting that fact as I came up. His rod was bent dangerously backward, pointing downstream. Following his line with my eye, out through the tip, I could with difficulty trace the crazy pattern of its course back to a hemlock limb, forward to a branch of rhododendron—it lost itself momentarily but I picked it up again —down to a broken projecting root, then back and away and down, in a long straight line to the water, where it disappeared. The Doctor was snagged.

He didn't see me as yet; his lamentation was a monologue addressed perhaps to himself, perhaps to all of nature in that spacious morning. Words issued from his lips in a kind of monotonous chant, like an obbligato to the theme of his deep distress. I could distinguish some of them as I came closer. They arrested me; I stopped in my tracks.

I had had a hint or two of the Doctor's profanity, mere sparks from the central heat of his anvil. But now I witnessed the white core of his iron; I heard, at my little distance, the hammer blows of his eloquence. There was mention of the minor saints, with obscene allusions; there were fancy names for rhododendrons and hemlocks which no upright botanist would dare to honor; there was a complicated but deftly handled conjuring of certain remote and private hells to which he was condemning for eternity his rod, line, leader, fly, and the whole ill-begotten vice of trout fishing. . . .

He saw me then.

"God damn it," he said, summing up.

"The epilogue is weak," I observed.

He sat down on a handy rock, keeping the strain on his rod, and mopped his brow with his red bandanna.

"First," I said, "ease your rod. Let a little line off your reel."

"I can't. It's all off the reel." He had no backing, and I realized we had neglected to tell him.

"What? Did you cast it all out?"

No. A fish took it out—and planted it in a sunken log back there. My backcast hit the water behind me and he took it."

"Well, walk back with the rod a bit."

"Then I can't sit down. And I need to sit down."

"Let's have your rod then." He gave it to me; I walked back the few feet necessary to get a little slack, and rested the butt on the bank with the middle joint athwart a branch.

At this point he arose, grunting, from his comfortable stone. "No," he said. "You came up here to fish, not to be gillie to a benighted idiot."

"You take the rod then," I directed. "It's easier that way."

I waded down to his snagged fly to tackle the trouble at the source. He stood there with the rod, like a man holding a skein of knitting yarn for his wife, while I freed his fly and gradually dissolved the complex geometric design his line had described in the streamside branches. When we were at last free I noticed three particulars which had escaped my attention. He was wet from head to foot, he was hatless, and he was not smoking his cigar. Somehow the first seemed to explain the second and third.

"I went down, up there," he summarized, indicating the fast water directly upstream. "I underestimated its depth and power and overestimated the traction I could get on one of those damned stones. . . . Had a little tangle in my leader. Tried to get it out in midstream, then decided to wade ashore and do a businesslike job, sitting down. But I waded the wrong way—toward the other shore because it was nearer. It was also deeper, and faster—"

"A roll in that water might have been bad."

"It *was* bad."

"I mean—a broken head or something."

"I *did* wham my head against a rock. The cork-lined hat saved both my skull and the rock from fractures. But I lost the hat."

"It'll float, all right. Must have floated down past me while I was walking up the bank. Maybe we can get it."

"To hell with the hat—it'll be good disguise for the first poacher who picks it up. What worries me is my sodden cigars. I've got 'em on a rock back there, in the sun. And you're a pipe smoker."

I reached into my shirt pocket and handed him a cigar.

"Great God," he sighed softly. "Did *you* foresee this—this contingency?"

"No. But Win did."

"Thrice blest be Win."

"A gentleman of foresight," I said.

"Or a belaborer of the obvious," he muttered darkly.

I didn't tell him that Win had given me *four* cigars with instructions to hand them out one at a time, in case the Doctor fell in the stream more than once.

Organized again at last, we went on upstream to the head of the fast water. "This time," I said, "try a light Hendrickson."

"It's just as well. This one on the leader is the last of my Hare's Ears until I get back to camp."

"Hmm. You *did* have trouble."

"I've been battling those bastardly rhododendrons all morning. Of a dozen Hare's Ears to begin with I hung up five in rhondodendrons and one in a hemlock, snagged three in the stream and snapped off two. Does that make eleven? Well, the twelfth is still on. . . . By the way, my dry cleaner for trout flies works as advertised." He had a small, wide-mouthed bottle of his gasoline-paraffin solution sewed into his jacket. "It takes the fish slime off and—"

"Hey, did you get a fish?"

The Doctor laughed in a single short grunt. "I wasn't going to tell you because I knew you wouldn't believe it. But it slipped out. Sure, I got a nice fish."

"Trout?"

"Do you take me for an eel-bobber, sir? Of course, a trout. Are not trout the *only* fish in this stream, between you and me? He must have been a rainbow because he was just like yours. But bigger, an inch bigger—an inch and a quarter, in fact, by my tape. Yours was eleven inches, as I recall."

"Right. Let's see him."

"Ah-h, that's the hitch. I can't let you see him."

"But—twelve and a quarter inches by your tape—"

"Exactly. And that's how I lost him. The damned tape, and my equally accursed hurry to see how big he was, before I even went ashore with him. . . . Do you see? He slipped out of my hands while I had the tape on him. In one moment, which I shall never forget, he was twelve and a quarter inches. In the next he was twelve and a quarter yards—away from me. He got away fast."

I gave him my condolences, as well as I knew how. "But at least you caught a trout," I added.

"It could just possibly have been fluky," he said, "and maybe I didn't deserve it. I was rather snarled up, you see. Some of the damned line between my reel and first guide got around one leg and a little more of it hooked on the buckle of my creel strap. I was trying to step out of it with one foot and loosen the buckle with one hand when he hit the fly."

"And still you could land him. I'll see what I can do about a plaque for the club living room."

"Listen—" He looked at me in an odd appraising way, as if wondering how much more I could take—" I fell down that time too. But the second spill—the one I told you about—was the one that really wetted me."

I left off my fishing to show the Doctor a few of the trade secrets. Possibly he improved a little in his handling of the rod as the day wore on. But he lost a number of items: three or four leaders, six or eight flies, and two authentic trout who rose to his wares perhaps merely to salute his colossal perseverance. Despite one or two subsequent bursts of high-explosive blasphemy and a desultory sniping fire of routine cusswords, I doubt that the Doctor's chance of salvation could be counted among the day's casualties. If that were lost it were lost long before.

The alarm clock never recorded a major or minor period. It was put out of action in that second roll, along with the cork hat and the cigars.

The Doctor tried to repair it that night before the fire. In an hour

he had achieved a complete dismemberment of the clock; in another hour all the members, except fifteen or twenty, were back in place. There being no abode of apparent promise for these the Doctor decided upon an impulse to gather up the entire mess and heave it into the trash can.

"I could have fixed it for you," confided Tom. Tom was scheduled to take up the Doctor's tutelage tomorrow. "But I didn't want it around, shattering the streamside peace."

"Oh, that's all right, thanks," the Doctor said. "I have another one. I am a man of infinite resource."

"You might better spend your evenings tying flies than tinkering with clocks," Bob offered. "There's an art you should learn, Doc. Just think, you could sit here at your little vise and replace all those eleven Hare's Ears, those four Hendricksons, those three Quill Gord—"

"After you quiet down, or preferably before, get me a drink, Bob, eh? You'll find my Scotch—"

Tom had a theory or two when he returned with the Doctor the following evening. One was to the effect that the Doctor should not, ever again, fish for trout. "He may be a good surgeon," Tom said, talking it over with Win and me afterward, "but I don't know—I'd be pretty scared if I knew my duodenum were to go under his knife tomorrow. If he tackles a man's guts the way he tackles a trout stream. . . . Do you suppose he swears at a fellow's kidneys?"

"Isn't he any better, at all?" Win asked.

"How do I know? I wasn't with him yesterday. But he couldn't have been worse. Today he broke two rods—"

"What?"

"Two rods. And a lot of terminal gear. Lost enough flies to keep me fishing a month—and another hat."

"Did he fall in again?"

"No. This evening, on the Pasture Pool, he got a bat in his head net."

"The hell he did."

"Indeed. That was when rod number two broke—in the excitement. When he got the bat out he was bleeding profusely from his right ear."

"The bat?"

"The Doctor. What do you suppose he said, when it was all over? Said he had read a story about bats in which they were called 'the surgeons' because their teeth were as sharp as lancets—so sharp you couldn't feel them when they went in. He didn't believe it, but he does now. He had no idea he'd been bitten until he'd gotten rid of that head net and his hat and the bat with it. Then he discovered all the blood spattered around. He was all admiration for the bat after that. But while it was going on—while that animal was slatting around inside his head net. . . . Well, I wish I could have transcribed his imprecations. They were beautiful, beautiful. I have the deepest admiration for his eloquence."

"Did he get any fish?" Win asked irrelevantly.

"Fish? My God, I forgot he was fishing—there was so much else going on all the time. No, he didn't get a fish."

But he got one the next day, under Win. How, I don't know, and Win's explanation was far from convincing to us. But he brought one back, a brown trout of twelve inches. Win and the Doctor were given the third degree that evening but no incriminating admission of worms or other sharp practices could be wrung from them.

That day under Win appears in retrospect to have been notable for its serenity and general lack of besetting tribulation. No rod was broken, only one leader was carried away, and the casualites among the Doctor's flies were negligible. The Doctor himself returned dry and whole, unscarred and happy. Maybe, we thought, he was getting the hang of it at last.

In the care of Bob on the day following, the Doctor netted a fish early. "Handled it neatly too," Bob reported. Bob is not given to figures of speech but he said he had thought for a while that the Doctor's rough trail of progress was emerging at last into the open.

But this euphoria was too beautiful to last. The session with Bob came to an explosive climax early in the afternoon. Having knotted on a new fly after losing one in a sycamore branch overhead, the Doctor was touching up the fresh fly with his dry-cleaner and floater fluid. Some imp among the Doctor's demons had set the stage for this ultimate coup with foresight and impeccable precision. A passing zephyr blew a hot coal from the Doctor's cigar smack into the wide-mouthed bottle containing his precious gasoline-paraffin formula. The bottle, encased in its neat sheath on the front of the Doctor's jacket, went off like a small hand grenade. He sustained a slight scorching of his whiskers, a blackened jacket and a lost button. He pooh-poohed these minor wounds but perhaps his pride had been touched at last. A little too much had gone wrong.

Rain, threatening all day, had come on in the afternoon, putting a merciful end to this most fateful of the Doctor's days astream.

That northeaster persisted for two days, intermittently drizzling and pouring down, slantwise along the constant wind. It provided for Tom, Bob, Win and me a welcome excuse to rest from our labors. We killed time before the fire in the big room, drying and dressing lines, replacing tippets, and going out occasionally to look at the leaden sky and the rising stream.

The Doctor, however, grew impatient. He who had labored harder than any of us wanted no rest of this sort. He had come up here to fish, he reminded us. The storm was only a heaven-sent opportunity to prove his fine rainproof equipment.

At noon of the second day he went forth alone. He returned a few hours later, miraculously dry under his fashionable watertight cape. He had one small trout and one large idea. He broached the latter to me:

"Tomorrow it's going to be clear, according to my pocket barometer." (That was one item of his equipment I had missed.) "It's your turn to fish with me, is it not? All right, listen. The stream down here is too high, and it will be too high tomorrow. But up above, in the headwaters of the south branch where the rain doesn't raise it much, it should be good, eh? Up where the public promenades the banks, what? Let us mix with our less fortunate fellowmen, upon the morrow. Up where no sign tells you to keep off. I'm tired of signs, even when they don't apply to me. It's making me feel smug and snobbish, just looking at 'em. Let's go where water is honest water and pools have no romantic names. I seem to lack a rapport with these lyrically labeled joints anyway. The Poacher's Pocket, the Monolith Glide, the Elbow, the Random Rocks have hardly fulfilled the poetic promise of their names. To hell with 'em. Let us go slumming tomorrow, my boy, up where a pool is just a pool, a riffle just a riffle, and some kindly native will lend us a worm if we need one. Eh?"

"I bow to your eloquence," I said. "I'll go."

The Doctor's barometer had called the turn. The morning was clean and fair, rain-washed and cool, full of the high tide of spring. We set off in the station wagon for the upper reaches of the south branch, ten miles away. In the swift passage of fishing days I had forgotten about calendars and the man-made sequence of time. Somehow it was a Saturday but I hadn't been aware of it until I saw the number of fishermen's cars along the road that climbs the narrowing valley.

"Looks like competition," said the Doctor.

We drove another mile up the valley and parked. The stream here was little more than a brook and the ranks of the Saturday fishermen had thinned a little.

"Let's fish wet flies downstream," I said. "We'll leapfrog around each other."

"We'll what?"

I explained the technique of leapfrogging and the major tenets of the code. "If you hit a likely spot it's better to stay with it a while than to move in and out of the crowd." I didn't mention keeping off the other fellow's water and giving a wide berth to anyone he passed. In such things the Doctor's instincts would guide him.

I had my usual misgivings about the sundry engagements with the foliage in which the Doctor would surely involve his gear. Rhododendrons were massed on both banks of the little stream, waiting for him. Hemlocks arched over many a pool. Space for a backcast was at a premium everywhere. This would be much more difficult fishing than any the Doctor had known to date.

I had him start below me so that I could work down to his troubles. For some minutes all went comparatively well. I could see him, occasionally, fifty yards ahead, but I couldn't hear him, and that was a good sign. I knew that if things began to go seriously wrong he would start consigning to his special crypts of Hades such of his appurtenances and physical environment as had found, in that moment, an affinity for each other.

And, for a time, things went well with me. I took a fat nine-inch native with my tail fly, a white-winged Coachman, on an early cast. I stayed with that little pool, practicing what I had preached to the Doctor. Nothing more came up but it was a pretty place and nice water to cast over, so I lingered with it.

The Doctor began erupting, mildly, downstream. It was a mere skirmishing on the outposts of profanity. A couple of routine maledictions drifted back to me. Nothing more than a lost fly, I surmised.

A fisherman wearing a straw hat and knee-length boots came down to the stream from the right bank, just below me, and started working up in my direction. This fellow was a steel-rod wormer and not a very good hand at his calling. And, I decided after a few minutes, he could benefit by a lesson or two in stream etiquette. He splashed closer, plunking his gob of worms upstream and letting it drift down. He came well beyond the point where I thought surely he would go ashore and around me.

A leader-crosser, I concluded—the first one I had met in years. He came into the very tail of my pool, his bait now dropping upstream from my two flies. I began, slowly, to get mad.

"Too close for comfort," I said. I wanted to say get the hell out of here you goddamned lout, but I am not thus constituted.

"So what?" That voice had never grown up in the country or the small towns hereabouts. It had a city sneer: it would be at home in a Lexington Avenue subway express.

"So you'd better go around me," I replied, wanting to add an appropriate embellishment.

He looked at me darkly, without moving. I took in his physical attributes then, as one will do in such moments, and saw that they were ample. He was taller and much heavier than I. His chest and arms filled out his bright yellow shirt. A little fat, but there was power under it. A two-day growth of black stubble smudged his chin. Probably he wrestled a big truck around the metropolitan highways.

"How's fer *you* goin' around *me*," he said. It was not a question; it was, I gathered, an ultimatum. He plunked the worm in again, three feet above my Cahill dropper.

"No," I said. "I was here first and I'm going to stay. And there's not room for both of us." I was aware that such talk would lead me up to a showdown and that probably I was going to get licked. But I was mad enough, now, to be beyond any great concern over that prospect.

At this point a new factor injected itself. The Doctor had walked back upstream, giving the water a wide clearance, and was now coming down to me from the rise of the left bank.

"Had a nice strike on a Cowdung," he began, "then hung the damn fly high in a hemlock. Only one I had with me. Could you lend a poor man a Cowdung please, sir—a number ten?"

Then he noticed my competition and looked at it a moment without speaking. Finally he said, calmly, to both of us, "Isn't it pretty close quarters—if it's any of my business?"

"It *ain't* any of your damn business," pronounced the wormer. "What are *you* buttin' fer anyway—you bastard."

The Doctor gave him a penetrating scrutiny for perhaps three full seconds. I glanced at the Doctor then, and I saw something go out of his face. I saw the face I had known leave him. What was left seemed to stiffen and go ash-gray, like a cooling metal.

"I see," he said. "So that's how it is." His voice was low and easy, almost conversational. He rested his rod against a branch, unslung his creel and landing net, took off his jacket, and carefully stowed them all beside the rod. I could scent trouble.

"Take it easy," I muttered.

The Doctor paid no attention to me. He stepped down to the edge of the water, opposite the wormer. "Put your rod down and come over here and apologize," he said, still in the same easy tone.

The big man showed a little surprise but mostly a surly amusement. His lip curled at the corner but he didn't speak for a moment. He was making some dull appraisal of the Doctor and concluding there was nothing much to worry about. The Doctor's avoirdupois was about two-thirds of his own, and the Doctor's waders and hobnailed wading shoes would hardly help his footwork.

"Ya wanta fight, uh?"

"I said apologize. If you'd rather have it *your* way I shall be delighted."

"Heh, heh. Th' little joik wants *me* t' 'pologize."

There was that curling sneer again as the man splashed across the stream where the Doctor stood, confronting him like a statue. I was worried. I stepped up closer, behind the Doctor. Two against one is not a sporting ratio but this thing didn't look like a sporting affair. It looked like plain mayhem. Then I thought for a fleeting second of what I had heard about the Doctor's former skill with his fists. I

186

hadn't much confidence in that rumor just then; anyway, this character was nearly twice the Doctor's size. It still looked like mayhem.
"Stay out of it," the Doctor snapped at me icily, without turning.
The big man threw down his steel rod, then took a step toward the immobile Doctor, started a right-arm haymaker from his knees and let it go. The Doctor's right foot went back, his body pivoted down and sideways from his hips as that terrific swing fanned the air over it, and came up behind his opponent's spent punch. The Doctor danced in, right foot, left foot, and got his own offensive into play. He was close up, inside the enemy guard, and his left fist was a twinkling blur of light like a burst of gunfire in that ugly face. I heard four or five thuds, too swift to be counted. The sneer was gone; in its place, just where it had curled the lip, blood was flowing.

The Doctor was shifty and elusive as pipesmoke in a morning breeze. He who had tangled his lines and leaders all week was tangling now in another way, a way he knew to the ultimate detail. The hammer blows of the enemy lunged at him again but he wasn't there. He leaned and ducked away, danced and sidestepped over the stones in his hobnailed wading shoes. What he would have been in fighting togs, on the level floor of a ring, perhaps only Terence Mullally and a few others ever knew. ... And then he eased in again, shifty and unpredictable, inside and under those flailing arms, and there came once more, full in the enemy's face, that snake-tongue action of the Doctor's merciless left.

The big man rocked back on his heels, staggered once, braced himself and tore in with a roundhouse left and right. The Doctor uncoiled like a steel spring, leaving the ground with both feet, sideways. The momentum of that tremendous rush and his unconnecting blows carried the man well beyond the Doctor. As he turned, the Doctor was inside him again. The Doctor's left, leading, licked out like flame at the enemy jaw three times, across less than a forearm's length.

I saw the Doctor's face, different now, but again as I'd never seen it before. It was smiling faintly, his only outward show of the joy of his mastery. It takes too long to tell, longer than all of the Doctor's beautiful action, of the revelation I had in that moment. Here at last was something he could do supremely well. He needed no profanity here. Here, and in one other place, he was king, and he could do without the compensations of blasphemy in both. In this little arena, and in that other one, that white still room where men came to his table with their hurt and eaten bodies, the Doctor commanded his genius. . . . He was on top now, after his days of bungling up and down our stream, his days of humiliation and defeat.

And when I saw his right follow the third of those trip-hammer lefts—when I saw it gather like a coiled snake about to strike, about to fade into that brushstroke of light and shadow—I knew that all of his floundering days astream were pent up in it. The rhododendrons were in it, the endless hang-ups and snags, the slippery rocks that had thrown him for a loss. The bat in his head net was in it, and so was the explosion of his dry cleaner for trout flies.

And only thought could encompass all those in the split second when the Doctor's right detonated under that bloody chin.

The big man swayed dreamily in his tracks and collapsed, slowly at first and then with gathering speed, the way an old rotten oak goes down on a windless day in the still woods.

The Doctor, untouched but puffing a little, stood looking down at his man. "My wind isn't what it was," he said. "I had to get it over in a hurry." That deadly gray in his face gave way to the slow tide of his old ruddy color.

And as he stood there his alarm clock whanged off in his back pocket.

"The major period," he announced.

"The end of round one," I corrected. "But the bell was too late to save him."

We doused his bloody face with stream water. Maybe the loud alarm had brought him to, for now he sat up. The Doctor donned his jacket again, took a folding cup from one pocket, a flask from another, and gave the man a long swig. Then he picked up the steel rod and laid it across the loser's lap. "You'll be okay in ten minutes," he said.

The man swallowed the whisky in two gulps. Then, surprisingly, he held out his hand and the Doctor took it. "Jeez, buddy, ya can use yer mitts. Where'd ya loin?"

As we left him I complimented the Doctor on his show. He said, "I'm kind of sorry now."

"He asked for it."

"I know, but look at his angle. We fish our private water, have it all to ourselves. He has to fish a crowded stream on a Saturday, the only day he can take off from his job. And he just might be a good guy withal."

"Look, if you hadn't known how to handle him he'd have murdered you, and me too."

"Well, yes. They all fight that way when they don't know how." After a moment he added, "And I'm afraid that's the way I fish. But if you'll give me that Cowdung, now, I'll try to do better."

Challenge at the Elbow 6

Roger Steele, not normally a praying man, thought seriously of praying now—for a three-day rain. A northeaster of that duration would interrupt his haying operations for nearly a week and raise the Big Stony above a decent fly-fishing level for the same length of time. After that he might safely be seen in the vicinity of the Elbow, where a corner of his employer's twenty-acre timothy field slanted down to the stream.

Decidedly Roger Steele could not safely be seen there now. Yet he had no practical means of avoiding the scrutiny of any fisherman —or, chiefly, of a fisherwoman—who might this morning be passing the Elbow on his way upstream or down. Lapping the big field in the tractor-mower, with the side-delivery rake hooked on behind, consumed about ten minutes. Thus six times an hour Roger Steele rounded, with a great noise of gasoline exhaust and a clatter of the trailing rake, that point of the field which juts into the hemlocks and hardwoods flanking the Big Stony at the Elbow. His mechanical racket, so dominant in the far upland quiet of the field, at this point fought with the roar of the rapids. Perched high on his vibrant seat Roger could hear the Elbow's rush and thunder grow in his ears as he approached the lower corner of the field, reach a crescendo as he made the turn and fade beneath the detonations of his engine as he climbed again the long slope to the northeast.

It was his first experience at mowing hay on a large scale with the implements of modern agriculture. Academically and in a detached way he didn't like it; he had, for a man of his years, an unusual complement of reactionary prejudices. And at the moment, banging and clattering down to that dangerous corner of the field for the sixth time this morning, he more than ever hated, with an unacademic and wholly specific bile, these mechanical conceits of modern agriculture, in particular the one he bestrode. A horse-drawn mower would take twice as long to lap the field and would be quiet doing it. He would touch in at the Elbow, then, every twenty minutes instead of every ten, reducing the danger of detection by half, and his approach—indeed his presence anywhere on the field —would not be heralded to every human soul within the radius of a mile.

But since such recrimination was idle he turned to figuring his chances under his existing handicaps. He noted that he had mowed in the six laps a forty-foot-wide strip of timothy. It would be wider, he knew, if mowed by an expert, for he was overlapping too much. Well, that was nearly seven feet for each lap. In six more laps— another hour—he would be forty feet in from his present position. In two more hours, eighty feet in; in three more, a hundred and twenty. It was hopeless. Mowing all day would still leave his track near enough to the stream to bring him within hailing distance if she should pass. ... Not if—when. For she would pass sometime. She had told him so, yesterday.

That prayer for rain, if he offered it up, needed to be answered. Looking at the sky, however, he concluded that it wouldn't be. The great arc from zenith to horizon held scarcely a perceptible gradation of color. The horizon was deep blue, clear and remote. A small flotilla of cirrocumulus clouds cruised out of the west, infinitely high. June was established at last. Perfect haying weather—it would hold for days. And the inscrutable old heart of his employer, Christopher Wintermute, could rejoice. ... Since that prayer could not possibly be answered he'd better not make it. No need to lose what little faith he had left.

He got safely around the turn and headed northeast again, up the long slope of the field, two thousand feet to the next corner.

He needed to think, to reflect a while in silence, to sop up in his body some of the country peace he had come here to find. Five hundred feet up the field he turned off the ignition switch.

The profound quiet of the June morning collapsed upon him like something palpable, like a giant tent that had been held up by the ridgepole of his motor. In the relief from noise and vibration he stretched his arms and took a deep draught of the soft air. He climbed down, walked to the edge of the woods and sat on the warm matted grass and dry leaf mold under a big oak.

Peace. It had been a structure, an edifice, laboriously to be built of flimsy materials in inhospitable surroundings. But here it was made solidly to endure; it stood open to him and had only to be tenanted. He considered himself a realist about peace. He had sought it deliberately and found it here, aided by a sympathetic if somewhat garrulous physician who had appraised the damage to his lungs and nerves resulting from an intimacy with chlorine gas and high-explosive shells one morning before Amiens.

(Roger did not like to recall that morning. Not the gas or the shells or any of the ruthless steel of war scratched and rasped in his memory, but an omission he had been guilty of, a momentary wavering of his character in one minute of that screaming dawn. A thing he could have done but didn't, an act of bravery good for a citation, the brief whisper of a challenge he had failed to accept. And a man, hopelessly wounded anyway, had died in that moment of his hesitancy. A case not of cowardice: the cool remembering years could never call it that; but a case of being a little short of some old and dim ideal. The delinquency, if it were such, had been seen by no one from his colonel down, and had long since slipped deep below the level of his conscious mind. Only at rare intervals would it be evoked by some passing remark or thought to be briefly unseated from the soft bed of memory, its rough edges scratching a little as it turned up again.)

In the garrulous doctor's office the old platitudes and shibboleths had been hauled out again, dusted off and made to do another stint of life-saving. "Country air is what you need, my boy. Higher air than you're getting in New York but lower air than you'd get in the Rockies. Country air, country food, quietness, a social setup approaching but not quite achieving solitude and enough work, not too violent, to give a physical purpose to your daylight hours.

"I trust you do not care a damn about money," the doctor had added, "or about the raised eyebrows of some of your hothouse associates when they learn that you wear overalls to business and get manure on your shoes."

"I don't," Roger had said. He had a little money and needed less, having no one to support. "And to hell with the eyebrows."

"I know a chap," the doctor had grown specific, "—happens to be the best surgeon in the world—who is a member of a fishing club up near Stony Forks—"

"I like the name," Roger had observed.

"—kind of a man who knows everyone within ten miles a week after you set him down anywhere. His acquaintances around Forks Township—"

"I like that name too."

"—include not only the members of his club but the poachers who infest their stream, the storekeepers and midwives of the village and every farmer in the township including one old coot who owns a long stretch of the Big Stony and leases the fishing rights to the club. This worthy agriculturist, name of Christopher Winter-mute, will, if my surgeon friend asks him, give you a job as farm-hand, with special stipulations as to working hours. Does it sound like anything to you?"

"I'll take it," Roger had said. "The stipulations to be as prescribed by you, in the interests of my delicate physique. No special privilege otherwise. I don't want to be any teacher's pet."

"It isn't delicate. It's 180 pounds right now. But it will be delicate if you work fourteen hours a day. Your pay may be adjusted in accordance with the stipulations, of course."

Roger had begun to feel militantly misanthropic. He would get away from people for a good while. And from business. He was sick of people, sick of his day-by-day acceptance of the ceaseless demands of his job. He had allowed that he would work for Mr. Wintermute for next to nothing. If the place names—and the visions they evoked—meant anything he would be paid fabulously in a different coin.

And he was. He was getting rich on it. ... Up there at the far corner of the field was Wintermute's house and his agricultural plant: the barns, silos, poultry houses, hog shelters and miscella-

neous outbuildings. One of the last was the present home of Roger
Steele. A one-room white clapboarded structure, it was complete
with cot, table, chair and a shelf of books. It was an outpost of
Wintermute's empire, a remote enclave in his far-flung domain.
Fronting it was the sweep of the timothy field, like a sea; behind it
were the hog shelters. The spring nights in Roger's little cabin had
been murmurous with soft porcine gruntings and the contented
mewling of new-farrowed pigs nuzzling and pawing at the great
udders of their dams.

Yes, he had been getting rich on it—until yesterday. He had lost
five soft pounds, developed an appetite like a black bear's in early
spring and, until last night, had known again the benison of dream-
less sleep.

And then, yesterday, he had met that girl, exchanged a handful
of brief sentences with her ... Priscilla Winthrop. A demure, a
chaste name. A name out of American history, a name for a Longfel-
low heroine. It had a far-off, early-grammar-school fragrance. But
her Puritan ancestors had been rebels, in their time and manner.
And she was one, in hers. Something smoldered under her ancient
pride: a spirit tense and eager as a sprinter poised for the gun.

The June morning was a low drone in his ears, the chant of the
oncoming summer. A hundred honeybees were plundering the
clover bordering the timothy field. He felt drowsy in the oak shade;
he leaned back against the great corrugated trunk and closed his
eyes.

Twenty-four hours ago he could have slept easily, here in this
place. But twenty-four hours ago he had never laid eyes on Priscilla
Winthrop.

He had seen her father, though, much longer ago than that. . . .
Against the deep red of his closed eyelids he pictured again that
brief encounter of yesterday.

Off duty just after lunch he had wandered down through Wintermute's thigh-deep timothy to the point where the field reaches
close to the Big Stony. He had gone up to the very edge of the water
at the head of the Elbow. Here was a little beach of stones, a nice
place to stand and look. The beauty and strength of the stream had
touched something unsuspected in him; he had been commanded
by its sheer power and movement and sound. Standing here close

to it, where it slid from a glassy smoothness into the tumult of the Elbow, he had heard it as he never had heard water before. It had a symphonic quality: its basic rhythm was full of secondary sounds, overtones, grace notes, watery comment as it sped by, like individual protests in the babel of a great crowd. The water had dominated him, held his almost complete attention. Once or twice before in his life the majesty of great music or of great prose had affected him in much the same way. This, he had thought afterward, was the age-old and forthright meaning of art, the simple answer to that question men had tried to make so involved.

He had been conscious suddenly of a movement along shore downstream, a flash of white in the corner of his eye. An elderly man and a girl, in fishing clothes, were coming toward him; the white had been the man's canvas hat or the girl's blouse above her waders. The faces of both had arrested him: the girl's for its startling loveliness, the man's for its odd familiarity. Roger and the man had looked keenly at each other; then recognition had come to both.

The man had advanced, smiling at Roger with a little puzzled smile, his hand outstretched. Roger had grasped it and all three had moved back from the bank, away from the uproar of the stream.

"I feel that I should salute you rather than shake your hand," Roger had said. For the man was none other than Colonel Winthrop, former commanding officer of the field artillery regiment with which Roger had served abroad.

"That is all over, my boy. Were it not over, the regulations would not be trespassed by a colonel shaking hands with a first lieutenant. I am glad to do so now, Lieutenant Steele. Think of meeting you here after so many years."

He had the same meticulous manners and speech, the same old-school dignity Roger had admired in war days. The counterfeit of that virtue is pomposity and is apt to desert a man under stress. But the genuine thing is present in all weathers: Roger had heard precisely these accents when the close and accompanying thunder was not that of the Big Stony's Elbow but of shrapnel and high-explosive shells.

The Colonel had presented his daughter then, but she had not held out her hand or nodded or acknowledged him in any way except with her eyes. Her voice had said "How do you do, Lieutenant Steele," because her father had introduced him that way. But the words had been proper and meaningless, a mere concession to the proprieties, discharging dutifully her obligation to recognize this exhibit of her father's. Her voice, Roger had thought, must be lovely when it spoke to those she loved. Speaking to him it had been carefully sterilized. But her eyes had seemed to betray it. They had looked up at him from their slightly lower level, blue and large, judging him quickly. At the verdict a look of relief or happiness had washed into them like a liquid, and the liquid had sparkled with the laughter in it. . . . And that night he had lain awake a long time trying to muster the forces of his reason against a pointless question his emotions had raised.

Feeling that his presence in the club preserve demanded an explanation, Roger had given a brief synopsis to the colonel. "It was partly my own crankiness, partly doctor's orders," he had said, summing up.

"The old sores troubling you still? It is too bad. Shellshock and gas are vindictive enemies. They are slow to forget."

"All this—" Roger had smiled to deprecate a gesture that implied all of the neighboring world, "has been good medicine. This quietness, and the simple chores I have to do."

"You didn't pick a very quiet spot here," the Colonel had said.

At that point his daughter had joined the talk. "After all, Dad, he didn't pick it for conversation," she had said. "For thought, it's as good as silence—when you're very close to it or in it."

Roger had looked at her. "It has a totality," he had suggested.

She had nodded agreement as if he had enunciated precisely her thought. "It's a lot like silence—not quite pure—full of its own little separate sounds." And it seemed to Roger that she had been listening to his recent reverie.

"I am not fisherman enough to have developed these finer sensory perceptions, perhaps," the Colonel had observed.

"Being too much of a fisherman might dilute that kind of perception. Two to one Mr. Steele isn't a trout fisherman," she had added, to Roger's amazement.

"Are you a trout fisherman, Mr. Steele?" the Colonel had quickly challenged her.

"No, sir."

"How did Priscilla know that? Do you read minds, Priscilla?"

Her mouth had been grave but the laughter had sparkled, still, in her eyes, looking full at Roger. "A trout fisherman wouldn't have been looking at the stream as you were, just now."

"Why not, may I ask?"

"Because he would have been thinking chiefly of how to cast over it and his preoccupation with tactics would have shown in his face."

No woman had ever said a thing like that to him. He had felt that he didn't like it. It was reasoning of a pretentious, facile and obvious sort, making small allowance for the subtleties and compromisings of the human character. Moreover it was meddling in his own affairs. . . . A mind reader, the penetrating, X-ray sort of woman who can't let a man have a thought to himself. Women like that could be unmitigated bores. He didn't think she was but the possibility had given him a valid reason—if he needed one—for dismissing her from his mind.

The Colonel had made the move to go, holding his hand out again to Roger. "Could we see you again, Mr. Steele? At the club, some evening?"

Roger had declined. Seeing the Colonel, alone, would have been pleasant enough. But with the Colonel's daughter it had looked too much like the beginning of an unpredictable and perhaps fatal sequence.

As if reluctant to leave the place she had stood facing downstream, looking back over the long fury of white water. "I love this spot," Roger had heard her say quietly, as if to herself. He had studied her face then, briefly. It was keen and spare without gauntness, shadowed in fine flat planes, its close-pored skin a little ruddy with the summer. It had known suffering, he concluded, and learned how to tell suffering to go to hell. Something of her father's polished iron was there.

"Do you have tactical preoccupations?" he had asked, and the sound of her phrase had made the question seem bold to him.

"Sometimes. Sometimes not. Tomorrow morning I'm coming down here without them. I may bring a rod but only for a very special purpose." Maybe she had a habit of talking in riddles, he had thought.

She had turned away to follow her father along the path. Then abruptly she had wheeled, as if by an act of will, and confronted Roger with a desperate earnestness. "May I see you then?" she had asked.

In that taut moment he had wanted to say yes without any equivocation. To have said yes would have charged his immediate future with something it seemed acutely to need just then. But he had kept command of himself. "I'll be mowing the field all day," he had replied. "You'll hear my tractor making the laps. Once in every ten or fifteen minutes I'll be down at this corner. I shall look for you."

He opened his eyes. The sun was brilliant beyond the oak shade, flooding the timothy field, flashing back at him from the shiny surfaces of the new tractor, that symbol of his duty which stood there abandoned and outraged, waiting for him. The windrows of cut hay, already wilting in the sun, were like long ground swells rolling in from the bright sea of the field. A couple of meadowlarks settled on the edge of the nearest row and moved along it, hunting, like shorebirds on the rim of the surf.

Probably she wouldn't come down to the Elbow this morning, after all. He could almost conclude that his equivocating acceptance of her invitation had been insulting.

For a moment he wished he had prostrated himself at her feet, protesting his inability to live through the long hours until the morrow. Perhaps he should go back now and look for her and apologize for his seeming indifference.

But no. He was glad he had not yielded to that momentary impulse. Emphatically he had not wanted to meet a woman in this place. In coming here he had wanted, above all, freedom from complications, particularly this kind which would embrace in devious ways all others. He had done well to reply to her with honesty.

Roger was not used to congratulating himself and the ensuing sense of smugness brought a strange reaction. For in that moment a flash of insight into another's character, such as he had never known, sparked in his brain like the instant of light through a camera shutter, revealing the loneliness of Priscilla Winthrop. It was gone at once but it left its clear and fatal impression on his mind so that he would forever see her as she had been yesterday, an

actress in a reckless role, concealing with her gay eyes a desperate
overture to one she had thought would respond.

A cynical small voice inside him wanted to contradict all that, to
deny the validity of his discovery. He ignored it for it wouldn't
recognize all he was beginning to see, his own loneliness and hunger. He had been simple enough to seek peace in mere physical
environment. And now that he had found it, it was not enough. It
was a fat, smug, squatting peace, a little insolent in its safe insulation
from the struggling world. There was something more; perhaps
yesterday he had seen its definitive form.

Take it easy, the cynical small voice said again. That sort of discovery would turn out to be a mirage. Men hopelessly lost, men
desperate for landmarks of any kind, would follow such beckonings.
Not he.

The meadowlarks were two flakes of brown far down the field
like a couple of dry leaves drifting with the wind. The shadow of
the oak had drawn into itself, compressed and deepened as the sun
climbed. Beyond it the world was blindingly bright, throbbing with
stillness and the noon heat and the hum of summer. The tractor and
rake stood stark and metallic out there, gleaming in the lush landscape like the curse of mankind upon nature. Heat shimmered up
from the bright steel. He'd get on it after a while, go banging up
the field to the house, have his lunch and resume his haying, round
and round in the dusty afternoon.

The bees worked ceaselessly in the edge of clover. Their hum-
ming almost merged with the far-off murmur of the Elbow. And the
steep intensity of his thoughts leveled off, became dilute and drifted
easily away.

When he opened his eyes he noticed at once that the round dark
pool of the oak shade was almost exactly where it had been. But an
appreciable interval must have elapsed because she hadn't been
there before, or anywhere near. He was looking straight ahead, his
eyes focussing again upon what had filled them the moment before
they had closed. Except that Priscilla Winthrop had not then been
in the picture. She was now.

She stood beside the tractor there on the edge of the incandescent field. She appeared to be giving it a curious and cursory inspec-

tion. He knew of course that she had seen him, and now as he watched her through his narrowed eyelids she straightened from her musing and looked directly at him.

He had an impulse to feign continued sleep. He could get rid of her thus. She would depart in a minute or two if he didn't stir, and that would end her so far as he was concerned. It was his chance, his easy solution. It lay still, within reach, ready to be grasped.

She stood erect in the white light of the field, statuesque and brilliantly young, her head turned away now and facing down the field as if she were deliberating her departure. He saw her full profile: she was hatless and her brown hair curved down to her neck and shoulders in a lush and classic wave. She was without waders or rod or creel. She wore a skirt of some tan woolen stuff, many-pleated and short and full, and a light-green blouse open at the neck. Her footgear was a pair of tennis shoes; above them her white legs were bare.

He knew in that moment when he could have lost her that if she started to go he would call her back.

He saw in her straight immobile figure a quality beyond beauty. It arrested him now as it had yesterday when she had turned in the path and spoken to him. It was neither pride nor austerity but something more basic than either. It might be an inbred awareness of power, the consciousness of a certain strength and certain perceptions useless now in a world which exalted the mediocre. She had that tragic knowledge and in it, he thought, the secret of her loneliness could be surprised. All at once she seemed like a child to him, a child in possession of a grown-up and intolerable truth. She had called out her need to him once. In his ignorance he had not replied.

He rose to his feet and stepped toward her. "Priscilla," he said, as if calling her name could discharge the accumulated storm of his thoughts.

She turned and looked at him and her eyes were laughing into his as they had yesterday.

"Hello—old sleepyhead," she said. "Shall I bring your pipe and slippers?"

"Excuse me," he muttered. He felt let down, angry at himself and at her.

"Of course. For what?"

"For—for calling you by your first name. For sleeping in your presence." He wanted to add, "and for thinking you were a goddess."

"In all this—" she indicated the great field and the encircling woods—"must we be formal? 'Priscilla' is supposed to make life a little easier, though I don't quite see how, for my friends and Dad's friends. Dad was so full of you last night I couldn't sleep. I was dreaming of war. Were *you*, just now?"

And there was that Amiens thing again, turning over and scratching in its nearly healed cicatrix. Had Colonel Winthrop told her? The Colonel may have known it after all and yesterday's encounter had brought it snapping back to the forefront of his mind, and last night he had told his daughter. . . . It annoyed him to meet with that thing again and it added a digit to the sum of his distaste for this girl.

"Just now I was thinking, not dreaming," he said. "I *was* asleep when you came up but just now I was awake. I was toying with a notion."

"Wouldn't it wind up, Lieutenant?"

"The spring seemed to be broken. It was about making believe I was still asleep. I gave it up—temporarily."

He was ashamed of his momentary idealization of her. His own loneliness, not hers, had let him down.

"It wouldn't have fooled me," she said, "the way you'd have done it."

"Why?"

"Because you wouldn't have been any good at that sort of trickery."

There was her probing and predatory insight again, so cocksure. "How do you know what sort of trickery I'd be good at?"

"Because you gave a little start when you awoke. Your head had been sagging and it snapped up, like this—and your eyes opened, then closed, or almost closed. You'd need a few rehearsals."

"That should have reassured you. It's the sort of thing a man ought not be good at."

"Right. If you had been very smooth about it I'd have been scared. I'd have run."

"No you wouldn't. If I had been very smooth you wouldn't have seen through it."

"Oh. A logician."

"Or a sophist," he said. "What are we talking about, anyway?"

She laughed suddenly when he hadn't expected her to, looking up the long reach of the field. It was the first time he had heard her laugh and the sound of it was like the look of it in her eyes. It eased away, leaving its memory in her smile.

"Won't you sit down?" he said.

"Where—on your tractor?"

"Under my oak—or Mr. Wintermute's oak."

They stepped back into the shade. He motioned her to the comfortable place against the trunk, where he had been. She accepted it, thanking him, and he sat beside her on the matted grass.

" 'Wintermute,' " she said. "I love that name. It's a log fire in a low-ceilinged room, and the smell of apples, and snow falling outside."

"That's good. I thought of below zero and Orion brilliant above a snowfield and a great horned owl in the edge of the woods. But the name is too easy of course. It's perfect onomatopoeia—is that the word?"

"It isn't, no. It's mere suggestion. But try something hard. Try 'Roger Steele.' "

"Too dreary, and I know him too well. You try it—same name."

"I'm too prejudiced by my father. You've got to take a name with no personal association, Mr. Steele."

"Roger," he corrected.

"Roger, okay."

"What is the personal association? You don't know me—our acquaintance is only twenty-four hours old. Listen, Priscilla, if Colonel Winthrop said anything ill of me he spoke the truth."

She looked at him sideways, curiously, and he was sure he saw only a mild surprise in her eyes.

"He said you should take up fishing."

"What else about me—in all the war talk?"

"I gathered you had been a good soldier. Why?" she added, as if she had seen a trout rise and was casting over it. "Did you do something conspicuously brave?"

"No. . . . There was a morning, near Amiens, when I could have gone into a shell crater and pulled out a man who was dying. It was fifty yards out and back and two minutes of my life if I'd made it. . . . I didn't go. . . . It was full of smoke and the man thrashing his arms. While I hesitated the smoke lifted and he was still, and there was no use going then. That's all. I'm trying to tell it as it lives in my mind but I don't know if I'm telling it right—I never heard it in spoken words before. . . . He'd have died anyway. But I didn't go."

She had a green oak twig in her fingers and was studiously peeling the bark off it with her fingernails, as if her verdict upon his confession depended upon the thorough completion of this little job.

"It was a long while back," she said at length, peeling the last shred of bark from the white wet naked twig. "In the years since, you've stirred it around in your mind until it's frothy. Dregs from the past are everyone's property—I have mine. Let them settle— if they ferment they can get poisonous. . . . Was my father there?"

"As it happened, he was with my battery at the time."

"Why didn't *he* go, then?"

"He didn't see it. Anyway, colonels aren't expected to—"

"Expected by whom? Are there rules of etiquette in war? Was not anyone else there—your whole battery? Why didn't someone else go, then? Why should God have pointed his finger at little Roger and said 'Lieutenant Steele, be a hero.' I declare, you have a worse conscience than mine."

Well, why indeed? There *had* been others. He could almost feel the thing receding.

"Why should I take up fishing, did he say?"

"He thinks you are the kind. With Dad there are many who shouldn't and a few who should."

"How does he rate those who fish here?" It was an easy, half amusing, loafing-in-the-sun line of talk. He could sit here a long while and listen to her opinions on all inconsequential things.

"Most of the March Brown members are shoulds. But some of their guests are shouldn'ts. You'll see everyone up and down the Big Stony if you watch long enough. Great gentlemen, small gentlemen and mediocrities by day, poachers by night. I've even seen, once,

Lank Starbuck, not a member but decidedly a should. But I didn't see him fishing. No one ever sees him fishing."

"Who is Lank Starbuck?" He felt as if he might be asking: who is Santa Claus?

"The gaunt ghost. The night prowler of the Big Stony. The beloved myth of the March Browns. The legendary trout charmer who materializes in the dark of the moon, seduces his three-pounders and vanishes into the shades. To my mind the greatest of them all."

"He sounds epic. Whom else may I see, perhaps?"

"Not Coolidge—he's dead. Not Roosevelt—he's a saltwater man. Hoover—you'll see him in time. Soon or late he's a guest at every club where trout are angled for. You'll see men who fish for the love of fishing and pompous souls who moralize about it as a means to an end, telling themselves how worthwhile are all sports which keep men of affairs in trim. Justifying it for the sake of their stuffy affairs instead of for its own sake. I like better the philosophy of Professor Kent who admits he'd rather fish than teach English literature. It's why, I think, he is one of the best trout fishermen in the world."

"I feel like cheering you for that," Roger said. An odd little subject, as all her subjects were, but she had given it a meaning. Her words elicited applause from his mind and he could understand that, but why they seemed to burn her brand into his heart he didn't know.

"I shouldn't speak of that philosophy as if I embraced it myself," she said. "I don't." Her voice had forsaken its earlier banter and had grown serious and tense as if charged with some urgency. "Very few women do. Mostly they are not anglers at heart. They are something else first and anglers second. Fashionable first, fishing in the right clothes second. Beautiful first, fishing picturesquely second. Socially ambitious first, fishing at a good club to talk about it later or be photographed doing it. That rot. . . ."

"Whereas," he interpolated into her little pause, "men are fishermen first, businessmen or professors or army officers after that. They plug away at their jobs so that they can get up here for their annual reward. It's why they fish better than women do. With men fishing is the flame, with women it is only the bellows to fan it."

"Very pretty, sir. And there you have the gospel, according to many apostles."

"Where does it hit you, Priscilla?"

"The surroundings, I guess. I can look at fast water, as you did yesterday, a long while—or at a black pool or a sunny shallow. Just look, whether trout are rising or not. Sport if they are, some kind of religion if they're not. Why try to describe it with a lot of banalities? I can look at a trout stream the way some people look at the sea. And it's not all dreamy and meditative. Sometimes it challenges me."

"How?"

"Well, there's a spot in the Elbow I've got to try sooner or later. A big trout rose out there yesterday but Dad wouldn't let me go after him. You have to get close, for a short cast, and that means wading nearly to the middle."

"Listen, you wayward child, I'm no fisherman but I've seen the Elbow and I respect it. Your Dad was right. If you ever went down in that water, and you would go down—"

"Not if I do it right." She *was* a child; her voice was eager and pleading now, like that of a small girl explaining some preposterous tale to her parent. "It looks impossible but it can be done. It's a trick. I've studied it from the bank. Taking off from shore you can make headway obliquely upstream, if you follow the right course, by keeping in the down-current lee of several big rocks. You can get out there and cast—the danger is in turning around to come back and in following the trail on the return trip. Doing an about-face in fast water is risky, likely to throw you off balance—and if you lose your balance out there you're done for. . . . No one at the club tries that place unless the water is very low. Professor Kent did it once but swears he never will again. Lank Starbuck does it in the dark, so the legend runs. . . . I want to. It dares me every time I go by it."

"A sign of extreme youth," he said. "Challenges and dares appeal only to the very young. Out of my great store of years and experience let me tell you of the futility of accepting them. Their acceptance leads merely to triumphs which are sterile, ashen, receptive only to the seeds of melancholy—"

He knew suddenly as she looked at him that she could have replied that their nonacceptance, by his own confession, led to endless remorse or something like that. But she didn't. She said only, looking away, "A dismal philosophy," and he loved her.

He knew she had seen the core of seriousness in the burlesque of his words. "It is," he agreed. "And it can't be yours." Somehow he was getting involved when he hadn't meant to. "I was quoting someone perhaps, though I forget whom. You don't believe him— and by God, I don't want you to."

He wondered at her curious mixture of wisdom and naïveté. She could speak like a sibyl one moment and like a school girl the next. But he was beyond wonder about himself. He who had doubted the fundamentality of every experience of his mature life had seen at last a clear and final thing.

She had leaned forward from the trunk of the oak and lowered her face into her arms, folded across her drawn-up knees. He saw the cascade of her hair and the straight plane of her neck, forward leaning.

"Never mind it all," he said. "I am tired of words." He put his arm across her lowered shoulders, leaned forward and kissed her hair. "I love you." The words seemed not his own, as if a volition outside him had framed them. He had no thought of their import; he only knew the truth they uttered.

She raised her head from her arms and rested it back against the tree, facing him, her head cushioned against the brown mass of her hair. Her eyes looked at him steadily and that laughter, that sourceless light, brimmed in them again.

"No," she said. "You don't love me. You mustn't try to. You don't know me." They were the old, old words, a dusty feminine formality pulled out of the past and used again. If they had ever had any decorative value it was faded and tawdry now. He paid no attention to them.

"I do," he asserted, looking at her squarely. "I know all about you. And you know I do. You knew it yesterday when we met on the stream. That's why you came up here this morning." He wanted to say much more: a crowd of words swarmed in his chest, rushing the locked exit of his voice.

She lowered her eyes, put a hand on his arm and shook her head. "I know, I know. But it mustn't come to this. You were lonely and

I took advantage of it and I'm sorry. You didn't want me up here. You thought you were safe from me, so far from the stream."

"That was long ago. I was a boy then. I'm a man now, and I know what I want."

"I know, too," she said. "You want peace. You want forgetfulness of people—of people like me."

"I wanted peace, yes, without knowing what it looked like." He spoke with deliberation, a little provoked at her. "But I know now. You can give it to me—and I demand that you do."

She didn't reply audibly but she shook her head and he thought he saw her lips form the word. In a quick little motion she lowered her head to his shoulder and immediately raised it. She laughed in a tight monosyllable, a half amused, half resigned laugh. He echoed it grudgingly, as if acknowledging with her their hopelessness.

"I'm going," she said. She stood up suddenly and smoothed her skirt.

"Where?"

"Won't tell you, nosy. . . . Yes I will—I'm going fishing, way downstream. My rod and gear are cached over there in the woods."

"Will you be back?"

"Where—and why?"

"Here—because I'll be waiting for you."

"Don't wait." She looked at him a moment, then averted her gaze across the field. "Never wait for me. You have a nice straight course to travel and I'd slow you up, looking into bypaths and loitering in the sun and accepting silly challenges and embarrassing you generally with my childishness. Forget *me.* Up along your road you'll find a mature traveler who can keep pace with you. That will be the meeting you want—the true union of minds and philosophies. And," she added, her eyes returned and full upon his, "of senses of caution."

"And if I don't?"

"Then you'll go on alone. For likely I'll have lost myself in some swamp where pretty flowers are growing."

She extended her hand to him in a sudden gesture and he took it. "Stay here," he said, to her lowered eyes.

He sat down again where he had been, still holding her hand, and pulled her gently down to her place against the oak trunk. He said, "if I didn't find that union this morning I'm going to quit looking for it. And as for my sense of caution—never mind all that rhetoric. I love you."

She didn't reply except with her eyes. They were direct upon his, oddly grave, neither offering nor denying what he sought.

"Priscilla," he said. It was the old sighing word, the command and the question and the plea all in one, the easy articulation of desire. His arms were around her, and slowly—her body resisting at first but then yielding and sighing the answer to his word—they drew her from the oak and gently to the matted grass. His left hand wandered as a detached being, an entity apart from him, upon the remote and secret pulsing of her blood under the cool curving continuity of her skin. Beneath his eyes the close shadowed grass and her hair seemed microscopically to intermingle. He felt her strength arching into his, and his roving hand, suddenly still and purposeful and again a part of him, abetted the pressure.

Dwelling upon it afterward he thought it might have been then that the ancient New England forefingers had come to point at her darkly and the ancient grave ghosts to remind her of hell fire. Or was it her own rebellious spirit taking command? For the tension of her taut strong body suddenly recoiled, arching back and away from him.

"No." The small syllable was vibrant with that feminine authority which—he reflected afterward too—only gentlemen respect and even gentlemen not always.

He respected it then without any reflection, a little angry at the respect he was showing. But he kissed her lips tenderly and drew apart from her and helped her to her former position against the oak trunk. "I shall not ask your forgiveness," he said, simply, seated beside her.

"I should ask yours," she said. "It was too beautiful for me—here in this solitude. . . . I can't take beauty—this kind."

"Or a challenge either, in spite of all you said about one." Immediately he wanted to take back the irrevocable words. "Forgive me, though, for *that*," he added.

She didn't reply, or look at him.

"Priscilla, forget that I said it."

She got up slowly from her place by the oak trunk. He stood up behind her and she turned to him.

"You try forgetting me, and all you've imagined." Her voice seemed tired like the resigned movements of her strong body, as if age had discovered it while looking for something else. Her eyes came up to his and rested there. The old laughter was out of them. In its place was something too flat and negative to be resentment or contempt.

She walked away, out of the oak shade into the white light of the open. He watched the rhythm of her figure until she was far down the edge of the field. Then he climbed on his tractor seat and turned the switch. The motor fired its machine-gun volley across the still, midday world. He looked back. Halfway to the stream she had turned at the sound of the motor. She stood facing him for a second. Then she was gone.

The afternoon had capitulated at last. Roger had laid it low on the timothy, beaten it down with the tireless slow persistence of the tractor. His circuits of the field had become gradually shorter, closing in on the center where an island of standing grass dwindled with each successive lap, like a reef when the tide is making. At the lower corner near the stream he had kept headway each time around. Scanning the Elbow from his high seat, as he swung by in the early-afternoon rounds, he had seen at intervals two fishermen, both unknown to him. And once he had seen the club guard go up the path.

But she might easily have passed without his knowledge. In his laps of the field he was in sight of the stream for less than a minute, and as his track had narrowed toward the center it had receded farther from the stream. Now his nearest approach was too distant to afford him sight of anyone fishing or passing there.

He had set six o'clock as the deadline when he would stop the tractor and go to the stream to wait for her. It was now ten minutes of six. The sun was still high over the line of woods along the Big Stony but the southwest length of the field was a stripe of shadow.

The routine of the infinite rounds was becoming unendurable. To hell with the next ten minutes to the arbitrary hour. They could hold only what the long afternoon had held, the ceaseless revolving and meshing of the cogs of his thoughts.

He shut off the motor. Even with the sun still high there was the imminence of evening immediately in the engulfing and violent hush. He heard the deep voice of the Elbow booming up through the woods like a shuddering of the silence itself. He descended from his high perch and walked toward the stream, stepping over the windrows of cut timothy. The new-mown hay gave up an ineffable fragrance as if his footsteps had crushed it out. It drew up from the field and seemed suspended in the windless air.

He'd wait for her on the little beach at the upper end of the rapids, where he had met her yesterday.

But before he came to it, while yet he was wondering if she would come, he saw her.

Well down toward the crook of the Elbow she stood thigh-deep in the central boil and fury, almost in midstream.

She had done it, then. She had taken that dare, entered the water from the far side and threaded the course she had explained to him.

She faced obliquely away from him. Her rod was bent and vibrant with the rush of water on the line. He concluded that she was fast to a snag. But it was immaterial except that it seemed to afford her a slight leverage, a delicate support in that furious current. What mattered was her grave and immediate danger. The strange tension of her figure, its backward-leaning angle into the assault of the water, was not the casual attitude of fishing but the grotesque defense of an untenable position.

He knew she was going to give way, and soon. She could neither advance nor retreat from the relative firmness of her anchorage, nor even hold her position for more than a brief time. He could see her press upstream, straining into the charge of water. And the long whip of the Elbow was below her.

The quick start of panic caught him in the throat like strong fingers choking off his breath. He fought it down with an effort. He tried to think quickly of a way out for her, but the ideas jumping in and out of his mind were futile and mocking. He couldn't reach her from his side or cross to try to reach her from the other. The nearest ford might be a mile upstream or a mile below. A rope, if he had one, but by the time he could get it she would be lost.

There was nothing to do but pit his own strength against the stream. He would enter it below her and try to reach her as she came down.

He was racing along the path, downstream, and yelling at the top of his voice: "Hold it—I'm coming." She didn't turn her head or give any sign of recognition, and he knew she had not heard.

He came abreast of her. Here a screen of rhododendrons between the path and the water kept him out of her sight. Fifty feet beyond, the path emerged upon the stream.

Here the water was fast and shallow over a sandbar for ten or fifteen yards out. Beyond that the central current churned by, the edges of its great waves diverging in over the shoal. Out there and for three hundred feet or more below, an archipelago of boulders, some completely submerged, others half out of water, studded the stream.

This was his place to enter, his only possible chance. He would work up toward her as far as he could go, shout to her to give way and catch her as she came down to him. It seemed too simple a plan to be any good, like the facile scheming of a child. He tore at the laces of his heavy shoes, getting them off.

As yet she had given him no sign. It was useless to call again, to try to make himself heard above the sustained thunder of the stream. Here it seemed that all the elemental sounds of the world were turned loose, rioting and storming in the long pitch of the Elbow. He glanced up at Priscilla and met her eyes directly upon his. She waved him back with a perfunctory gesture of her free hand. He couldn't read her eyes at his distance but he felt them to be holding the expression he had last seen. He waded in, giving his attention to the immediacy of the water.

He had misjudged both its depth and power at his point of entrance. It deepened to his thighs a few feet off shore, and even here on the outer flanks of its offensive he sensed its strength. He pressed against it slowly, diagonally upstream, feeling it out. It was like something alive and muscled, trying its power against his. So far, it was not equal to him. He tried to estimate his reserve, the margin he would have left for the final and furious attack of midstream. Over the middle of the sandbar the depth and speed remained constant. He noticed a few surface bubbles, a few derelict leaves jump into the outer limits of his vision and shoot by.

At the edge of the central wave-crested turmoil he paused, leaning into the flood, digging his feet into the sand. He would rest here a few seconds, give the situation a little study.

A hundred feet upstream and nearer the other shore Priscilla Winthrop held the set fantastic posture of her hopeless defense, her line still taut and knifing into the racing surface. She swayed a little, against and with the current. Exhaustion was catching up with her; once, when she eased back from her upstream slant, she struggled to keep her foothold.

He remembered what she had said about the difficulty of turning. She could lift neither foot and pivot on the other without foundering at once. Indeed the delicate pressure she could apply to her rod seemed all that held the balance in her favor.

She caught his glance again, shook her head and smiled. He saw it as a resigned smile, with an overtone of defiance. He knew what it meant.

But his own helplessness maddened him. Desperately he put one foot out ahead of him, sliding it along the bottom. It went down, taking a sounding on a slippery stone six inches below the other foot's level and meeting an onslaught of water that jerked his leg downstream in an arc. He regained with some difficulty his roots in the sand.

Something else then, centuries old but only in this instant catching his eye and mind, came to him like an inspiration, offering a desperate move out of the stalemate.

Just below Priscilla a boulder barely above water split the midstream current like a wedge in a log. If she could throw herself on the stream well out to her left—and she could do it without turning for she was facing that way—she would carry down to the left of that rock and be swept within a few feet of him. How he could reach her even then, he didn't know. A long surface plunge might do it if he timed it right. But if she could swim well—it would have to be extremely well with her waders on—she might even win her way over the sandbar on which he stood. If she could do that he could catch her as she came by and haul her ashore. If she couldn't do that—if she swept past that boulder on the other side—she was lost. And so was he. . . .

He shouted to her again with all he had in his lungs. He waved his arms wildly at her, pointing out the way. He traced with his arms her course to the left of the boulder and down to him, and held his arms wide to receive her and closed them upon her imaginary form, and pointed to the bank. She *must* understand. The tumult could stop his voice but his pantomime could get through.

But she only smiled at him again and shook her head. She motioned him back again, pointed behind her whence she had come and looked at him steadily. He knew she had understood his signals but had another plan, and all at once that plan was clear to him. Keeping her pitiful support—that exquisitely gauged pressure on the rod which if overstrained an ounce would snap her leader—she would attempt to retrace her steps, backward.

While he watched in a tense and rigid fascination she took the initial step, lurched slightly in the press of water, seemed to hold firm an instant, lurched again, lost her balance irrecoverably.

And as she fell she turned in the water and seemed to plunge as far as she could to the right.

He didn't understand at once. There had been a chance of safety the other way, to her left. He was dreaming perhaps: the mad situation had taken on the incongruity of a nightmare. Then, in the lightning idiom of thought, it came to him.

Death was no stranger to Roger Steele. He had looked upon it in various forms. He had seen it settle upon hurt and exhausted men like an evening mist on a landscape, and he had seen it fell strong men in full stride. But always it had been in accord with such physical laws as he could understand. Death had come to those men; they had not sought it.

But for this thing before him now he was unprepared as a child. The shock of witnessing a suicide of which he himself was the cause fell upon a part of him that was untried, tender, infantile.

She had taken the far side, then, to discourage his attempt to save her. . . . So that he could stand here and watch her go because it was hopeless to try. So that he could save himself by his own cowardice, eh?

Yes, he could exercise, now, what she had called, with a tone that had bitten into him like the slow application of a hot iron, his sense of caution.

He lost sight of her for a second after her plunge. Fifty feet downstream from her takeoff the Elbow gathered the forces of its final and abandoned fury. Dark water turned suddenly white there; solid waves, three feet high, were comminuted into spray against the upstanding rocks, and the spray drifted back and across the stream like a luminous mist, crossed with a rainbow in the late-afternoon sun. Through a rift in that vapor he saw in midstream what appeared to be a log heave up slowly in the cauldron and go down again. But as it sank he saw the wader shoe on the end of it and the momentary flash of sun on its hobs.

Yes, he could watch her die. He could play again his role before Amiens, in a different setting. He laughed in some incongruous happiness that came upon him, seeing the end of his keepsake from the war.

He tried to keep himself high as he plunged, to win distance along the broken surface.

But the current took him as a fast-moving train takes a man who hops it from a station platform. The extent of his headway across stream was the length of his body before the charge of water fully countered and turned the force of his spring. He ascended, head and shoulders high, the crest of a driving wave. He looked where he thought Priscilla would be but all he saw was the white mad career of the Elbow, the turn immediately below and the pitch of foaming water below that. At the end, he knew, was the miracle of surcease, the length of a quiet pool. Then he was down, wrenched under in the scissors-hold of an eddy. . . . It would be a minute through the entire stretch. No more. Dead or alive, in one minute he and Priscilla would be through it. It was far away, a lifetime away, but it was only a minute. . . .

He tried to swim in what he thought was the general direction of Priscilla but achieved only an absurd thrashing of his arms and legs. He gave it up. . . . She had been justified in her belief that he would not follow her. No one but a fool would have. . . . His lungs were beginning to want air. He had been down a long time. But no, it couldn't be long—he kept that minute in his mind. Keeping his eyes open he was aware of dark huge forms shooting by. The rocks.

214

One loomed ahead in the underwater gloom; he shot up to it expecting to crash it but the water took him to the surface and it slid by beneath him. He drew breath in the momentary upsurge and then he was down again, turning over and over. He could see the bottom spin upstream, clear stones and pebbles before his eyes. They faded in a gathering darkness. He must be way down: it was dark all around. He could feel his feet and his knees hit hard, cutting against stone. Then his right hand, trying to ward it off. But his momentum doubled up his arm, brought his hand punching into his chest. He closed his eyes, tried to get his left hand in front of his face.

The blow had cut him somewhere in the head; he tasted blood warm in his mouth. But it hadn't knocked him out, by God. That was a fact to cling to. If he could stay with that idea he could stay conscious. He repeated it in his mind, and he thought drowsily of how much of that minute might be left.

But the minute didn't matter anymore, now that he was in this tunnel. The tunnel was so long he could see no opening, no point of light at its other end. It sloped ahead in infinite perspective, eerily lighted and full of moving shadows and the roar of wind and a pressure that would burst his lungs. The light faded and the wind died and he was gathering speed, falling into a darkness that was ultimate and still.

He had been an eternity in that tunnel before a light grew in it again, the faintest gray washed into the totality of black, like the dawn of a winter morning when fog is heavy over melting snow. The light grew around him and now he saw its source, the opening ahead where he would emerge. His velocity had slackened almost to a halt. He was drifting in the growing light and he knew a peace he had never known before.

Out there near the source of the light he heard voices. He was content merely to hear them without making the effort to understand. That they were voices, the sound of humankind, was enough. He had thought, entering that tunnel, that he would never hear voices again.

The light grew stronger; it was a little too bright after that impenetrable darkness and it hurt his eyes. Once, in a particularly vivid flash, he saw directly before him a wide surface of pine boards. He closed his eyes against the light but they continued to hurt. His whole head hurt, and other parts of him—his right hand and forearm and his right leg from the knee down.

The voices were clearer out there, but quiet—a dull monotone against which the sharp edges of his pains seemed silhouetted. He tried to follow the sense of the words, to fit the words together. He would find a place, perhaps, where he could join in.

A man and a woman owned those voices and the man's had a lot of profanity in it. Roger liked that. All at once it made him want to laugh; it made him happy to remember about laughter, about things in life being funny and people laughing at them.

"You get over your damned worrying." That was the man's voice. "He hasn't a fractured skull anymore than I have. A bad concussion and that's all."

"Why doesn't he come out of it then?" It was the woman's voice again and it was familiar to him.

"He did for a moment. It's like sleep—good for him. He'll be out of it again shortly."

"Damn it, don't hide anything from me. Will he stay out, then?" It was Priscilla's voice. He had heard it another time like that, electric with eagerness. It had a sound like fire running in dry grass. But it couldn't be Priscilla's voice. Priscilla had been in some awful danger. She had died in the Elbow or something like that.

"He should stay out long enough for you to tell him you love him. After that let him sleep. He was knocked cold and got a bellyful of water. That's all, other than a few abrasions. All easy to cure—like cancer—if you get 'em in time. As for you and your worrying, you little idiot—"

"Call me anything you please, you big bully. You saved him and you saved me. Your privilege to call names is practically a blank check."

But it *was* her voice. She hadn't died, then. He reached for it, out through the fog, and got hold of it and brought it up close and clear. . . . This man with Priscilla, whoever he was, had pulled both of them out of the tail of the Elbow.

"Luck saved you, not I. Jesus, think of you coming through the

Elbow with a scratch or two. If I had *your* luck—and *his*—in my fishing—"

"Your destiny is to succor the helpless—a nobler destiny than to catch trout."

"A damned dismal destiny. I wonder, sometimes, if the helpless are worth succoring. Whereas the trout are always worth catching. A nice brown was rising to me when you two came barging into my water."

And here he was, Roger Steele, on someone's cot, with someone's pajamas on.

He raised himself a little, the pressure hurting his right elbow, and opened his eyes on a pine-walled room and Priscilla and the man. There was lamplight in the room and at each of the two windows the dusk was a blue curtain.

"See," said the man. "He lives."

"I like it," said Roger.

"He likes living, Priscilla. He'd better, after the sweat I got into pumping water out of his guts."

"I mean—I like this place. What place is it?"

Priscilla got up from her chair, limped over to him and sat beside him on the cot. "The bailiwick of the March Browns," she said. "A quarter-mile above our little swimming hole."

"Um-m-m. I remember. Hurt?"

"No. Better ease down. You banged your head. Feel fairly good?"

"Stiff. All tied up. Look, I *am* tied up." He saw that both his arms were bandaged.

Priscilla and the man laughed. "You have a few others," she said. "So have I." She lifted the left leg of a pair of gray slacks to her knee, exposing the wrapped tape from the ankle up. "Mr. Steele, let me present Doctor Hatch. He's a bully. He called me an idiot just now, but we can't get on without him. You've already been presented to him, in the pool below the Elbow. Feet first, he tells me."

"She *is* an idiot, Mr. Steele," Doctor Hatch said. "Any woman is an idiot who tries to wade that lick of the Elbow. Is there another name for it or is idiocy, perhaps, the right one?" He glared at her. "You madcap, you—I'll tell your father on you when he comes in tonight."

He stepped over to Roger. "Take it easy with that head of yours.

I'm old-fashioned about bad concussions. Twenty-one days flat on your back. Lay up here if you want to. I'll fix it up with Winter-mute."

"Believe me, sir, I'm grate—"

"Never mind. Thanks are hard enough for a well man, forbidden to my patients. If you'll both excuse me, I'll go back and look for Priscilla's rod. A bare chance, somewhere along shore."

When he had gone Priscilla said, "One of the great of this world. He swam out in the pool—and he's not much of a swimmer—and hauled you ashore. Then he came back for me. I was about done. I couldn't have made it alone. Then he hauled us both back here in his station wagon."

From his pillow Roger studied her profile. It was a little worn and pale, strange and lovely to him.

"You and your challenges," he said.

"You and yours." She looked down at him gravely. "Do you understand—everything?"

He nodded.

Her voice was low and tense and her eyes blazed upon his. "I thought it was all over. Your side of the rock held the hundred-to-one shot that I could make the sandbar. But if I'd taken that side and failed to make the sandbar you'd have come after me anyway. And it would have been hopeless—"

"So you tried to retrace your steps backward."

"That, too, held a slight chance."

"A thousand to one against *that*. Because when you fell—and you knew you were going to—you couldn't head my way. You *had* to take the other side of the rock then."

She nodded agreement, looking away from him. "It looked hopeless on that side. It looked so hopeless that I thought you *might* not follow."

"I understand all that. I understood it the moment you gave way."

Her eyes came back to his and she looked wonderingly at him. "But you *don't* understand this—the instant I let go I knew you *would* follow." She turned away and shook her head and dabbed at a tear that was starting in her eye. . . . "I had ordered you to kill yourself and I couldn't take back the command."

"You told me this morning to guard my realities," he said. "I was trying to."

Exhaustion had him. He felt that he lacked the strength to keep his eyes open or to utter another word. But that was all right now that he knew everything he had ever wanted to know.

Before his eyes closed they looked straight into Priscilla's. They saw the afterglow of her tears. Or was it the old laughter, brimming there again?

Old Poacher's Return 7

The long train curved out of the narrow valley and swooped across the expanse of the meadow. From his window in the rear coach Lank Starbuck could see the leaning locomotive, far ahead, rush upon the widening landscape. He could see the churning piston and three revolving drivers and, far beyond, way down the sweep of the rails, a little cluster of buildings. Now a white plume trailed from the locomotive's whistle and its low and distant wail came back to him: Number One's warning for the crossing at Stony Forks. He unlimbered his long body from the plush seat, took down his felt hat and his old black suitcase from the rack above and lunged up the aisle to the door. The train ground to a reluctant and patronizing halt, complaining in all its journals and underparts.

Lank Starbuck got off. The train sighed through its dusty length and labored away, straining up the valley, leaving him there absurdly alone in the wide and brilliant afternoon.

In odd moments during the past five years of his exile Lank Starbuck had contemplated cheering at precisely this point. But now that the time was at hand he couldn't cheer anymore than he could have cheered inside a church. There was a solemnity in this country peace which he either had forgotten or had never known until now. It smote him like a silent wave washing over his gaunt and tired frame, hushing the little surge of his gladness. It was like a benediction to the infinite fatigue of his spirit. Lank Starbuck was a religious man in his own way; he stood there for a moment with his head bowed, and his lips moved faintly with his thoughts.

Then he looked up and around him, taking in the familiar scene. He saw with relief that the village of Stony Forks had suffered no vital change since he had left it. Its physical shapes were intact: the dun-colored depot, the general store, the post office and the quick lunch. The feed mill stood apart on its siding, and the two freight cars basking at its platform might be the same cars that had been there one May morning, five years ago, when he had boarded the train for New York. It was all there, drowsing in the sun as of old. The years had blown by, high over the little village, but only the echoes of their tumult had impinged upon its immemorial peace.

The road he would take to his home crossed the tracks, slanted south over the broad meadow to the Forks bridge and made a long ascending turn around the base of a knoll to the westward.

Lank had an impulse to follow that road at once. Then he thought better of it. He couldn't get away unseen. Dave Strouthers, the station agent, had no doubt seen him already. Dave saw everyone who got off Number One at the Forks. And Dave would have it over half the county in no time. . . . His movements would be suspect anyway, as they had always been at this season when trout were in everyone's mind, but they would be less so if he made known promptly and openly his return to the Forks.

He went into the station and hailed Dave Strouthers, agent there since time out of mind. Dave looked up from the ticking of the telegraph key. "Well, bless me 'f 'tain't Lank," he said, as if surprised. That sly and knowing look, familiar to Lank Starbuck, was in his eyes. Others who knew Lank looked at him with a similar expression between the first of April and the thirty-first of July and, not infrequently, before and after those dates. He had missed it during his five years in the city and he was glad to get back to it again. He felt at last that he was home, restored to his proper sphere.

"Don't be actin' startled, Dave," he said. "You saw me climb off of Number One."

"Didn't recognize ye, though. I'd as soon have looked for the Dook o' Windsor to get off of Number One as for you. God almighty, we been mournin' ye for lost around here. The county's poor have got resigned to troutless Fridays." Dave poked among some freight waybills and express receipts on his desk and added, "An' the fishin' club members have been celebratin' their release from the depry- dations of the past. How ye been, Lank?"

"Older'n I was, Dave."

"You better take care of yourself, at your age. They tell me the stream's still cold as a spring brook. Mark Herring—he's down with rheumatism fishin' up above the Rattlesnake two weeks ago. You won't bother it none up thataway though, I guess, eh?"

Dave accompanied his question with a wink. But Lank needed no such accent on the implication of Dave's words. The Rattlesnake was a brook that fed the Little Stony a mile above the Forks. Up there it was public water. Below the Forks, for three miles, the Big Stony was leased to and posted by the March Brown Fly-Fishing Club and closely patrolled by the deputized guard of that organiza- tion. Those three miles had been the fishing water of Lank Star- buck, man and boy, for nearly half a century prior to the year of the club's intrusion. And in that year Lank had sworn a solemn vow that those three miles would continue to be his fishing water until the day he died. Dave Strouthers knew that, as did everyone else in Forks Township. Yet it was a subject never openly discussed with Lank himself. It could be hinted at, as Dave was hinting at it now. Such innuendo was within the bounds of good manners, indeed it was considered a complimentary recognition of Lank Starbuck's exploits. But the tight little code of amenities in Stony Forks permit- ted no trespassing beyond the line of inference.

Lank Starbuck crossed the stretch of cinders behind the depot and entered Caleb Wilson's general store. Caleb boomed at him from the redolent cool shade in the rear.

"Saw ye comin', Lank—the last of all critters I expected to see. Want some number four Sproats I expect, eh? Or hev ye turned purist after all this time in the big city?"

"Guess I don't need any hooks right now, Caleb."

"No? I've damn near went out of business sence you ain't been here to buy hooks in the springtime. You never been much of a fly-fisherman."

"I've never been one to let sentiment interfere with what a trout needs."

"What about spinners, or an ar-ty-ficial mouse? I hear there's some big browns feedin' below the bridge, nights."

"Who said I was aimin' t' fish below the bridge?"

"Wait now. I was goin' to add that maybe them big browns 'd run upstream some."

"Nope. I just don't want any tackle right now. For one thing I'm short of money. For another I'm seventy-two next month, and Dave Strouthers tells me the water's colder'n all get out. I'm a mite oncertain about my fishin' this year, Caleb."

"Shucks. Your credit was always sound in this here tradin' post. I'll sell ye a pair o' boots that'll keep the misery out'n your legs—nothin' down an' a dollar a month."

"No thanks. I'm walkin' up home an' I don't want t' be burdened with luggin' boots additional t' all the baggage I've got with me now."

"I'll drive ye up, boots an' all, soon as my boy gets back with the truck."

"Nope. Much obliged. . . . Thad might've met me. But I guess Thad's too busy gettin' seed in."

"Thad ain't farmin' this spring, Lank."

"He *ain't?*"

"No. Thad ain't turned a furrow. Sold out his stock, chickens, implements—the whole works—'bout a week ago."

"Well I'll be damned."

"Didn't ye know? Didn't your own son ever write to ye?"

"Practickly never. But then, Thad ain't much of a hand to write."

"Does he know ye're comin' home?"

"Guess so. I wrote him t' that effect. . . . Thad ain't farmin', eh? Well I'll be damned. What *is* he doin'?"

"Don't know. Don't anybody know. Course it's only a week sence he sold out all his stuff—and whatever he's doin' it ain't had time to infiltrate into Stony Forks society. If he had a wife, now, the womenfolks 'd git hold o' the lowdown on Thad's doin's. But he don't have ary wife."

"No. He's got his points, but. . . . 'Tween you an' me, Caleb—and maybe I hadn't ought t' say it about my own son—no sensible female's likely t' take up with Thad."

" 'Twon't get any further'n you an' me, Langtry." There were moments when Caleb Wilson took the trouble to pronounce Lank's given name. . . . "I don't know—I can't figure that boy. He's smart enough, in a way. He's been a good customer o' mine an' paid his bills when due. I don't know what 'tis about him." In his heart Caleb despised Thad Starbuck, without quite knowing why.

Lank was leaning against the counter, his long legs stretched out before him, gazing down at his shoes. "I know what 'tis," he said. "It's his lack o' visible vices. It's his damned petty morality."

Caleb didn't reply. There was no need to embellish Lank's stark and truthful utterance. Lank was a shrewd devil—he could find words for things. He could bring a thing out of the fog in the back of your brain and show it to you clearly, just with a couple of words. . . . Thad's lack of visible vices. Lank was right, by God. Thad never smoked, wouldn't take a snort of whiskey even in the dead of winter. Why, Thad wouldn't even swear. If he banged his thumb with a hammer he wouldn't say "Damn it to hell" like any good Christian man. He'd say "Jupiter!" or "Thunderation!" Lank had seen that much. But Lank was fond of his only child and maybe he hadn't seen what Caleb had always suspected: that somewhere, hidden among Thad's visible small virtues was the shadow of a great vice that one day would take form. Thad's Jupiters and Thunderations kept in some poison that a good oath would have let out into clean air.

It was a half mile from the town to the Forks Bridge, an easy half mile, gently down-sloping across the wide area of the meadow. Lank took it in his stride, his suitcase on his shoulder. A sharp inner compulsion acted perhaps as a propelling force. For now that he was on the road at last, his social obligations paid off at the village, he was impatient to see the Big Stony again at the bridge.

As he approached the bridge he could smell the stream. He could smell the cool damp of the wash of fresh water over stones, the wet leaf mold of the shady banks where new ferns and fat-leafed skunk cabbages stood moist and supple with their sap amid violets and dogtooths. He smelled May and trout fishing, for the first time in five years. And now he could hear the stream: the eternal soft voice that had told his youth and manhood about fortitude and peace and a trust in the verity of God.

Then he saw it. He took the bag from his shoulder and put it down on the bridge and stood leaning on the rail, gazing down at the familiar features. A long and constant riffle, stream-wide and shallow, ran out from under the bridge, sloping easily into a black and rock-hemmed pool two hundred feet downstream. At the head of the pool the water narrowed a little and poured like curved glass over a solid rock bottom, smooth as a floor.

He gazed at it all for several minutes. His gray angular face bowed again, over the rail, and his lips again were murmurous with his thoughts.

The reverent moment passed, his head straightened from his little communion with his God, and his eyes began a keen appraising scrutiny. In a moment Lank Starbuck knew that he was going to fish that water—tonight. It was right, if ever he had seen it right. Its color, its pitch, and something else—a quality he couldn't define though he could sense it—spoke trout to him in words he could not ignore. It might not have been just so yesterday; it might not be just so tomorrow. But now—it was. It had the once-in-a-season bloom, the transitory peak of sheer perfection. And while that held he was bound by every dictate of his conscience to accept the gift.

But he was in a dangerous spot. Anyone else could stand here and look, but if Lank Starbuck were seen here, studying the water, he would be suspect. Two signs, one on either side, faced the bridge squarely from the downstream side:

PLEASE KEEP OFF
POACHERS AND TRESPASSERS
WILL BE PROSECUTED

March Brown
Fly-Fishing Club

It was a nice polite sign, not hardboiled like some others he had fished under. But it had teeth. Lank Starbuck had never felt them but he knew others who had.

He crossed over to the other side of the bridge and went down to the stream. No sign was here: upstream from the bridge the water was public. The fork was in sight immediately above, where the Little Stony came in from the right and the south branch from the left. He dipped his fingers in the stream. It was cold—no doubt of that. It was damn cold for this late in May. On one count this pleased him: it supported his preference for night crawlers. On another it did not, for he was pretty sure he'd have to wade wet.

He was on his way again. Another half mile stretched before him to his house, all of it upgrade. About midway of this distance Lank put the bag down and rested a minute. Already he was planning tonight's foray, considering his old lines of ingress and his strategic routes of withdrawal. After five years he might be at a disadvantage. His once smooth technique might be rusty from disuse. Certain old paths and hideouts and places for secreting tackle or trout might not be there anymore. The club guard likely had altered his schedule. Perhaps there were two guards now. The thing would need all his old-time cunning. Despite his long absence from the stream he had no doubt of his fishing skill. In the five-year famine he had kept fishing alive in his mind and spirit. He had thought of the feel of the rod in his hand and the pull of Big Stony's currents on his line; night after night, in that mean little city room, he had wooed sleep by conjuring detailed tableaus of secret raids on the forbidden waters. In his heart he had kept alive Big Stony's riffles and pools and back eddies, its snags and stones, the endless diversity as he had known it of old and in more recent years had seen it by moonlight or felt it in the total dark. It wouldn't be strange to him anymore than his wife's face would be strange if he could see it again.

He sensed the change upon the little farm as he came around the last bend of the road and saw the small white house a hundred yards ahead. At this point always, in the spring of the year, he could see his Holsteins knee-deep in the timothy and clover beyond his line fence. But now the gate was open upon a wide and cowless field. Burdocks and daisies were a spreading rash on the green breast of his old east pasture. The little margin along the road, between the road and the fence, had been newly and neatly mown. That was like Thad, he reflected—neat where he thought neatness would show.

He could smell the emptiness, the abandonment of the place. The barn held no sign of animal life. A ghostly odor of cows lurked in odd corners, but it might have been only imagined. The combined reek of a disinfectant and of crank-case oil was too real to be thus haunted. A rubber tire hung from one of his old cow stanchions. No thumping of hooves came from the horse stall. The silo was open at the bottom, bright with sun on its clean-swept cement floor. The poultry yards were unpeopled and already rank with pigweed.

He went up the path to the kitchen and found the door locked. He had a key and he applied it, wondering for an instant if the lock had been changed in the general upheaval. But his key went home.

The kitchen was neat in a man's way of being neat. His wife— Thad's mother—would have had flowers around and a bowl of fruit on the kitchen table. She would have had a fire in the stove and a pot of something stewing on it. Thad's stove was studiously cold, and Thad's strictly utilitarian appurtenances hung on their proper hooks. Well, Thad had always been efficient and tidy. He shouldn't be unjust in his thoughts about his son.

The house echoed with his footsteps. He looked into the neat front parlor which smelled almost antiseptically clean, and looked away. The dining room had lost its heavy old table; the pine cupboard which Lank's father had built into one corner had been removed. In their venerable places were a bright golden-oak table and a glass-doored china closet. Chairs and a sideboard of the same cheap gleaming veneer stood precisely spaced around the walls.

He went upstairs, sick with a queer nostalgia. To his immense relief he found his old room just as he had left it. Its door was closed and it had the smell of a place long untenanted. Dust lay on every flat surface like new snow before footprints get on it. Thad had scrupulously cared for every room in the house but this one. That was because Thad was indifferent to the things of his father. Lank knew it without defining the thought. His room had been closed like an out-of-the-way closet where some foul and shameful thing is stored.

He opened the windows to the south and west, letting in the fresh tide of the late afternoon. The dust could keep for a while. He went to his closet and a big chest inside it, like a hound to a holed-up rabbit.

He dragged the chest to the light of the window and raised its heavy lid. His stuff was all there, thank God. The sight of his old treasure, after his long time away, created an uproar in his blood.

This kind of thing, this boyish thrill in the mere sight and feel of trout tackle, he had thought a deceased capacity, buried deep under the old years, and now he was a little embarrassed in the strange recurring glow. He took his rod out of its cloth case and velvet-covered form. It had been a beauty in its day, costing him half of one month's milk check in that spring when the Big Stony had been taken over by the March Brown Club. He had chosen it as a specialized instrument for the work he would have to do from now on: six short joints so that he could carry it, taken down, inside his trouser leg. He had rewound it with his own hands, in his own scheme of colored silk, on that long-gone day when he had brought it home. He remembered how his wife had ransacked her sewing baskets for the shades of thread he had wanted, and how Thad, then twelve years old, had looked over his shoulder with a rapture he had hoped would live.

Lank Starbuck assembled the joints, sighted along the rod's length as along a gun barrel and rotated it slowly. It had had a little bow for years from the pull of Big Stony on his heavy night crawlers. But it had grown no worse in its long incarceration. He swished it back and forth in the room, happy in the response of the good bamboo.

He took a quick inventory of the rest of his gear. A couple of level enameled lines, wound carefully around a cylindrical oatmeal container, were still good enough. A tin box held his reel, divorced of its click for professional reasons and well oiled in its cloth sack. It held, too, the flat tobacco can he used for a bait box, two or three candle stubs for finding night crawlers, a few large wet flies, a simple collection of spinners, half a dozen #4 Sproat hooks, eyed, and his fish knife. His leaders were useless but he drew from a pocket an envelope containing a few level six-footers, heavy-trout, bought in New York. His folding landing net had been left assembled and the cords were still sound. He cut off the dead elastic thong, drew from another pocket a five-foot length of new elastic and attached it in a big loop.

That left only his boots. Greatly patched and brittle with age they were beyond further repair. He would wade wet as he had expected. It wouldn't be the first time.

Working fast and with something of his old mastery of detail he fetched two rubber bands and two short lengths of string. He took down the rod, placed all the joints side by side, lashed them together lightly at one end with a bowline loop left on the cord, and at the other end with a rubber band. The handle and folding frame of his landing net were similarly tied. The joints of the rod would of course go into one leg of his trousers, the landing net in the other, with the loops of cord around his suspender thong on either side, preventing rod and net from dropping while allowing them freedom to swing, inside his pants, with his stride. He stowed the velvet form and cloth case in the chest. He knotted a hook on each of three leaders, wound the better of the two lines on his reel, and he was ready. Then he thought of the defiant notes he used to leave on the stream. Just in case, he'd take a pencil and a piece of paper in an upper pocket where they wouldn't get wet.

The sun was lower in the west window. An oriole in one of the old apple trees was a brilliant recurrent sound against the fundamental stillness of the late afternoon.

As yet, no Thad. Lank arranged his gear for an immediate getaway—all except the leaders. These he took downstairs to the kitchen and soaked under the tap at the sink. An inspection of Thad's larder revealed bacon and eggs and coffee. Lank kindled a quick fire in the stove.

His supper consumed and the utensils washed, he went back to his room and changed into his fishing clothes, his old corduroy pants, a flannel shirt and a denim work jacket with four pockets in front and one large one across the back. He stowed the tied rod joints in his right pants leg, the net in the left, and pocketed the rest of his gear, amused that he remembered precisely his old system of certain pockets for certain items. He patted his pockets and pants legs in a final checkup and went below.

If Thad didn't want to come home he needn't. The hours of fishing waited for no man.

Outside, the sun was already under the ridge to the west and the world was blue and quiet with the dusk. The song of a wood thrush in the old orchard was a smelting of bright silver in the twilight. The gentle contours of his acres heaved and dipped away, blurred in the soft wash of the fading light. The wall of the distant woods stood vague and motionless, curving out to the road ahead of him. A cottontail sat in the roadside dust and loped off at his approach. A star was suddenly coined in the high east straight ahead.

He came cautiously to the left turn where the road heads north, verging into its down-slope to the Big Stony. He listened for cars, horses, men, any traffic to which he might be suspect if seen headed toward the stream, particularly if such traffic happened to be the club guard himself, Foster Prentiss. A decent enough man, if you stayed off the club property, though of course a lackey and bound by the lackey's point of view. Lank wondered if Foster still kept to his old schedule. If so he would be on the prowl, this time in the evening, in his Ford. He should have passed here half an hour back and he would pass again in another half hour.

He hated himself for his slight nervousness. But he was long unaccustomed to secrecy: his old inurement to the skulking philosophy of all hunted things had slipped from him in his five upright and dismal years in the city.

Feeling like a target for some ambushing fire, he made the turn and proceeded north along the sloping road. The old keenness for fishing was rising in him too, along with his little fear. He was eager to feel the press of the water again, the weight of a brown trout on the far end of his line. . . . He would get over that dread of detection. One or two more raids and he'd be immune again.

Just ahead was his old cutoff, now almost invisible to any casual or unsuspecting eye. He veered into it from the open road. The dark woods and a warm flood of reassurance engulfed him. The little path looked the same as it always had. Under his feet he felt its firm friendly texture.

The long twilight thickened almost imperceptibly. Even here under the tall trees the dark would not be complete for half an hour. He had ample time.

The path sloped down, northeastward, to the stream. In a moment he saw the glint of water, an area of a quiet pool through the trees ahead, and heard the murmur of the riffle above it. He stopped, tense as a panther, peering into the empty and silent, radiating aisles. Then he took his rod out of his trouser leg, removed its cord and rubber-band lashings, assembled it, attached the clickless reel, threaded the line through the guides, looped on a leader, drew the hook back and inserted it in the cork grip. He removed the landing net from the other trouser leg and undid the cord lashing but left the rubber band on.

Thus prepared, Lank Starbuck disappeared around a mass of rhododendron to his left. In a minute he returned, empty-handed, and started back up the path.

Back to the road, up to the southward fork, a quarter mile over the hill and a few steps through a strip of woodlot brought him out, in less than ten minutes, upon the cropped surface of a golf club fairway. Going in that direction, away from the stream and unencumbered by even the indication of a fishing rod, he was above suspicion.

The darkness was not quite whole but it would do. He took a candle stub from his pocket and lit it. Bending close to the earth and holding the candle low, he proceeded slowly along the edge of the grass, giving it a microscopic scrutiny. Fifty feet of the fairway yielded to his tobacco tin a dozen fat night crawlers. He doused the candle and hurried back.

It was dark now and he felt his way into the cutoff. Coming up to the place where he had assembled his rod, a thin vein of apprehension threaded the almost solid structure of his confidence. Things had gone too smoothly perhaps, and it were well to keep his guard up.

He stopped, suddenly, to decide whether his imagination or his physical ear had heard a voice in the darkness ahead. It came again. Two voices. Lank knew, even, whose voices they were. Mr. Stokes and that college professor—Lank couldn't recall his name—who was by all odds the best fisherman among the members of the March Brown Club.

Lank knew where they were sitting too, and at the thought he chuckled quietly to himself. But he would have to wait until they left, and get himself hidden at once. They wouldn't come up *his* path. There was an easier one, a little to the left, which he had avoided because it was the usual exit of fishermen. But they would come near his path and they'd have a flashlight.

Testing each footstep before giving it his weight he eased his way twenty feet into the woods to the right.

Both Stokes and the professor, Lank knew, had been fishing flies this evening. They always fished flies unless the stream was over its banks and then, usually, they didn't fish at all. They embraced some queer artificial faiths, strange codes of self-denial. When the night came on and the chance of snagging into a big brown was really good they were coming off the stream.

They had come off the stream now and were resting a minute, and that was all to the good. Down there, at least one big trout was not interested in flies tonight. In his gallery of mental slides Lank could see the dark two-foot-long form cruise into the shoals on the night prowl for its prey. A big streamer, presented in just the right way, would perhaps fool him. A six-inch chub would be ideal. But the night crawler would do. He could divert that fish, the way he'd offer the worm. . . . And almost certainly it had not been frightened by the fly-fishermen. Stokes was a quiet careful angler and the Professor didn't disturb the water anymore than a ghost would.

Yes, his luck was holding. But he couldn't relax for a second. His vigilance was and always had been the key to his success.

Crouched there in the brush he thought briefly of himself as a poacher, a man outside the law. The public water above the bridge had offered the way of safety and most of his fishing acquaintances around Stony Forks had followed it. But his gnarled old pride had been too tough to let him confine his fishing there. The best moments of his life had been sneaked, in a sense stolen from other men. On that point, on all points that touched his fishing, his conscience was clear. If he had had to skulk from the sight of men he had never been furtive from the bright eye of his God. He had no remorse about the trout he had lifted from the club water, in season and out, or over the number he had taken upon occasion in excess of both club and state limits. On the public water above the bridge he had always respected the closed season and the state bag limit because that water was the property of other plain men, his friends. But from his forays below the bridge Lank Starbuck had distributed club trout among the needy people of the countryside in all months from March to October inclusive. And he was aware that the club members knew it. The cardinal sin was waste: a trout killed but not eaten. And the cardinal error was to let himself be caught. As yet he was guilty of neither.

Mr. Stokes and the Professor were coming up their path. Their flashlight made jerky silhouettes of the intricate patterns of the woods. Lank drew into himself, into the intimate earth and the undergrowth, like a grouse before a bird dog, as they went by in the woods to the left. In a minute their voices were no longer audible to him. He stayed under cover a minute more. Then he felt his way back to his path and followed it a little distance toward the stream. He diverged from it again, left, where he had turned off earlier. Under his mounting anticipation he was aware, for the first time tonight, of the fatigue of his body. He came up to the hollow log on which Stokes and the Professor had been sitting. Reaching into the butt end of the log he drew out his assembled rod and his landing net.

The cold water shocked him at first. In five years he must have forgotten how cold the Big Stony could feel. It took his breath but he went resolutely in. It would recognize him after a while and warm up to him, like a woman with a stranger. It always had.

He remembered the lay of the bottom at this point. But it would have changed some. He tested the bottom step by step, wading quietly and steadily out. At this pitch of water it should grow deeper and stronger gradually until it reached his thighs, then level off in midstream and shoal again to his knees on the far side. It did.

This was the point he wanted for his right-handed downstream fishing—a rod's length out from the north bank. The deep run eased its pressure here, flattened and widened below him over a broad gravel-bottomed rippling shallow. The encroaching trees gave way from this expanse. Above him was the night sky, luminous already with the prescience of moonrise.

He let the big worm go down into that shallow drift below. The whole of the Big Stony held no better night-feeding ground for big fish. There was depth below it and depth above, day hideouts for the large browns, and between them this two-hundred-foot shoal for the night range.

The guard appreciated the strategic importance of this place— called the Poacher's Pocket by the March Brown members—and gave it extra vigilance on his rounds. For a trespasser it was the most dangerous water of the club preserve. Lank would go down it slowly with forty-foot roll casts across stream, letting the current effect the wide arc of his bait downstream and back to his side. He'd let the worm hang in the gentle flow a moment and then ease it back and let it drift again. Moonrise was still minutes away. Before it came he should hook a fish here; then he'd play it into the dark water below.

His heart pumped a little against the biting chill of the water. Or maybe it was in remembrance—and anticipation—of the feel of a big brown trout's strike in the dark.

For that would come to him again in these next few minutes. Without sentiment, now, he could appraise that simple thing, that moment just preceding and containing the strike. He could look at it in relation to the sum of his life and see its constancy and truth. It had survived because it was fit and honest and pure, along with a handful of little memories and beliefs, such plain things as pride and love and his hardy faith in his son, and the clear quiet memory of his wife. As he stood there in the night and the stream, just before moonrise gave back to him the familiar identities of his ancient haunts, the deep vessel of his years evaporated at last and left this simple residue of its ebullition.

Returning from his professional rounds Thaddeus Starbuck warped his shiny roadster into the end of the cow barn. He shut off the ignition and lights, jumped out and slammed the door behind him. Standing at the barn door he surveyed his property—as he liked to think of it—in the early moonlight. Several nicely groomed conclusions came out for encores in the forefront of his mind. He visualized it as it would be when at last his industry and thrift had shaped it according to his dream. With the old barn torn down and a cinder-block fireproof garage erected in its place, with the chicken houses out of the way and a neat cement path instead of the rickety old flagstones going up to the house, the place would reflect the fact of his success.

He glanced up at the house and was relieved to see it completely dark. The old man had not come then, after all. Thad had guessed that it was mostly talk and would subside if he ignored it. Congratulating himself on his judgment of men in general and of his father in particular, he walked up the path. His gait was at once springy with his twenty-nine years and conscious of the new dignity attaching to him. He let himself in at the kitchen door and snapped on the light.

Quick chagrin tightened his apple face at the flick of the switch. For he smelled the evidence of his father's arrival, the remains of the recent fire, the bacon and eggs.

For all his full-bodied roundness Thad Starbuck had the instincts of a ferret and they had been sharpened in the recent days of his new employment. His khaki-clad and putteed figure stood still a moment, then abruptly marched upstairs and entered the old man's room.

He saw the chest first, where Lank had left it, and it was all he needed to see. But as a routine confirmation, as a detail of a thoroughgoing professional job, he raised the lid of the chest. . . . If only he had acted on his impulse, this very morning, and done away with his father's rod and tackle while still there was time.

No emotional conflict stirred in Thad. In that moment, looking down at the evidence, he was conscious only of his duty to his employer. In a later moment, when launched on his course, a little question was to disturb him. He needed an interval of time to grasp the implications of a given set of circumstances. He was the ideal policeman in that respect. Duty spoke to him with a peremptory voice, crowding out of his ears the whisperings of conscience other men may know at such times. Hearing the voice now, he acted without question. He patted the badge on his chest and the gun in his holster without looking at them. He had formed that habit in his few days on the new job—to make sure always that the gun and badge were there.

The ways of the father's poachings and trespassings were familiar of old to the son, and just now this knowledge gave Thad an advantage of which he delighted to avail himself. He backed the car out of the barn, turned it quickly and was off down the road in pursuit. He went by his father's old cutoff slowly, looking it over in the light of his headlamps but not stopping. He kept on across the Forks Bridge, parked his car just beyond and made his way on foot along an easily traveled wagon road, his beat on the north bank of the stream. His father had had many points of entry but Thad remembered the one he had liked best, and he thought the old man would use it now on his first attempt in five years.

That single two-hundred-foot stretch might take two hours of his father's fishing if no strike rewarded him. Then he, Thad, had plenty of time. He knew the old man could not have started until the dark was complete, for Mr. Stokes and Professor Kent had been on this very point of the stream at dusk.

He felt a quick pang of something like dismay. Had *they* apprehended his father? . . . It subsided. Of course not. The old fox was not to be snared that way. . . . But it thinned out into a dull misgiving, the first of two which were to nag him briefly. It brought to him, in due time, the realization that his arrest of his father might be embarrassing to himself. Conceivably it might cost him his new job of club guard which he had applied for and obtained after the recent resignation of Foster Prentiss. For his employment by the club, he suspected, was partly predicated upon his own statement that his father probably would never return to Stony Forks. Thinking of that declaration to the club members a few days ago he recalled that it seemingly had caused Doctor Hatch to wink at Mr. Harlow and to mutter something about "preferring his ghosts unlaid," to which Harlow had replied, "That's one ghost who *can't* be laid." . . . But Thad hadn't understood. The club members, particularly Hatch, were always saying things that made no sense to him. He stopped in the trail to ponder his problem and as he stood there in the sifted moonlight the alternative dawned on him, giving him slowly the solution. For he certainly could not take a chance on *not* arresting his father. If he let him go, tonight, the old man might be at it again tomorrow night or the night after. Someone might see him eventually, and it would come out. . . . "No," he said, half aloud. "I've got to take him without any fuss."

And then that other misgiving made signs at him. Suppose you can't? it said. Suppose the old man got tough about it? He was capable of it; he had gotten tough with other men before. Thad recognized, without understanding, his father's contempt for uniforms and badges, for any authority that sought to shackle the dictates of his private convictions.

He patted the gun in the holster and went ahead. A minute's walk brought him to the long flat where he expected to see the old man. In the flood of moonlight he should be distinctly visible to anyone looking for him. To other eyes he might be another of the several boulders ranged about on shore and in the water. The old man could be companion to the rocks, as motionless as they.

Thad strained his eyes at the moon-flushed expanse of open stream, focusing intently upon each boulder and the in-between spaces of water. There was no slightest movement, no sound except what the stream and the woods made in the nights of May. He crept to the water's edge and sprayed his flashlight beam over all of the water within its range. His father was not there.

Thad returned to the wagon road and followed it quickly and quietly downstream. There was another point, and he didn't think it would fail him.

There it was, at last. Lank knew he should not have to wait much longer. That immemorial pull, that age-old signal of the big brown. . . . Again.

Lank Starbuck struck. He put his rod high and gave out line grudgingly with his left hand. The trout took it from the clickless reel—out, way out, seventy-five, a hundred feet. Lank braked the fish gently and went downstream with it into deepening water, wondering if the old line would hold. This fish was big—as big as any he'd ever known. Five pounds, he thought. The strain seemed insupportable but he must turn it now, with most of the line gone and deep water ahead. He held his breath in the long moment of crisis. Then, as the great fish turned and raced upstream, winning yards of slack, he stripped in line like a man possessed, and as the fish came opposite and bored past, upstream, he fed it out with added pressure. He forgot the ice-cold band where the water level girdled his thighs; he forgot everything in the waxing conviction of his mastery. He was licking the biggest trout that had ever grabbed his bait. He had known that something big would be in this shoal tonight—he had been certain of it, this afternoon, when first he had seen the river from the Forks Bridge—but this one was beyond his farthest hope. And he was beating it down, for all its size—his first feel of a fish in five years.

Twenty minutes passed. The tempo of the battle had slowed almost to a halt. Lank had worked the fish down near the narrow tree-arched water to land it out of the moonlight, out of sight of any prowling guard. And now in the final stages of the struggle the old man stood still, fighting his tiring adversary direct from the reel. The rushes of the great fish became feeble; it was surging heavily near the surface now. Lank's droning monologue, always a part of his battles with large trout, died to a whisper as the strength faded from his fish, and now it had almost ceased.

"Easy, easy now. Easy, easy now," he kept repeating, and that was all that was left of it. He was bringing in that mammoth brown trout, slowly and with exquisite care. "Easy. . . . Easy. . . . Over the net. . . . Easy."

Slowly over the net and out.

So far, he had won. But his victory was never complete until he had retired safely from the stream. It looked simple at this moment —go ashore back there in the open, write his note and hang it on a bush, knife his fish and return via the wagon trail to the road and home. But that was against all the tenets of his code. Guards liked that spot too well. It was easy for them to wait there and nail you as you came out. Retracing his steps to his point of entrance would be risky too, now that the moon was up. And wading upstream was too noisy. . . . There was another way, harder but safe. It meant wading a hundred yards downstream, most of it up to his waist, and crawling out to high ground through a rift in the rhododendron jungle, and curving a course through the woods to home, avoiding roads. He hoped that little exit was still as it used to be.

The big trout was half out of the net, head down, gulping air with its convulsive exhausted gills, full of a spasmodic dying power. Lank gripped one hand around the net below the protruding tail, held it high to avoid splashing and started downstream.

Immediately he was glad he had followed his rule and not gone ashore. The sound of footsteps came to him from the path on his side, approaching from upriver. He had a quick impulse to crouch but his old experience denied it in time. He proceeded as rapidly as he could without splashing, gaining the end of the wide and open stretch of water and entering the deep narrow run under the dark trees. He was out of the moonlight just in time. The footsteps ceased behind him and in the stillness he kept going, feeling his way in the deeper water. In a moment he was aware of a ghostly illumination moving under the trees. Instinctively he stood still; then, as he realized he was out of range, he turned and saw the point of the flashlight and the beam searching out the surface behind him.

He kept on. The water was an icy belt around his waistline, making him gasp audibly. His escape could not be effected on the far side: the Deeps started just below and the Big Stony for a quarter mile downstream was too deep and fast to wade across. But he felt safe. The guard had made a routine search of that part of the stream where searching was easy and would follow the path to its next emergence upon open water, well below Lank's exit. By that time Lank would have vanished behind him. . . . He smiled in the darkness and looked back. The light was gone.

After the guard had gone by he'd write his note and leave it on the trail. Not here—it could give away this useful exit. In his mind he had it nicely worded: "A five-pounder Mr. Stokes and the Professor missed. Poacher's Pocket, moonrise May 18. Thanks."

The trout struggled and lunged once or twice in the net. Holding the heavy fish high was making his arm ache. The freezing girdle at his waist had slipped an inch or two down but the cold was beginning to paralyze his legs and the chill rose like a mist up into his chest. But he'd be all right if he could get out in a minute—if the guard would hurry and get below him. The walk home on dry land would warm him up. God Almighty, he hoped Thad would have a fire in the stove.

Groping along under the high bank, in what little moonlight sifted through the trees, he came at last to his old outlet. A four-foot boulder just off shore and a great leaning sycamore identified the spot. The tree had almost collasped in the years since he had last seen it; it leaned now precariously, half its roots heaved up from the earth. His little path, negotiable only on hands and knees, went up the bank from this point, joining the wagon trail above.

He worked up between the big rock and the bank. He would go quietly ashore and sit by the sycamore's upthrust roots to wait. If he could kill his fish quickly he'd be saved a lot of trouble. Drowning would be difficult with a fish so large, sure to make a splashing and would risk losing the trout. As he came up to the steep bank he put his rod down and reached for his knife. Operating by the sense of touch he pressed the long blade deep where the back of the head and body joined. The great fish welled up against the strength of his left hand and wrist, and lay still. Lank transferred it to the back pocket of his jumper and buttoned it in. The tail end protruded a foot out the right side. And at that moment the expected footsteps were on the trail above him, approaching.

The flashlight could pick him out here, for keen eyes, despite the underbrush. He took up his rod again and crouched low behind the high bank. The water, circling his waist again, took his breath in a gasp that might be audible up there on the trail. But the guard's footsteps didn't miss a beat. They came on fast; they would go by in a minute. . . . His luck was holding; he had killed the trout in time.

That regular, almost measured tread halted abruptly above him where his little path came out on top of the rise. Squinting over the rim of the bank he saw the light go on again. He ducked below the edge, sinking a little deeper into the water, and immediately the beam shot down the path, flooding the area of stream behind him. In the tense stillness the water flowed into the circle of light, crossed it and disappeared into the darkness downstream. The light veered a little and came back to its focus; and above him were renewed footfalls and the rustle of underbrush. The guard was coming down the path.

Lank Starbuck, half submerged, pressed into the wet earth of the bank. In the intense cold his breathing was quick and labored but it wouldn't be heard until the guard finished fighting the brush and stood still on the bank above him. In those few seconds, noisy with the guard's progress, he took the deep loud gulps of air his lungs were crying for. With the full intake of breath he regained a measure of mental poise, and the reality of the situation seeped into his underlying disbelief of the whole affair. He knew he had not been seen and certainly no club guard could have anticipated his exit here. Foster Prentiss had never known of his use of this place nor had any other man so far as he could remember.

Yet here was the guard coming right at him with a light. In a minute more he'd be seen. In the darkness and the cold and the ebbing of his strength, that was clear. He had a minute, at most, for a getaway or a fight.

There had been a time when he'd have stood and fought. He considered it now but so briefly that it was only an irrelevant reminder that once he, Lank Starbuck, had been young and strong. . . . Let it pass. Age and exhaustion had him now, and the cold water.

The flashlight beam, brilliant directly above him, flickered once and died. In the ensuing smother of the dark Lank heard the guard stop still in his thrashing down the path and say "Jupiter!" distinctly into the stillness.

There was no other voice like it anywhere in the world. And no man on earth but Thad, his own son, would have said "Jupiter" in just this moment.

The voice spoke again into the darkness: "I'm the guard here now. If you're there, Pop, surrender to me. I'm armed."

Thad, his son. . . . His crazy crowding thoughts had a kind of core, a central master thought about which all the loose tag ends of related notions revolved. Thad was a gamekeeper, a servant. His own son, reared in the wide freedom of his farm and brought up to be, above all else, proud, had hired out as a lackey to other men, had put the cheap delegated authority of a uniform and a badge above the will of his individual soul. The conviction carried a deep hurt to the old man, a sense of some fatal omission of his own, never recognized until now, some dereliction in his training of the secret and quiet boy.

And yes, he remembered now: way back in the past he had told Thad of this hidden path, this secret outlet. And Thad had stored that bit of knowledge through the years and uncovered it tonight for this bright, vindictive employment. Lank Starbuck understood it with a deep wounding insight that was not surprise but an ancient buried awareness. All men had their scales of loyalties, and perhaps he had always known how Thad's was graduated.

Thad was armed and so, in his mind, his father should surrender to the odds of the policeman and the law.

But he wouldn't be taken. He had never been, and he wouldn't be now. If there could still be a conflict of allegiance in his son's heart he could eliminate it for Thad by removing the cause. Thad would never find him; Thad need never know. He could go now, with his record and his conscience whole. . . . The revealing moments of his life had ever been dark moments, and this one held the final apocalypse. His time had run out. He had come up short to the end and it looked all right to him. He had no reason, anymore, to stay. The knowledge came into his mind, easily and without shock, that tomorrow's dawn had no meaning for him, nor did all the dawns to follow. He knew all that they had to tell. Let the young quick eyes have them now, the eyes vulnerable to their wonders as his own once had been.

He saw reason and comfort in the prospect, beauty and peace and the fair proportions of any fitting thing. The Deeps of the Big Stony could have him now, and the pure record of his poaching.

Sink into it low, quiet. Push off shore easy, into the strong deep current, and keep down. Never mind the long breath—it couldn't be taken anyway.

Old Glory's Trout 8

On the morning of a fateful day Tom Garrison took the special-delivery letter from the boy who had bicycled and walked it all the way to the March Brown Club from the post office at Stony Forks. Before opening it Tom looked at Professor Kent and me, who were getting into our waders. His glance had a lift of anticipation.

"It's from Doc Hatch," he said. The mere announcement, if you knew Doctor Hatch, founder, chief sustaining member and perennial renewer of jaded morales among the March Browns, was enough to spark your interest in the immediate course of events. For Hatch was not the man to write a special-delivery letter to tell you his wife's peonies were budding.

Tom opened it and read: "Englishman I met in El Alamein during the war—by name Brigadier General Edgerton H. Blake-Carrington—is in town looking for peace and not finding it. I'm sending him up to play with you guys. He has some fishing stuff but I haven't had time to see it. Putting him on Number 3 for the Forks on Wednesday. Meet him, one of you, and drive him in. A man of good will—and he damn near turned Rommel back from Alamein all by himself."

"Brigadier General Edgerton H. Blake-Carrington." The Professor intoned the syllables. "The name itself sounds like an artillery barrage. Wonder what the H stands for."

Tom knew a little about the General. "As it happened," he said,

243

"he was Colonel of a British Eighth Army tank regiment in North Africa when Hatch met him. The word 'met' is hardly just. Hatch was over there with some other medicos on a government-sponsored look-see to find out about war wounds. At the time things were tough—Rommel had the British backed damn near to Alexandria. The then Colonel B-C was brought in with a leg torn up by shrapnel, the wounds full of sand and crank-case oil and whatnot. The British, who had discovered penicillin, didn't have any. Doc Hatch did. And Hatch considered B-C important to victory. Also, he liked B-C."

Tom fluttered the letter in his hand. "You can see by this that B-C didn't die."

"The Doc picks up the damnedest people," Professor Kent said, threading his line through the guides. "On Wednesday, his letter says. That's today. And Number 3 is due at Stony Forks at seven thirty, yes?"

"Yes," Tom said. "This very evening."

The Professor said he would meet B-C. Poor Hatch, someone had to look after his global waifs. Never a season went by but what the Doctor found a refugee from the world's brashness and sent or brought him to our sanctuary on the Big Stony.

"The March Brown Protective Aid Society," Tom muttered to himself. He was knotting on a small Iron Blue Dun. "Why can't we have a little privacy now and then?"

"Somehow they never can fish worth a damn," the Professor said.

"That's why Hatch brings 'em up here," Tom observed. "By comparison with them his own fishing looks almost professional."

This eminent surgeon, Hatch, though his enthusiasm for fishing knows no superior, is not notable for outsize trout, or indeed for trout. In his earlier seasons he committed every angling sin in the book, some so incredibly grotesque that, according to Tom, no one but Doctor Hatch could have committed them. The Compleat Tangler, Tom had named him, as I said on another page.

But this story concerns Doctor Hatch in a vicarious and absentee fashion. This time he was away, he hadn't fished with us for nearly a week, and only his ambassador from overseas was there to stand figuratively in his waders.

This is a story, first, of a trout, a kind of rebel among brown trout, who hit my marabou streamer early that very afternoon. That proved him an individualist, for brown trout of this one's dimensions are supposed to attack marabous and other minnow imitators only at night. Most browns have been, I think, regimented: they surface-feed when they're supposed to surface-feed, nymph when they're supposed to nymph. A dreary conformity has fastened upon the once unpredictable tribe of *Salmo trutta* or *fario.*

Just now they were supposed to be doing nothing. They had had word from their fuehrer about a disengaging action. But this heretic was able to defy all official edicts; maybe, indeed, he was the fuehrer himself. For by my poor standards he was a big brown. I saw his head, his dorsal fin, his tail, all at once, at the end of a thirty-foot cast. His head was bigger than your fist if you're not a longshoreman or Joe Louis. His dorsal fin was a forearm's length abaft his head, his tail another forearm's length astern of that.

Tom and the Professor, wise fishermen, had gone in an hour before. My dark Hendrickson and others hadn't drawn a rise in an hour. There was streamside heat and a sabbath stillness and slack water devoid of insects or the bulges of feeding trout.

At this point a consultation of the manuals would have divulged a lure but would have revealed nothing about the pleasure of retiring from the stream at such a time.

Fifty yards upstream was the modest clubhouse of the March Browns; downstream were a thousand yards of the Big Stony which I could fish without poaching on the next fellow's water. I had those two alternatives to cope with, and the former was not without its casual enchantments. Our house has a screened porch with rocking chairs, overlooking the stream. Already I thought I could hear the creak of the rockers and the tinkle of ice in glasses. ... And yet, maybe a few of those thousand downstream yards, with wet flies or nymphs or something, before going in.

I found myself taking off the Hendrickson or whatever it was. Somewhere I had read that a small Black Gnat, wet, would draw 'em in the slack motionless hours. Okay, maybe those disciplined browns had had word from their chief of staff about small Black Gnats.

I'll never know. Something else in the box caught my eye. Under a felt flap attached to the lid lay that siren of a marabou, that blonde witch whom I fancy as a potential retriever of days which are duds. Her white semblance of chastity is beguiling in sentimental or desperate moods.

She was on as quickly as you can hum the first bar of the Lorelei. She was on too quickly, in fact, for I didn't even pause to change my 3X leader for one stout enough to hold the kind of prospect who might be interested. A grave error, of course. I knew it but I let it slide. Roll-casting the marabou across the lower reach of the Club Pool would be what it had usually been, a nice exercise in tactics, nothing more.

A sunken log lay against the far bank, thirty feet from where I stood in midstream. On the first business cast after getting her wet the marabou came down over the log, the current had her at once and I started the little jerky retrieve, keeping her close under the surface and watching her swim, tracing the shimmering silvery course—

At first, when I saw it, I didn't believe it. There was a split second of incredulity, of downright denial of the whole affair. That fish coming out from under the log was too big for anyone to believe. I saw him whole—his head and his open jaws, his topline, dorsal fin and upper tail. He assaulted the marabou in a single and savage thrust amid a great surface swirl of water.

I struck—after the moment of disbelief had passed and realization had seeped bright and hot into all this make-believe fancy. I felt an immovable resistance for an instant, and then the break and the weightless emptiness, and looked over my shoulder to see my line and part of my leader written all destitute on the surface upstream. The ripples were spreading away from the scene of the crime; otherwise I could have believed I had dreamed it all.

Back at the house, five minutes later, my story was accorded an almost militant indifference.

"Pour yourself a drink," Tom said. "How big d'you say he was?"

"I have my ideas of course, but you wouldn't subscribe to them."

Tom yawned and made small circular motions with his glass, tinkling the ice around. "Well, *about* how big?"

"Twenty-five inches. A minimum guarantee of two feet. And heavy."

They were unimpressed. "Suppose he had been twenty-eight

inches," the Professor remarked. "It's tougher to lose a twenty-eight-inch fish than a twenty-five-incher, any day. You're not so badly off."

"Your lot could be worse," Tom echoed. "You might be unemployed, with twelve kids. Cheer up, my friend."

You would think that a subject so devoid of fascination as my hypothetical fish would be dropped. There were other things to talk about, certainly—the labor situation and the Democratic primaries and the probable rise in agricultural purchasing power. But one or two desultory attempts to switch the talk onto some such vital topic got nowhere at all.

"Probably seventeen inches," the Professor said after a while, as if talking to himself.

"What's seventeen inches?" I inquired.

"Oh, er, your fish."

"Listen, you damn cynics—"

"I assume you're going back after him," Tom said, "after he has had time to quiet down."

I said that I was, tonight, and if anyone messed around the Club Pool before then—

Tom drummed his fingernails on the arm of the rocker and addressed the Professor in a resigned voice. "Here we are up here on a respite with this—this extremist. Expenses, fun, responsibilities, pleasures—all are split three for one. If I hook a dollar bill with my fly each of you gets 33 cents of it. But now we run up against what may be a fair fish and—"

They shamed me out of it with their innuendos, feints and oblique sorties around my poorly defended flanks. I surrendered the rights to that fish to each of them: one hour apiece on the Club Pool before I should again try it myself, they to toss for choice of time, and the same hour-apiece sequence to continue, with rest periods between, until the fish or our patience expired.

The Professor won the toss for the privilege of opening the offensive. Mindful of his mission in Stony Forks he chose the hour of six to seven P.M. Then he would meet the General and return to camp with him about eight o'clock.

Tom allowed that he should be on hand when the General arrived so he chose the hour of nine to ten. That left me with a late-afternoon hour (too soon) or a midnightish one (too dark). I opted for tomorrow's dawn. If I had pricked that trout badly the longer rest would be helpful.

Fishing with his usual precision the Professor drew a goose egg in his evening hour and departed to meet General Blake-Carrington at Stony Forks.

Tom and I had supper and at eight o'clock the Professor drove in with the General. The Professor introduced us and when no one was looking he winked at me solemnly. Doctor Hatch's North African find was an upright and formidable soldier, a giant of a man who seemed at first glance imbued with the physical attributes of the tanks he had shepherded across Libya's and Egypt's sands. His face was the color of a desert sunset. If you thought of his wounds at all you could judge when he walked that the repair of the leg was complete. Hatch had run the show when they had put the odd pieces of that leg together. This job, you had heard from Tom via the esoteric world of medicine, and you knew it now in your own terms, was one of Hatch's best. You wondered how the hands which had managed that piece of surgery could so bungle a dry-fly cast. And you loved the Doctor a little more for that bungling which was so specially his.

General Blake-Carrington smiled down at us, put out his great hand and disarmed at once the vast formidability of his presence. He protested his utter lack of trout-fishing knowledge but conceded that the sport might be jolly. He had brought up what he called a "hybrid and possibly quite wrong" outfit and hoped to try it in the morning. Would we look over his gear later, when he had unpacked, and advise him on the fundamentals of fishing?

I accompanied Tom to the stream for his postponed hour, to kibitz his operations from the bank and to give the General time to get settled. Halfway through his allotted time Tom took a twelve-inch rainbow who danced all over the Club Pool in the course of the fight, so disrupting that placid stretch that Tom finished out his period in the long riffle upstream. "Anyway," he said, "how do we know he'll stay where he was?"

Well, how did we? That shallow run above the Club Pool is a place for a big brown to feed in the hours of dusk or dark. And maybe dawn.

Maybe dawn. . . . I thought about it as we walked back to the club. British people, I have heard, are early risers. British literature is full of dew and dawn mists and the cock's shrill clarion. It would be just like General Blake-Carrington. . . .

The Professor met us outside in the firefly-studded dark. "Wait till you see his stuff," he said.

"Nice?" Tom inquired.

"His surf rod's a beauty," the Professor said, and I remembered his wink when he was taking the General's gear out of the car.

General B-C was well settled, except for his fishing things, when we entered. Smoking a large pipe before the fire he was surrounded and besieged by a mess of the strangest oddments of fishing equipment ever seen on the Big Stony's banks. British understatement had been implicit in the General's recent appraisal of his tackle. "Hybrid and possibly quite wrong" was no fit way to describe the awful heterogeneity of gear to which he introduced us. A hybrid is a blue-blooded aristocrat compared with the many-sired rabble which the good Briton offered for our inspection. Saltwater rods were married to freshwater reels and these were wound with yards of Cuttyhunk. A four-ounce pyramid sinker and a #12 Parmacheene Belle kept company as the terminal gear of one rig; at the end of another yardage of stout seagoing string a nine-foot tapered leader was attached to a three-way swivel. Neatly arranged on the mantelpiece was a goodly complement of surf squids, cork floats, #20 nymphs, more sinkers and a bottle of dry-fly oil.

"Where's your swordfish pulpit, General?" Tom asked.

The General admitted that he had seldom, if ever, fished before. "This paraphernalia," he explained, "was loaned to me by a number of friends—"

"Friends?" I echoed.

"—of diverse fishing habits. Some are saltwater fellows, others seem to like frogging about in ponds. I took whatever was offered. Last night in my flat I tried to put bits of it together. It does appear, now, that some of my rigs are ill-conceived, indeed perhaps quite unworkable on these waters."

"Quite," the Professor agreed. "Do you mind if we unhook 'em and fix up a good one for you?"

The General seemed profoundly relieved to place himself and all his borrowed angling goods unreservedly in our hands. In an hour we had unscrambled the ill-mated pairs and set up the best fly-fishing assembly that could be effected with the stock at hand. Two simple rigs on level leaders: one a wet-fly combination of Cahill dropper and Coachman tail, the other a plain Mickey Finn. Some dry flies and tapered leaders we let alone, fearing to get the General over his depth on his first try.

Tom suggested a worm if the fly rigs proved troublesome. We gave the General a few hooks and advised him on handling a big fish and other tenets of the lore. Also, we told him of the lunker we had marked down in the Club Pool and the details of our campaign.

Though no fisherman the General was instinctively sound in his perceptions. "It's as serious as that, eh?" he said. "Of course I'll keep off this pool then."

I hurried to invite him to fish any and all of our water, feeling a little awkward at his show of deference. He wouldn't take that trout in a century but the chance of his disturbing the fish concerned me.

I overstayed the alarm in the morning, and to save time decided to forego the bacon and eggs. A pot of coffee, half full, was on the stove, apparently left from last night though I didn't remember it. I heated it, gulped a cupful and went to the tail of the Club Pool as the dark thinned and the first birds became vocal. The sort of morning I wanted was easing in out of the night—windless and warm and full of a gray mist that didn't augur rain but was just part of the dawn trappings. Already, as I rigged up, three fish of twelve inches or so were rising within casting range. It was a temptation to go after them, to rig light and fine with a small gold-ribbed Hare's Ear. But the presence of these lesser fish was of course a fair sign of the absence of the greater one.

I thought again of the shallow run above the Club Pool. In that lower part of it which I could see from here no break was apparent anywhere on its surface. It might be just the place and the time. I tied on the best 1X leader I had and started up there. The lure could wait. Maybe I'd see him show or gather otherwise some inkling of what he might be up to.

The Big Stony curves above the top of the Club Pool and as I walked along more of it became visible to me. I had covered part of the distance when something caught my eye a hundred yards up river.

A man, a tall, rubber-booted, tweeded and curve-stem-piped man stood knee-deep in the stream, slowly reeling in line to his dangerously bent rod. It was, I saw, the Briton, the Carrington, that Blake. He had been up ahead of me; had neatly made breakfast while I slept, and left the coffee for me.

A tremendous slow surge on the surface, forty feet below the General, showed momentarily the flanks and fanlike tail of a great trout. I hurried toward him along the stones of the bank.

That fish was done; the General, somehow, had licked him many minutes before, there in the predawn darkness. The level leader had so far held. But the job wasn't over. There was still the yard-by-yard operation of bringing him home, and the landing. I thought of the final exhausted surge that has won many a big trout its freedom, and at the same time I noticed that the General had no net. Fortunately mine was big, bigger than I almost ever need.

"Easy," I said. "Lower your rod a little."

"He's played out, quite, poor fellow," the General observed casually. "An absurdly long tussle, really."

"They're never safe until they're on dry land. Get him into this quiet water and I'll net him for you."

"Net him?"

"Of course. There's no good beach here—and even if there were . . . ." I prayed for that leader, and it held. "That's it—a little more. Easy." A great heavy fish, as long as an axe handle and with spots as big as nickels, he was resisting still with his last strength. The net went under him from down-current, came up and lifted him clear.

With the sudden slack line the General's hook and the remains of a gob of worms came free. "I tried the flies at first," he explained, "but they became desperately tangled in the shrubbery."

Well up on the bank I put the trout down and stood feasting my reverent eyes on his heroic dimensions. The General seemed delighted with his success. Then I saw something in the corner of that great mouth. "It's him," I said.

"Eh? Who?" General Blake-Carrington was comfortable about ignoring my grammatical slip.

"The trout we told you about last night. Look." Working gently

251

I extracted my marabou streamer from the trout's lip. "He hit that yesterday."

"Oh, he is really yours, then."

"Like hell he's mine. I lost him, you got him."

And as I released the marabou I saw something else, or what was left of it, deeper in the big jaw. Another lure, a bucktail about the size of my marabou but it wasn't like anything any of us used. It had red, white and blue wisps of deer hair still clinging to the long hook shank. It had been there for days, I judged. Some poacher's bucktail no doubt, a badly tied job. To extract it would be a major operation so I snipped the hook. The General asked to see it and when I handed it to him he regarded it closely, for a long moment.

"I say," he said, "he really won't live much longer. Don't you think, before he expires, we'd better put him back?"

"Back?" It was a sudden and unforeseen turn of affairs. The General had felt pretty good about that fish. "God, General, you're sporting," I observed.

"Sporting? How, sir?"

"You've seldom fished and maybe you don't know. But in this country, and I guess in yours, it's sporting to put a trout that size back in the stream. Not only sporting but maybe foolish. They're terrific predators on smaller trout."

"I see," he said slowly. "Well, he has earned his freedom. He fought me to a standstill for twenty minutes before you came with the net. And he's dying. Are we sportsmen, eh—you and I? And as to his predations, well, we perpetrate ours too, I dare say."

Of all fish, this was one I didn't want to see lost. There were those two unbelievers, asleep back there in the club. But the General was challenging me now. And I'd have to answer him quickly. There was a dying labor in the great gills, and a slow alternate expansion and contraction of the fins.

"Look, General," I pleaded, "you've seen haddock that large in stores. They're fish—so much a pound. But a stream-caught trout this size isn't a fish, it's a miracle. This one you have here—I'd give my right arm for. Oh hell, never mind. He's the prize of a lifetime, that's all. And he's yours. I'll knife him now for you—"

"I don't want him," the General said, very simply.

I was annoyed a little at the futility of trying to persuade this rock of a Briton. "What's the real pitch on this?" I asked. "Are you giving him up because you think he's rightfully our fish—because of what we told you last night?"

He didn't answer at once and, when he did, his reply seemed evasive and hesitant. "It *is* rightfully your fish," he said. "You chaps run the show up here, have your scheduled campaigns all nicely arranged. Your hearts are set on this fellow. And I'm just a visiting amateur—I didn't angle for him as you would."

He didn't sound convincing. Few more if any such fish were in the Big Stony but some good ones were left and General Blake-Carrington thought we were fishermen enough to take them. There was another reason but for the life of me I couldn't track it down. Maybe, like some other soldiers who have killed men in war, this one wouldn't kill game or fish for sport. There are such men. But I considered that a moment and decided it was no good.

I took out the thirty-inch tape I brazenly carry and laid it along the trout's length from the tip of the lower jaw to the center of the tail. "Twenty-six and a quarter inches," I announced.

I would extract whatever thin juice of moral triumph might be left in the core of defeat. "General," I said, "before we put him back do you swear that you will bear witness that this is the true and exact length of this brown trout, to any and every one who may question us on same, particularly those two skeptics in yonder cabin?"

He avoided my direct look for a second, then he turned to me squarely. "No," he said, "not to any and every one—not to your two friends. I am going to ask—and I must insist on this—that you never tell Hatch I caught this fish. Don't let him ever know, directly or indirectly."

"Okay. But why?"

"It might—it might hurt his pride. A swashbuckling fellow, this Hatch, but under it is something fine and vulnerable. I, for one, wouldn't hurt that thing."

I thought I saw a light.

"Doc Hatch really saved your life, didn't he?" I asked.

The General answered quietly: "He did, sir. And with anyone else in the world on that job I'd be a helpless cripple today, if alive at all. Anyone else in the world, I say . . . Hatch was lucky, indeed, that he didn't lose his own life while mending me."

I looked at him inquiringly. The Doctor had never intimated this to any of us.

"The hospital tent, if you could call it that, was under heavy fire. Two orderlies, helping Hatch, were killed."

I asked, after a moment, "Did he ever indicate, if I'm not too inquisitive, that never in all his fishing life has he caught a really distinguished trout?"

"I gathered that, yes. But look here, Doctor Hatch has had a distinguished trout *hooked*—and very nearly landed."

"So?" The single word must have asked where, when, how, everything.

"Indeed. Last week when he was up here with you fellows. A distinguished trout, sir, by your own admission." He pointed to the fish at our feet. "That trout," he went on, "was very nearly Doctor Hatch's fish. On this—" He held up the remnants of the red-white-and-blue bucktail. "Hatch tied this himself, called it 'Old Glory.' Ever see it before this morning?"

"Never." I could only look, very blankly, at General Blake-Carrington.

"Exactly. Hatch is like that. His queer pride, you see. You chaps would have ribbed him. Same way with the fish—if he had told you of his half hour's battle, and of losing the fish at the end, you wouldn't have believed *that,* he thought."

I still couldn't find any clear words to offer the General.

"But he told *me,* for I'm a worse blunderer than Hatch himself. He needed an audience and I was a safe one, what? But if he knew that with all my vast incompetence *I* had caught this big one that he lost. . . . Let's save Old Glory's' trout for Hatch. A sort of reverse lend-lease, eh? Maybe Hatch will hook him again. Or one of you chaps, in your scheduled periods. Any of that would be all right. But for *me* to take him—no."

I looked down at the trout again. There was still time but not much. "All right," I said. "Wet both your hands in the stream, gather up your fish and wade out there with him. Don't drop him in; ease him in very gently."

He did as he was told. I stood beside him as he lowered the huge trout into the stream. The fish hung in the current for a moment as if unaware of its freedom, then the tail and the fins moved and the great form faded slowly downstream.

The General watched the V-ripple spread out. "I've seen an almost spent torpedo make the same show," he said.

He looked at me and smiled a half-embarrassed little smile, like a boy. I could see that he felt much better about the whole thing, not with any smug pride but in a way that was private and warm. He had been in a spot, as I see it now. He could have let me find my own reasons for his decision to release his fish. It might have been easier that way. But B-C had taken a decent course without letting Hatch down. If his simple loyalty was without logic, so are many of the profound convictions of men. It had truth, as the dark reasoning of the heart knows truth.

Wait till I see Hatch, I was thinking, who sends his agents, his foreign spies, to find his fish and save them for him. . . . Then I remembered I'd committed myself to secrecy for all time. And suddenly I knew that if ever I should land that trout I'd release it. The Doctor just *might* hook it again.

"I'm sorry about *you,* sir," the General said, as if reading my thought. "Could we go up to my room and have a drink to that fish —and to our bitter little secret?"

Midwinter Night's Dream 9

Along about Thanksgiving I exhorted Tom Garrison to do something constructive with the winter months. "A flytier of your eminence," I observed, "should start now instead of waiting, as you commonly do, until two weeks before opening day. Now, with four months ahead in which you'll do nothing but dream about the Big Stony—"

"I'm planning to hibernate this winter," Tom said. "Like a bear. I told the telephone girl to ring my number early in the morning of April first."

"Okay, I'll hibernate with you. But we'll have your vise and some mandarin necks, peacock herl, all that stuff—and a couple of tall glasses. And come April we'll be set with forty dozen slatewing Coachmen, Quill Gordons, Hare's Ears—"

That was how it started. We would amass a sufficient backlog of the dull orthodox patterns that seduce the Big Stony browns to keep us in business a whole season.

While the snow rustles against the window April, May and June are far off and fabulous, and fishing looks as easy and unworried as things remote in the future always look. I would put another log on the fire and watch another quill body sprout wings in the little vise ... and every pool of the March Brown Club water would hold a two-pounder who would come up, slow and deliberate, to engulf my floating fly.

Tom would finish the last dab of stickum to seal off the final turn of thread around the hackles of a Wickham's Fancy, loosen the vise jaws, drop the fly on the green felt tabletop to see how nicely it landed, relax in his chair, take a draw on his pipe and say, "So." The single syllable was eloquent with accomplishment. Another fly tied, another trout as good as caught, another step toward the sum of our preparedness for April.

It was nice and comfortable for a while. Because I don't tie flies very well my function was to keep the fire going and to provide a certain moral support to Tom's industry.

But one evening, after a month of building a small stockpile of Cahills, Hendricksons and others of that drab, murderous ilk, Tom was suddenly fired.

"Look," he said. "Let's try something different. A red-squirrel body, nylon-quilled, a mallard tail, indigo hackles and wood duck wings, eh? Do you want it long-shanked or short—number ten, twelve or fourteen?"

And it came finally to flower, looking like no trout fly we had ever seen. Tom said "So" again; we gazed at his conceit under the magnifying glass, floated it in a transparent dish and looked up at it from beneath with the trout's-eye view, and told ourselves in all seriousness that it was good for a twenty-incher. We could think again of the wood-thrush-haunted dusks along the Big Stony and how the Pasture Pool would look, black below its murmuring riffle. A lunker just had to be there, all primed to grab this fantastic hybrid of squirrel fur, mallard tail, wood duck, indigo.

"I'd rather catch a fish on that baby than six on a Cahill," Tom said. "Let's try something else, a bit different. I'm fed up with the theory that a fly has to be dull to be smart. Imagine such beautiful things as the Parma Belle and Silver Doctor being out of fashion, mere museum pieces."

We decided to spark a renaissance in fly-fishing. We would bring color, judiciously of course, into our flies.

And we started judiciously enough. But as the winter wore on we were like anyone else with a foul habit. One fall from grace leads to another, the moralists say; and a couple of hackle feathers, dyed a pale indigo, can and did lead to whole cockerel necks dyed royal purple, emerald green, cerulean blue. Nature ran out of colors early in our campaign, and those we improvised with dyes would have set any barnyard flock to screaming. We made an orange-and-black flamboyant fan-wing on a bass hook and called it Old Nassau. When the dyes ran out we pushed our experiments into the field of design, achieving ultimately a double fly, a four-winged, two-tailed job seeming fixed in a mating act, and called it Wickham's Ecstasy.

Tom took a hundred such steps to April, announcing each with a "So," as he let the fly drop on the green felt. It was like checking off on some tabulating machine the step-by-step passage of the winter.

And we believed in them all while the snow eddied outside. All of fishing is so easy in that off-season interlude. Winter is the angler's time to dream, and in his dreams his flies are right and his casts true. There are no hang-ups or snags in this winter fishing, no aching legs and wrists, no waders full of cold water. There are, in a word, trout.

But spring came, as it always does, like an alarm clock on Monday morning. Spring, with her spurious reputation as the time of poets and young love, is the realist among seasons. There was suddenly a noontime when March was running the last of winter down the gutters and a tackle-store window brought me back to fishing. Here in these bright new gadgets was the real thing again—fishing as it is, full of its hope and striving, promise and pain.

I didn't need any flies of course, after our winter's industry. But once inside I took a look at them anyway. Here they were again, like moths out of their winter cocoons. I pored over the neatly labeled trays, looking for something new. Had the flytiers, for once in their lives, used their imaginations as, for instance, Tom and I had used ours?

The labels didn't indicate it. Here were the ancient standbys as I had seen them every spring for more years than I like to count: the March Browns, Cowdungs, Royals, the he and she Beaverkills, the Whirling Duns and Ginger Quills. The old recital of names. Beautiful names, yes, but—

What about that green-and-gold thing Tom and I had made the night of the blizzard—the one we called Brodhead's Incomprehensible? Why wasn't something like that here—at eighty cents apiece, nine dollars a dozen? Could it be that no demand for it existed because it wasn't likely to take a fish? And all that stuff from the magenta-dyed neck—the magenta-hackled, silver-bodied spiders?

I tried to remember how good they all had looked when the thermometer said ten above outside and a great feat of natural chemistry had yet to melt a foot of snow and bring the buds on the forsythia and the geese on the south wind. How long and dreary a stretch, then, before our fancy flies could feel the bounce of an April riffle.

But suddenly the time was at hand and the killers were speaking to me again, from their show cases, of the gross satisfactions of a weighty creel. "If you want to get trout," they said, in their special idiom, "here we are, and you'd better respect the wisdom of the years." . . . Come to think of it, maybe Tom and I should have paid more attention to the orthodox flies. Our theory about the fancy stuff was pretty, yet we shouldn't slight those members of the old guard who have a way of bringing home the bacon. . . . "If you want to get trout—"

I didn't revert whole hog to the extreme right, of course. The winter fancy died harder than that.

April came in warm, low water, dry-flyish looking. Just to be stubborn I would start with one of our fancy Dans.

A sparse hatch of a yellowish fly was astir as we approached the stream. "See that?" Tom said. "A light Cahill is my baby, to start this season off."

An old meat-in-the-pot fly, the Cahill, at whose eminence in history Tom had sneered, if I remembered rightly, last winter. I reminded him of that and added that I'd back the lavender and tea-rose job we had named Campbell's Lunacy.

"Oh, *that*," he said. "Well, I kind of think the light Cahill—for the first fish, you know. After that maybe I'll give some of our beauties a play."

I called him a sniveling coward but he pretended not to hear.

An hour with the Campbell's Lunacy was pleasant enough. Nothing happened, but it was nice just to cast again and to feel the press of the stream after the long months away. And my gamble with the C.L. proved me of course a man of character, a sportsman able to resist the easy tempting thing.

But as to trout. After all, I did come up here for trout.

I sat down, eventually, on a streamside rock, took out the fly box and looked inside. A lot of good old stuff there, from last year. Four or five light Cahills, for instance.

Behind me a voice was audible above the sound of the water. "Any luck?" The voice belonged to one of the younger members of the March Browns, on his way upstream.

"Nothing—yet," I said, with the inference: But give me time.

"No? What fly you using?"

"It's a little invention," I replied feebly. "It hasn't any name, I guess." Of course I should have confronted this upstart like a man, asserting, "I am fishing the Campbell's Lunacy, sir, whose exquisite genius I have kept out of the manuals for beginners. It tempts no fish under three pounds." But I didn't.

"Got any light Cahills?" the youth asked.

"Yes. I was about to change to one."

"You should. They're hitting 'em." His tone had a youthful deference but it hardly obscured the smug authority every man somehow achieves when he has trout in his creel.

"You do any business?" I asked academically.

He lifted his creel lid and drew out a thirteen-inch brown and a twelve-inch native. "Both on the light Cahill," he reported, confirming his unimpeachable wisdom.

That ended my go with the Campbell's Lunacy. Indeed it almost ended my whole winter's dream, the sum total of our hours of industry at the vise.

But not quite. There came a time, before the trout season waned to its late-summer slack, when one of our private brands did have its moment. With a backlog of four trout in my creel—victims of one of the meat flies—I could afford to speculate that evening. It was the rare moment that comes in my fishing, when the weight of my creel allows me to gamble. Now, when all my conservative instincts told me a Pale Evening Dun would draw a rise from the darkening pool upstream, was the time to get out a certain pink-bodied, emerald-hackled, spent-wing beauty from last winter's harvest. Tom had said "So," after this one, for perhaps the ninety-eighth time. "It's some kind of a dun," he had added dreamily over his glass. "Let's call it the What Have We Dun?"

It had looked trouty then; it could *be* trouty now. For a brief period of every year, usually a few days in June, the Big Stony's browns exhibit a sort of holiday spirit, an irresponsible abandon in their choice of food. Here was a soft June dusk, the streamside woods wet and clean and steaming after a shower, the wood thrushes vocal high in the washed trees. A good trout rolled up lazily, unwarily, thirty feet away, exposing his spotted flanks as he went down. . . . If there was ever a time for the bright coinage of our winter it was now. Let the pork-and-beans flies stay in the box. This trout was playful rather than hungry, a little drunk with the fat and easy living of June. The What Have We Dun? could be a nice liqueur after a full meal.

Play up to his mood, I told myself. Don't make him work by casting below him where he'll have to turn and rush for the fly as it floats down-current. Put it above the point of his rise so that he can take it lazily as it comes opposite.

A few minutes later the miracle had been wrought. A pound-and-a-half brown actually had taken that dream bug, that caprice in feathers, that absurdity of a winter's night. In five minutes I was bringing him in, a tired fish now, fair-hooked by the What Have We Dun? I eased him over the net, lifted him clear, took him ashore and administered the coup de grace. Laid out with the tape on him he was sixteen inches. I stowed him in the creel.

Maybe this was the way, after all—the bizarre thing that no one ever uses. A fly I had ceased to regard as legitimate had killed the best fish of the day.

I looked forward to answering Tom's "What'd you take him on?" A dozen times I had met that inquiry with one or another of the old expected names: "On a slatewing Coachman" or another of the elect. It was never news, never a surprise. But now, at last, it would be.

In a few minutes Tom came up the path accompanied by an elderly angler, a March Brown member who used to fish the Big Stony before we had a club there.

We greeted one another. Then Tom said, "Well?"

I opened the creel. They looked inside where the big one lay on top, and said, both at once, "What on?"

I gave them the name, held up the What Have We Dun? still on

261

the tippet, and watched the swift incredulous surprise jump into Tom's face.

The old fellow said, "Let's see that fly." He took it in his fingers for a close scrutiny, turned it around, held it up to the waning light. "Yep," he said, as if thinking aloud. "That's just what it is." Then, to me, "What was that name you called it?"

"The What Have We Dun? It's a crazy thing Tom and I dreamed up last winter, and we gave it a crazy name, just for the hell of it."

"I'll say you did," he said. "Craziest name I ever heard for the old June Witch."

Tom and I looked at him, then at each other. "You mean," I said —"you mean it's a real fly?"

"You bet it is—or it was. Haven't seen one on the Big Stony for a long time. But years ago we used to see 'em, only a small hatch or two each year and always about this time of June. Then, for some reason, they disappeared. But when they came on, in the old days, they were the hottest thing you could use. I've tied dozens of 'em, about like yours. Your hackles are a little too bright a green."

That's how to take the edge off a miracle, I was thinking. In all our fabulous production Tom and I were bound to imitate nature, without knowing it, as least once. The What Have We Dun? had lost caste as a dream bug. But it had gained on another count. A sixteen-inch brown is no slouch of a fish, even in the Big Stony.

Maybe our winter project hadn't been completely futile after all. And maybe the brown trout knew their flies better than we did.

When All the World Is Young 10

The road to school took him past the things he loved to the things he hated. It took him, first, past the white house that had been the home of old Lank Starbuck who had taught Chris how to fish for trout. Chris had been glad when Lank's son Thad, had left, and he hadn't wanted anyone else to move in. If it was empty he could go by it and think of old Lank, but if someone else moved in it wouldn't mean old Lank to him anymore. A house wasn't just a house, it was who lived in it. If the man who lived in it was your friend the house was your friend too. But when a stranger moved in the house became a stranger and you had to get to know the house all over again, by another name. He hadn't liked it when Dr. Martin had moved in there, last summer. Dr. Martin, they had said, was needed here. There wasn't a really good doctor in Forks Township and the nearest help folks could get for a sick person was fifteen miles away. Maybe so, but he hadn't liked it.

But thinking now about how he hadn't liked it at the time, he could see how foolish he had been. That was a kid thing—standing pat on what you have and seeing no good in something different. When he had begun to change was the day Dr. Martin had called on his dad, early last fall, just after Dr. Martin had moved in. Chris had been scared that time. He hadn't known what was the matter but any time his dad went to bed in the middle of the day it was scary. But after Dr. Martin had seen his dad and had come downstairs and talked to him he wasn't scared anymore. He didn't remember what the doctor had said. But he knew his dad was going to get well and that everything, the whole world, was all right again.

After that he felt like looking again at the old Lank Starbuck house when he went by.

And he had even got to thinking of it, now, as the Martin house, thinking easily of it that way, not with homesickness, being glad to hook up the name Martin with it. The first day of school last September a yellow-haired girl had run out of the Martin door as he had gone by. "I'm Rosemary," she had said. "I'm going to your school. Can I go with you?"

The road took him, second, past the bridge over the Big Stony, the bridge just upstream from the March Brown Club water and just downstream from the junction of the Little Stony. He wasn't allowed to fish the water below the bridge, though his dad owned it. That was a hard thing for Chris to understand—it was a grown-up thing—but he was beginning to get it now. He had met two of the March Brown members and he liked them, and that made it easier for him to understand the rule and to respect it, as he had, now, for nearly a year. Those people paid a lot of money to fish his dad's water. The idea of paying to fish was something he hadn't thought of until lately. You didn't pay to play ball or fly a kite though you paid for the ball and the kite cord. You bought a fishing rod but not the use of it. He had no money to pay for that and he knew he wouldn't pay for it if he had because he could fish the entire Little Stony for nothing. The fishing wasn't as good up there but it was good enough if you knew how to go after 'em. Trout were in there. So far this year he had taken twenty-eight, in ten tries, counting only keepers of course. And that, he knew darn well, was double the number Sticks Hooker had caught, in twice that many tries. Sticks lived up the Little Stony on a back road, with two kid brothers and a baby sister, in one of the several houses Chris's father owned in Forks Township. Living right on the stream, Sticks had all the chance in the world to fish. Sticks didn't pay for his rod even—he cut it in the woods. And he thought Chris a kind of stuck-up dude for fishing with a bought rod. . . . Sticks was all right, though. Chris liked him in a way, but Sticks was just enough older and bigger to try to bully him a little—and he liked Rosemary a little too well.

Chris wanted to be friends with Sticks, but something—he didn't know what—got between them like a wall. Maybe it was his fault, maybe Sticks would like to be friends with him, too.

It took him, finally, to school, to books with dreary words in them, and to windows with dingy red-brown shades under which his eyes would stray to the outside world of blossom and birdsong and wind-filled trees and, over there, beyond that hump of a pasture, the little valley where the dark stream ran. It took him to the smell of chalk dust and old paper and of children who do not get enough baths, the school smell, the smell of the Hooker kids. It took him to Miss Spencer, standing in her straight black dress at the blackboard with a long pointer hovering over long rows of figures and suddenly lighting on one like a fish hawk spotting a chub, or tap-tapping over states on a down-rolled map and coming to rest on a yellow one near the middle—Miss Spencer who would say much less than she thought but make you think she meant a lot more. "To what capital of what state am I pointing, Christopher, and what is its chief industry?" And he would answer "Topeka, Illinois, and they make glassware there," and she would lay down her pointer slowly on the eraser shelf, as if giving up the whole thing in disgust, and say "*Chris*topher *Win*termute." That's all she'd say. But she'd mean "You, the son of the richest man in Forks Township, do not know that Topeka is the capital of Kansas and that they never heard of glassware in Topeka." And all the class would know that was what she meant.

He gave the whistle that May morning to Rosemary as he went by. Their private signal had been decided on some time ago, after a good deal of deliberation. Rosemary knew the bobwhite call of the quail and had wanted to make it that. But Chris had overruled her —there were too many real bobwhites whistling in these fields in the spring and summer, and he didn't want any false alarms bringing Rosemary to her door. The whistle of the greater yellowlegs, the *whew-whew—whew-whew*—a one-note, two-syllable, once-repeated call, would be better. That was a sound heard from natural sources only in April and September around here, and not often then. It was easy and it carried, but it wasn't loud. It wouldn't stir up grown people or bring dogs running when you didn't want 'em.

And besides, it was uncommon: it gave him a chance to explain to Rosemary what the greater and lesser yellowlegs were. . . . Bet Miss Spencer never heard of 'em and wouldn't know one if she saw it. Schoolteachers, who were supposed to know everything, didn't know important things like this at all.

The front door of the Martin house opened as if his whistle had made some secret contact with its lock. Rosemary took the porch steps in two strides and ran down the walk, her bright hair flying. She had on a white dress—a high-waisted thing with ruffles—and a sash the color of her hair.

After they had walked a little distance she said, "Want to run? Look, I'll race you to the bridge."

"Aw, no. You couldn't keep up with me. No, I want to talk to you. Let's walk."

"You're 'fraid I can beat."

"All right then. Give me your books so you can run free. On your mark—set—go!"

He let her draw away from him in the first fifty feet, then he spurted a little and kept an even distance between himself and the flying heels and the white dress and the streaming hair. She made the left turn onto the bridge road and gained a little on the down-slope to the stream. For a girl, she could run. He hadn't expected her to hold the pace and now he had a momentary real fear that she would reach the bridge ahead of him. The heavy schoolbooks, a strapped bundle in each arm, handicapped him. But he put all he had into a final sprint and beat her to the log rail by a stride.

They sat on the lower rail, on the upstream side of the bridge, Rosemary flushed and panting, Chris trying to keep his breath even.

"You can run," he said.

"But boys always beat. I wish I was a boy."

"If you were—who'd you want to be?"

"Oh-h-h. How do I know?" She tried to make a circle in the roadside dust with the toe of her shoe. But her legs still had the running in them, they were trembling and unsure. "If I was Sticks Hooker I'd be tall and strong—the best ballplayer in school. If I was you I'd have a rich dad, and I could get things, nice clothes."

"Listen, my dad isn't rich. He's got a lot of land so people think he's rich but he's land-poor. He's worried about taxes an' rents he can't collect—I heard him say so. But don't tell that—that's a secret, like our whistle."

"I won't."

"Anyway—"

"What?"

"Is that all you'd have?"

"Is *what* all I'd have?"

"If you were me. A rich dad—if he *was* rich?"

"Oh." Rosemary erased the circle in the dust with her shoe. "You're nice, Chris. I like you."

"Better'n you like Sticks?"

"Maybe . . . I like Sticks, too. He brought me a trout yesterday."

"One?"

"Um-h-m-m. That's all he promised."

"How big?"

"Eight inches. We measured him on my ruler. Gosh, he was good. Had him for breakfast this morning."

Chris got up from the lower rail and turned around and leaned against the upper one and looked for a long moment at the stream flowing under the bridge, and his eyes followed it slowly upstream, as if studying each foot of its dark fast surface, to the point where the Little Stony comes in from the north. Rosemary stood up too, and looked from Chris's face to the water and back to Chris's face, and kept silent, respecting something she felt to be going on in his mind.

"Look, Rosemary," he said finally. "I'll get you five trout, none under eight inches, maybe some bigger." He looked straight at her blue eyes. "Five. Maybe one will be twelve inches."

"Five? Altogether—at once? From Little Stony?"

"Sure, from Little Stony. Why?"

"Sticks said you fished the club water sometimes because your dad owns it—an' that's why you catch more than he does."

Chris pondered that for a moment. It was why, maybe, Sticks didn't like him. Then he looked squarely at Rosemary again. "I *have* fished down there—two or three times—last year. But each time I had to sneak it, past the guard. I'm not allowed to fish there. When I fish there I'm poaching, and Sticks can do the same thing anytime he wants to try it. An' I'll tell him so. . . . Today," he added, "I'll fish Little Stony only. Word of honor. . . . Believe me?"

"Yes," she said.

"The water's right, Rosemary. I can get 'em from Little Stony."

"How do you know? Is that what you were looking at, so long— to see if the water's right?"

"Yes."

"How does it tell you?"

"I don't know. Right pitch, right color. An' the day's right— cloudy but it won't rain an' it'll stay warm. . . . It all smiles at me when it's right—it looks friendly, like you look when you smile at me." He had heard old Lank Starbuck say that, years ago, and he had never forgotten it.

"But maybe, by the time school's out, it won't be right anymore."

"It's an all-day job, Rosemary. I won't go to school."

"Oh-h-h. But you can't do that. That's hooky."

"Sure, hooky." He said it casually, with an offhand assurance that puzzled her, made her think he had done it before.

"But you can't," she persisted, to draw him out. "Where's your fish pole—and what do you do with your schoolbooks? An' if you go home to get your pole now, and your dad sees you, what'll he do?"

"He'd do plenty. He'd look sad an' he'd *be* sad. No one else could see he was sad but *I* can. An' he'd be calm. He wouldn't rant at me —he'd talk easy. An' then he'd whale me. Gosh, you don't know how he can hurt. . . . But he won't see me. 'Cause I won't go home. . . . You know what a cache is—I told you."

"Um-h-m-m. I remember—the time you left the muskrat skin for my fur collar by our back fence."

"That's right. Miss Spencer wouldn't tell you, 'cause she wouldn't know. Well, my rod—don't call it a pole, it's a rod—my rod is cached up along Little Stony. I leave the books there, pick up the rod, leave the rod there when I get through fishing and pick up the books an' take 'em home."

Rosemary looked at him admiringly. There was enough deviltry in that technique to appeal to her. She wanted a part in it—but she was only a girl.

"I won't tell," she said, with satisfaction. That gave her a definite role, however small, in the plot. She elaborated it: "Look. If Miss

Spencer asks me where you are I'll tell her you started out with me but you got all out of breath at the bridge and decided you didn't feel like coming to school today. Is that some kind of a lie—a white lie?"

"Nope. It's true—except I didn't get *all* out of breath. I can run farther than that. I ran all the way to school once. . . . But that's good —you tell her that, before class begins, hear? Then maybe I won't need an excuse from Dad."

"All right. . . . But hooky—that's wrong."

"Why?"

"I don't know. It just is—like stealing."

"No it isn't. I'll tell you sometime. . . . 'By, Rose."

He headed into the woods along the north bank of the stream. When he was up to the confluence of the Little Stony he stopped and looked back to the bridge. She had gone. The road north of the bridge was not visible through the trees except for one short stretch where it topped a rise two hundred yards away. He laid his sight on this spot like a barrage, and presently the white dress and the yellow sash and the yellow hair crossed it, walking fast.

He wondered, now, why he hadn't kissed her good-bye. He had wanted to. It had been the moment, when he had left her—she had been "right" then, as the stream was right for fishing. No good, now, to call to her to stop and to run to her. The moment was past; he had lost it. . . . He could take the stream for fishing, always, when it offered itself, as he was taking it now, even at a good deal of risk, for he knew the chances to be better than even that his truancy would be found out and punished. But he couldn't take her who presented no risk at all. If his conscience had called it wrong he could understand. His conscience called plenty of things he did wrong and kept him awake at night thinking of them. But his conscience approved this and still he was afraid of it. It bothered him, like a buzzing fly he couldn't swat.

Well, he'd swat it tonight, once and for all, and clear the air of the thing. When the time came for him to leave her this evening, after giving her the trout, he'd claim his reward. It would be another right moment, on her front porch with the dusk drawing in, and this time he would grab it.

A narrow path led him along the northeast bank of the Little

Stony, upstream. A fisherman's path, it was never far from the water in its gradual climb up the valley. About a quarter-mile above the bridge Chris turned off it to the right and entered a little swale grown thickly with birches and witch hazel. A woodcock whistled up out of it, a native bird, fat with the spring worms. An ancient oak stood in the middle of this small area. Chris stooped and reached into an opening at the base of the great hollow trunk and drew out a cloth-cased steel rod and a willow creel. He opened the lid of the creel to see that all his gear was intact—his double-action reel with the enameled line on it, the packet of leaders, the cork full of eyed hooks and the tobacco can for worms.

A flat brown *Geography,* a blunt green *Practical English Grammar,* a stout red *Elements of United States History* and a thin black *Graded City Speller,* well strapped with a double loop of webbing, took up the occupancy of the old trunk where the rod and creel left off.

A good trade, he thought.

Occasional hooky was not against his conscience either, anymore. It had been, once. His father had talked to him of the duties and responsibilities of men and of what men owed to their society and to the world at large. A duty was something that was unpleasant now but paid you some sort of reward later on. You got an actual reward—money, perhaps, or maybe only a better character—at some future time by doing something unpleasant now. God paid you, in some way, for the duties you performed. Education was one of those rewards and going to school the duty that got it for you. It had sounded right, even brave, the way his father had put it. But thinking about it later, in the dark of his room, when the ring of his father's words had died out of his ears, he thought he could see something selfish in the pursuit of duty. If you were after a reward anyway perhaps you could take your reward now—have fun now instead of later. It all came to the same thing in the end; God paid it anyway, now or afterward. That hadn't decided him, though. That wasn't strong enough—it was only his little kid idea against the ancient wisdom of his father which had proved itself too many times to be doubted. That had been one of the times when he had wanted a mother's opinion too. He had felt that a mother's judgment would have some nameless tenderness, be less severe and easier to live with, no matter what it was. But he didn't even remember his mother, who had died when he was two years old. His father had to do.

But one day last summer when he was poaching on the club water, sneaking around a big rock at the head of the Pasture Pool, he had met face to face, head on, a princess. His first instinct had been to run, for anyone met on that private water was probably his enemy. But he had looked into her face, met her eyes, and known at once that he had no need to run from her. She was grown up but not old, and not a real princess of course, but she looked like the princess in the fairy-tale book he had at home. She had asked him his name and given him hers, Priscilla, and told him to call her that. He had thought of "Princess Priscilla" and the words had seemed to fit, to swim together. She was the daughter, she had said, of a real army colonel who had fought in the war and was a member of the March Browns. She had asked him to sit down on the rock and talk with her awhile. The Pasture Pool was an open spot where the guard could see him if he went by, but that would be all right, she had said, she'd take care of that. The talk had turned to poaching and had gotten around, as he had known it would, to the question of whether it was his duty not to poach. "What do *you* think?" she had asked. And you had to answer her straight, you couldn't just answer the way a nice boy was supposed to. That was the way you answered Miss Spencer at school, but not her. She had a face and a voice you couldn't lie to. So he had turned the thing over in his mind for a couple of minutes before replying, trying to line it all up with what his father had told him of duty.

"In a way," he said, finally. "It's my duty to poach."

"How?" she had asked.

"Well, it takes a little nerve to poach here—I have to be a little brave about trying it. That's hard. And being careful not to get caught—sneaking—that's hard too, if you do it all day. But sometimes God pays me with a big trout, bigger'n I'd get upstream."

She had seemed to think about that for a long while. Then she had said: "I like that, Chris. I like you for saying it."

They had talked for an hour or more, there on the rock. She hadn't advised him to keep off the stream or to go on it again, but had left that for him to decide. "Another duty is having fun," she had said, and it had sounded like his father's words in reverse, "so long as it doesn't spoil other people's fun." She had told him to have all the fun he could while he was a boy and to keep on having it when he was grown, fun in his mind when his body got too old for it. "The great men are simple men," she had said. "They never quite get over being kids."

Since that day he had never again fished the club water.

But playing hooky was his own affair. That didn't spoil the fun of a single soul on earth.

He took the steel rod out of its cloth case and stowed the case in the hollow trunk with the schoolbooks. He collected some worms by kicking over grass hummocks on the far side of the swale, put them in the tobacco can and headed upstream.

The Hooker house was three hundred yards above here, well back from the other bank and partly visible through the trees. Just opposite the Hooker house his path would come out high above the stream overlooking one of the best runs of trout water on the whole of the Little Stony, a place where he had taken more than one good fish. If this were a Saturday he would give it a look but on a school day the smart thing was to leave the path before he came in sight of the house, make a wide detour through the woods, and return to the path at a point well above. For if one of the younger Hooker kids saw him he would tell Sticks afterwards, and Sticks might tell the teacher.

He heard their voices across stream as he worked his way past through the woods. Regaining the path above, he proceeded almost a mile before he stopped and assembled his gear. This was his favorite place to start. A little riffle spilled into deep fast water between two boulders below which a dark pool arched down to a flat undercut rock at its lower end. With luck he could take two fish here, one in the fast run and one from under the rock below.

Crouching well back from the bank above the head of the run Chris let the worm go into the dark water, deep, with a little slack to keep it down. For a second he could see its course in the riffle, then he lost it. The current straightened his slack—the worm should be between the rocks now. He held his breath for the strike and it came. He hit back, felt the strong resistance of the trout, guided the fish up through the fast water, lifted him clear and swung him to the bank. A deep ten-inch native and a good start on his day. He bent back the trout's head, gathered some ferns and laid the fat fish on them in the creel.

Another try in the same water was part of the technique he had inherited from Lank Starbuck. He went through with it, gave it plenty of time, but nothing happened. The slow center of the pool, sometimes good for a trout, yielded nothing either. He crossed the stream, wading over his knees, for it was necessary to fish the undercut rock at the pool's tail from the other side. He backed away from the bank, crouched low, waited a minute, two minutes, up to the limit of his patience. Then he put on a fresh worm and swung it gently into the slow current upstream from the rock. It was out of his sight below the rock's edge, drifting deep in the black water, just the way he had wanted it to go. In a moment the drift of his line halted though the current all around it kept on. He knew what it was: there was nothing to snag him on that smooth bottom. His line, the part of it he could see, started upstream then, gaining speed. He struck and felt at once that he was into a bigger fish than he had dreamed of hooking up here. The trout raced for the head of the pool, taking line from the reel, then turned and bored downstream. The lip of the pool was a shallow curving wash over a flat rock bottom, only inches deep. The trout thrashed into it, exposing its great proportions, seemed to roll once or twice and slid back into deep water again as Chris's line went suddenly slack.

A curious and empty quiet was all through the woods and over the water. If any birds had been singing they were still now. The little pool had lapsed to its former expressionless calm. It might never have held a trout, and this one, just lost, might have been only imagined or dreamed. That vacant sense of stillness was inside Chris, too, in the region of his heart. He had known it before, many times. It was pure loss. No word or act could, at the moment, answer its thrust. Only time could put it behind—an hour's fishing with its new problems, new hopes and perhaps new success.

He reeled in. His hook and half his leader were gone. He cut the frayed end of the leader cleanly off and tied on a new length of gut and a new hook. By noon he had regained control of his day and could look back on the loss of the big one and see it as a definite part of fishing. Three trout were now on the ferns in his creel, an eight-inch native and a nine-inch brown added to the first one. He needed two more to keep his promise to Rosemary.

And he'd get 'em. He'd get one extra, six in all, so he could keep one for himself. They were coming, and when they were coming he could take six if he were very careful. This was the day, perhaps the best he'd see this year. The high tide. It came once in every season, and he had spotted it. It was worth the risk he was taking, worth being caught and all that that would entail.

A wood thrush sang into the noon stillness. A gray squirrel sat on a windfall ahead of him, jerked its tail twice like a mechanical toy and raced down the log at his approach. In a wide backwater which he had to cross on his way downstream a muskrat plowed straight as a tugboat, towing a leafed branch. He was happy in the way a trout fisherman can be happy when all the world is young and the day is right and confidence is with him. He had that rare fishing happiness which can forget for a while mere keenness for the chase and indulge itself with the quiet asides of angling. He sat down on an old stump and spent half an hour watching the water and the woods on the far bank, and thought about the little unseen lives that lived and died there, year by year, while boys went to school and men worried over taxes and their duty to a society which worried as much as they.

Then he went back to it, fishing carefully, approaching with great caution each likely run and pool on his way downstream. Another native and another brown, ten inches each, were in his creel before three o'clock. His promise of five trout to Rosemary was kept. . . . Wait till Sticks hears about this.

But he needed another and he wanted it to be big. He had mentioned a twelve-incher to Rosemary. The one he had lost had been well over that but he couldn't say much about "the big one that got away." Even Rosemary, who knew nothing about fishing, had heard that tale too many times to be impressed. She would laugh at it and the effect of the five good trout might be lost in her scorn.

The big one, if he got it, would be for Rosemary, and that would free one of his ten-inchers for his dinner tonight. Bringing home a trout would need no explaining: it could have been caught after school as some of his others had been this year. . . . His stomach, without food since breakfast, was beginning to talk to him, to nag at him, interrupting his fishing now and then with its assertions. He began to think too much of the dinner he would have. Trout or no trout, it would be a good one, as it always was. Old Sarah, his dad's cook, could turn it out. There would be a big ham and baked potatoes and peas—or maybe a great smoking stew with dumplings —and a tumbler of milk filled twice, and all the fresh bread and butter he could eat, and an apple pie. And he could feel how sleepy he would be after it and how good his bed would feel as he lay in the cool sheets just before sleep caught him, looking up at the ceiling at the angular shadow cast by the dim hall light beyond his half-open bedroom door, and feeling the spring night fanning his cheek. . . .

The Hooker house was just below him now, on the opposite bank. He had come to the point where he had rejoined the trail this morning after his detour around the danger zone, and if he were to retrace his steps he should leave the trail here. He stood still in the path, to ponder the question a moment and to listen. The vicinity of the Hooker house was still a no-man's-land to him. It was not yet time for school to be out and his presence here on the stream would give him away now as surely as it would have this morning. Sticks wouldn't be home for half an hour at least. The other Hooker kids were making no sound. They were in the house or far off in the woods, for when they were nearby you could always hear them. He might just possibly get away with trying that good run of water directly opposite the house. It was a desperate chance —it made him feel as poaching on the Big Stony used to make him feel—but today his reward might be there.

The path from here on climbed gradually above the stream; just above the Hooker house it emerged from the trees into an open slashing, a badly exposed position for anyone sneaking it as he was. But it held an advantage: its altitude above the water gave him a penetrating view of the sand-bottomed run. There was something about that run he never had been able to understand. Its straight fifty-foot stretch was devoid of windfalls, rocks or overhanging banks. It had no trout cover worthy of the name, and certainly it could offer little underwater food. Yet it was a place where large trout loved to lie. The small fish, he knew, were afraid of its bright exposure.

If a fish was in sight he would maneuver down to it; if not, he would leave the trail at once and go home.

He studied the house—as much as he could see of it from the shelter of the woods—before he dared the open trail ahead. A blue column of woodsmoke stood up straight out of the chimney. But no sound came from the house and no one was in sight. If the Hooker kids would stay indoors while he did what he wanted to do, he might yet get by with it.

Once beyond the cover of the trees there was no need to crouch for he could be seen out here, crouching or standing, and crouching would make him look more suspicious. So he walked erect along the high open trail to the vantage point where he could scan the bright water below.

He had to look sharp; a few vague shadows were on the bottom, and a waterlogged stick or two. For a minute he saw no sign of a fish; then, as if his straining eyesight had created it, a large trout was there, directly below him, its tail fanning almost imperceptibly in the gentle current. He wondered that he hadn't seen it before, it was so distinct now. A rainbow—all of sixteen inches long. He could see its pink stripe and its myriad tiny spots. A great trout, strayed up from the club water probably—the biggest trout he had ever seen in the Little Stony.

He faded back up the path to the woods, walking backward, his eyes on the fish. Then he sneaked down the wooded bank to the stream and baited his hook with the worm he had been saving for just this chance.

Well upstream from his fish, Chris put the worm in with a short gentle flick and let the easy current take it down, drawing out the slack between the reel and first guide. Though he would do his best to keep the worm drifting as long as possible he knew it would sink and come to rest on the bottom fifteen or twenty feet above the trout. It would be better to work it a little nearer but he dared neither a long cast nor a closer approach. Alternately feeding slack to the current and raising his rod top to keep the worm up, Chris could feel it along the line when at last the worm settled into the sand. His line, soaked with the day's fishing, submerged itself gradually upstream until only a few inches of it were visible between his rod tip and the surface.

Now he had only to crouch and wait—and control himself, if he could. He was a little ashamed of his agony of expectation and the way his heart and his hands were affected by it. Even this fish—the biggest trout he had ever deliberately angled for—shouldn't make his heart pound or cause his hands to tremble so that he couldn't hold his rod steady. He tried to be cool and thoughtful, to figure the chances of that rainbow seeing his worm and coming upstream to take it if he did see it, and the possibility of his leader escaping notice. To lose his terrific excitement he tried to discourage himself. But it was no good: despite all his reasoning there was still an outside chance of that giant taking hold, and this nearness to such success as he had never known might prove too much for him to bear.

His rod had caught the trembling infection from his hands. The little length of visible line between his rod tip and the water jerked back and forth in the slow current. He watched it steadily as if trying by the very intensity of his gaze to make it still, and as he watched he discerned a movement in it which even his trembling hands could not have caused. The visible short stretch of line lengthened a little downstream, came five or six clear inches out of water, straightening itself in a widening angle from the rod. It lapsed back, almost to its former position, then straightened again swiftly, six feet of dripping line knifing out of the surface below his rod. Chris Wintermute stood up and struck. . . .

He tried to recall that battle afterward; once, when she was in a mood to be still and listen, he tried to give Rosemary the details out of the long view which retrospect should have made clear. But he could never quite track it down. His memory of it remained a confused picture of a surface shattered like glass, a surface erupting all over at once with a great trout bursting from each eruption, a memory of spray and the noise of breaking water, a memory of a frenzied dream, of something that couldn't happen in real life, and a slow awakening from it as the fish tired, a gradual return after an incredible time to the familiar world on which he could plant his feet and feel safe. . . . And of his happiness at the end, when he eased the exhausted trout up the slope of a little sand beach at the lower end of the run. But there were no words for that and he had never even tried to give that part to Rosemary or to anyone else. That was for himself only, to think about sometimes when he was alone.

Just then, as the fish came up on the sand, he didn't believe it. He had known that there were rainbow trout in the world as big as this one, but that one so big should be his own, caught by himself, he didn't believe.

Neither did the two Hooker kids who had materialized from nowhere, on the opposite bank, in time to see Chris beach his fish.

"Sucker, ain't it, Chris?" one called across. "Big sucker—I seen one in here."

"Sucker, my eye." Chris was looking for a short stout club, for this fish was too large to be killed by the usual method. "He's a trout— a rainbow."

The arrival of the Hooker kids annoyed him. Up to this moment his adventure had been a success. To have taken this trout quickly and have gotten away unseen would have made his day perfect. But now he was discovered. The Hooker kids didn't know what playing hooky meant but they would tell Sticks they had seen him, and Sticks would know. And tomorrow it would be all over school, and tomorrow night his father would have it.

"Aw, trout ain't that big. Sticks said they ain't."

"Because he can't get 'em that big." Chris was beginning to get mad.

"He could so—if they grew that big." The youngest Hooker boy was loyal to his big brother. The other, the next younger to Sticks, seemed to hold certain doubts. "Shut up," he said quietly. "Maybe Sticks can't. Sticks ain't so good at fishin'. Let's go see it."

Chris found the right club and killed the trout with two blows on top of its head. The Hooker kids, barefooted, rolled their faded blue overalls to their thin thighs and waded in. They had legs like those that had given Sticks his nickname. All the Hooker kids could be called "Sticks," he was thinking.

"You ought to have sneakers on, or somethin'," Chris said. "Some of those rocks are sharp—and there's some glass and junk around here."

"Aw, we ain't got shoes," the larger one replied, thrashing across.

"None of th' kids in our house got shoes but Sticks. Sticks needs 'em 'cause he goes t' school."

Chris looked at them, coming across. The thought of their being without shoes, having nothing at all to wear on their feet, hurt him deeply like an insult, as if someone had called him a damned fool for ever thinking the world was beautiful. The thought, he knew, would never be far from him. In the nights, in the alone moments when he got out the thoughts he loved, this thing would come breaking in on them and leering at them and chasing them away.

He held up the big fish before their wide, devouring eyes. "Is it a trout?" he said.

They stood looking in silence, trying to make their minds believe the story their eyes had to tell.

"Right in our own front yard too," the smaller one said, finally. "Betcha Sticks would have got 'im if *you* hadn't come by."

"Like ta have 'im for my supper t'night," said the other one. "Boy, would he taste good!"

"Um-m-m. Better'n ol' cornmeal mush."

"I like cornmeal mush all right," Chris said. "I have it for breakfast sometimes. You don't have it for supper, do you?"

"Sure. Supper—breakfast too. All meals."

"Gosh. You must like it better'n anything."

The two Hooker boys looked at each other and smiled in a little superior way, a mutual acknowledgment of a bit of information not known to Chris.

"We hate it," the larger one said. "Wouldn't be so bad 'f ya could have a lotta milk on it. 'Thout milk it's dry—gets in your teeth."

"But—if you don't like it—why, why do you eat it so much?"

They exchanged the same look a second time and the larger one spoke again: " 'Cause there ain't much else in our house t' eat. Mom planted some beans an' pertaters but they ain't up yet. She gets dandylions an' wood herbs. But they don't fill ya—ya can't eat much of 'em. Fried dough fills ya—we have that, some."

"Once in a while Sticks gets a fish," the smaller one put in. "We try to but we don't get none. Been tryin' all mornin' t' snare some suckers. No luck. ... Fried dough fills ya *too* much," he added quietly, as if talking to himself. "Made me puke, las' night."

"You make too much noise," Chris said. "That's why you don't get any fish. I heard you this morning, on the way up." He uttered the words but he wasn't thinking them. It was as if someone else had put them in his mouth merely to keep up the talk while he thought about something else—about cornmeal mush, day after day—and why Sticks's legs and his brothers' legs were so thin—and about having no shoes—

"Get any others, Chris?"

—and about fried dough and dandelions, and Mom who had planted beans and potatoes but they weren't up yet—Mom, whom he had never seen but whom, he thought oddly, he could love—

"What does your Dad do?" he asked suddenly, seizing on a forlorn shape that had come out of the gloom in his brain.

"Pop? He ain't home," the small one said.

"I mean—doesn't he work? Doesn't he make any money to buy food?"

"He was workin'," the older one said. "He worked in Post's garage over at th' Forks. But he don't now. He lost his job. Get any other fish, Chris?"

A faint complaining cry drifted down to them from the house across the stream.

"What's that?" Chris asked.

"The baby. She's sick."

The forlorn shape receded back into the murk of the cornmeal mush, the fried dough and the shoeless feet, like something that slowly heaves up and goes down again in roiled water.

"Did you—did you get any others?"

"Five others," he said.

"O-o-o-h. Can we see them?"

Chris opened his creel and they crowded up to it and their eyes seemed to crowd into the trout- and fern-filled cavity, staring and eager and hungry. The smaller one touched some of the trout with his fingertips, daintily, as if to be sure they were real. "Gosh," he muttered after a moment. "You're a good fisherman."

"You roll 'em in cornmeal or flour," Chris said. "An' fry 'em till they're brown on both sides. Put salt an' pepper on while they're fryin'—"

A visible trickle drooled out of the mouth of the smaller Hooker.

"Tell your Mom that," Chris added. "She might not know."

"Aw, she can cook a trout. But we don't have any. Did you think we had any?"

"You've got these," he said. "I'm giving 'em to you." . . . It was out now, and no more thinking about his promise to Rosemary would put the words back in his mouth or keep the trout in his creel.

Their eyes wrenched away from the trout and up to Chris's face, unbelieving, then sought each other's for some confirmation, some assurance that it was true.

"All of 'em?"

"Sure. Look, I've got to get home, fast. Can I see your Mom a minute, right away?"

"Sure. . . . Gee—six trout for supper. Come on, we'll give 'em to her. She can cook 'em. Yay! Boy—oh—boy!"

They went into the stream again, shouting "Mom! Mom! We got six trout. Mom! Chris Wintermute gave us six trout!"

Chris followed through the knee-deep water of the lower run. The uproar from the kids had brought Mrs. Hooker to the door. During the noise attending the display of the trout Chris stood a little apart, looking closely for the first time in his life at this house he had always avoided on his trips upstream. It was going to collapse. Its roof sagged in the middle and a lot of shingles were gone from the roof. Those places had been patched with scraps of tar paper and pieces of tin fashioned out of flattened oil cans. If the old boards had ever had any paint they had long since lost it; they were gray and naked to the weather. In the four front windows several panes of glass were out, replaced by squares of cardboard or brown paper. The entire structure leaned as if tottering with its own weight. There was not a straight line or a right angle: the vertical and horizontal planes all slanted in ways that looked dangerous.

Sticks, living in this place, came into his mind and suddenly he found himself admiring Sticks in a way that was new and strange to him. Sticks had been able to go to school every day from this house which was dying, and come back to this house at night and go to school again and play the best baseball of any kid there, and get good marks, and fish with a pole he had cut in the woods, and give a trout to Rosemary when he was starving for it himself. . . . Sticks had guts.

But when the kids had gone inside with the trout and quiet had come again over the little square of clean-swept dirt which was the front yard, and Mrs. Hooker stood there in the leaning doorway, in a little area of sunlight as if framed by the old house behind her— Chris knew that the house was *not* going to collapse, after all. Mrs. Hooker held it up and always would hold it up. Mom . . . Mom was where Sticks got his guts. He didn't go to school from a dying house. He went from Mom and he took something of Mom with him to make him good at baseball and to get him good marks.

No one could call *her* "Sticks." She was tall and broad in her blue gingham apron and her hair was a gold-gray, neatly drawn back from her high proud forehead. She stood straight and clean, a brave and kind figure, looking at him. Her mouth was straight across, as if set in a fighting position against something that battled her from inside, but her blue eyes had sunlight in them and they were smiling at him.

And suddenly he knew he could not say what he had come to say. She was too proud, too strong, to take it from a kid. No. . . . He would have to tell his father, later. And that would mean confessing that he had been fishing here today. But he couldn't tell Mom. She would talk him out of it and he didn't want to be—he couldn't be —talked out of it. If he were talked out of *that* he'd want to take his trout back. It would be the end, the complete and final ruin of a day that had suddenly cracked up on him anyway.

He returned her smile and tipped his cap to her. She took a step toward him but as she did so the baby cried again from somewhere in the old house. Chris saw her step halt and retrace itself. He saw a little wincing look cloud the sun and the smile that had been in her eyes. She turned from him, and her fine straight back disappeared into the gloom of the leaning and rotten doorway.

He walked away, down the path. He crossed the stream again, hurried back to his hollow oak trunk, stowed his rod and creel, took up his books and started home.

There was no fishing left in his mind now—none of the high hope of the morning. That moment, only seven hours ago when he had left Rosemary at the bridge, seemed now an age away, back in his early childhood. Something bigger than fishing had taken up all the space in his brain and his heart, a thing he gotten hold of and couldn't drop, a tremendous thing that was heavy, perhaps too heavy for him to handle. A man's thing. It didn't make him sad except in a small way, in its revelation of a certain loss to himself. He could not define that loss but he knew what it was. It was the loss of a kid's pure joy in fishing and in life. For it *was* lost now. He would fish again and do other things again, and get fun out of them, but behind them always would be this thing he had seen today, this thing that was poverty and famine, something he had thought of vaguely and heard of from his father but had never really believed until this afternoon. It was not particularly the Hookers on the Little Stony but the Hookers who—he knew now—were all over the world.

That thing had made him older. It was perhaps that boundary line in his life he had often wondered about. There was a line somewhere, he had told himself, that a kid came up to and stepped over, and when he stepped over it he was a man. This was it, then, and he had stepped over it.

The day had done that for him, at least. In all other ways it had licked him. His promise to Rosemary was broken. His truancy would be found out and surely punished. And Rosemary was involved in that, too, since she had given an excuse for him to the teacher. He would be in bad with Rosemary, his father, the school, everyone. But along with all that mess of failure the day had given him a man's job to do. And he had begun on that job and would finish it when he got home.

And maybe those ways he had been licked were kid ways, and the way he had won was a man's. He didn't know. As he walked up the long drive to his house he wondered how his father now, and Rosemary later, would take his separate confessions, and whether he could bear up, proud, in the way that Sticks was proud, in the way that took guts, if they should condemn him for what he had done.

His father was nowhere around, outside. Perhaps he was in his little office off the sitting room, at his ledgers, as he often was at this time of day. Chris opened the door, tossed his cap on the rack in the long hall and looked into the adjoining sitting room and his father's office beyond it. Both were empty. He called upstairs, "Dad."

Sarah labored heavily in, on her flat pads, from the kitchen, and the early nebulous fragrance of a dinner's beginnings followed her through the opened door.

"Yo' Dad ain' home, Christ'pher. He an' Harry Stack taken Ol' Korn over t' Long Holler t' wait on some cow."

"Did he say when he'd be back?"

"Dinnah tahm, reckon. He said not much befo' then."

Chris went upstairs to his room, took off his wet shoes and stockings and lay on his bed looking up at the pattern of the ceiling paper. He wanted his father to be home right now while his mind was made up to tell him what he had to tell. Time was against him. It was almost four o'clock and if he had to wait until dinnertime to see his father he might find reasons to go back on his plan. For if he didn't tell his father he might still get away with the hooky at least. The chances were pretty good. The excuse he had told Rosemary to give Miss Spencer might hold, after all, and if it should then Rosemary was not mixed up either. . . . Perhaps it were better, that way. Let the other thing wait a week, until his absence from school should be well forgotten.

But that would give Mom Hooker a week longer to worry. She looked as if she could take it, but because she looked that way he didn't want her to. . . .

No. As soon as his Dad came in he'd tell him.

He got up after a while, put on dry stockings and shoes, unstrapped his schoolbooks and tried for half an hour to master the six pages of his *Practical English Grammar* which, he guessed, would be the lesson for tomorrow. He liked it—alone among all his studies —and ordinarily he would have had it cold in fifteen minutes. He left it at last and went to his window and looked out on the fading unpeopled afternoon. And as he stood there his father's big truck turned in between the gateposts and crunched up the gravel drive. Harry Stack was driving and the big Holstein bull, Sir Piebe Korndyke Segis Colantha—affectionately known to the household as "Old Korn"—rode with majestic dignity in the rear, home from another seeding in a far country.

Chris heard the truck stop and then go on again as Harry Stack drove it back to the barn. He heard his father come in at the front door and walk through the sitting room to his office. He stood there at the window a few seconds more, then turned and went down-stairs.

As Chris entered the office his father looked up from an entry he was making in a ledger marked "Bull Services." He turned his craggy inflexible countenance up to his son. It was a large face of promontories and furrowed cliffs, with eyes of a color hard to de-fine, so deeply shadowed were they under the great eaves of the brows.

"Well, Chris," he said, "how'd it go at school?"

"I wasn't at school today, Dad."

"Eh?" That rigid and chiseled face showed little if any change: the emotions worked deep underneath it but only a terrific upheaval could disturb its surface rock.

Chris sat down in the odd chair at the side of his father's big rolltop desk. "I played hooky, Dad."

Christopher Wintermute, Sr., looked at his son studiously for a moment and returned to his entry on the ruled page. "I'm sorry, Chris," he said. "I've felt good today and I don't want it to end like this. You know what my stand is on hooky."

"I know. I felt good this morning, too. The stream looked right —it was a peach of a day—and I knew I could take 'em. I promised Rosemary five and I got six."

"Of course." His father blotted the entry, closed the book and regarded his son keenly. "That was the temptation. This afternoon I could have charged old Amos Kinsey twelve dollars for a service and he'd have paid me. That might have been a temptation too. But I charged him eight. . . . We have been all over this before. It seems that a father's words have no weight in this day. . . . Well."

He sighed and got up from his chair, closed the door and the single window. From a corner of the little room which the door had concealed while it stood open he procured a short thin cane. No woodshed formality attended the elder Wintermute's administra-tions of justice. "My stand on hooky is the same as it was last time," he said. "Hooky is hooky, even when you confess it like a man. . . . Loosen your belt, Chris, and take 'em down."

His father had never shown him anger. He could call him Chris, the affectionate contraction, even when he was about to flog him. The whippings were as impersonal as a lightning bolt except for the expression of wounded and betrayed trust which always preceded them and the deep forgiveness which came afterward. That would follow, tonight, after Chris had gone to bed. His father would come upstairs, enter Chris's room, take Chris in his arms and kiss him. He would speak but a few words and they would be shaky, and the dim hall gas jet would make a blended pattern of light and shadow on the uplands and valleys of the great face, like moonlight over a landscape.

Chris stood before his father, small and white and naked from his waist to his knees, his embarrassment gone in the deeper tide of his apprehension of pain. He had steeled himself for the sting of that lash, the increasing agony of the repeated licks. The last time he had not cried out until the ninth, with only one more to go. There were always ten, never more nor less.

"I'm ready," he said. "But before you start can I tell you something—something awful important that I found out today?" He felt a little ashamed of himself, as if he were begging for mercy, as his father stood looking at him in a faint surprise.

"Well?"

"Dad, you own that old house up on Little Stony—the one the Hookers live in?"

"I do. Why?" The elder Wintermute was impatient as if he, too, had steeled his will to the task his conscience had imposed, and dreaded that time might blunt the fine edge of his decision. "Make it quick," he said, "and let's get this over with."

"How much rent do you charge 'em—if you don't mind telling me?"

"Ten dollars a month. . . . What is this, Chris?"

Chris felt the warm nudge of confidence, sensing that his first sally had scored.

He followed it up: "Do they pay it?"

"Every cent, promptly when due. What is your interest in the Hooker house?"

"Would you—do you need that ten dollars a month?"

"It is business. I have a right to it and they need the house. But—"

"They need a decent house. That thing—you wouldn't keep your cows in it. Listen, it's—"

"The lease stipulates no repairs, at that rental. And anyway, what
—"

"Have you seen it lately?"

"No."

"Well I did, today, when I was up there fishing. Dad, it's falling
down. It's rotten—the paint's gone—the shingles are off—windows
busted and patched up with cardboard."

His father took this in silence. What had been faint and far-off was
with Christopher now, and full-grown, the knowledge that he was
going to win. Beating or no beating, he had his man on the run.

"It's falling in on 'em, I tell you. Four kids in there, and the littlest
one sick . And the old man—Mr. Hooker—lost his job. They haven't
any money. I mean *no* money—not a cent—'cept what they might
be giving toward your rent. The kids have no shoes to wear—only
Sticks has shoes, the big one, 'cause he has to go to school. An' not
a thing to eat but cornmeal mush an' fried dough an' dandylions an'
wood herbs that Mom—Mrs. Hooker—picks. She's got potatoes an'
beans planted, but they're not up yet—"

"Before you go any further, Chris, pull your pants up. A man can't
talk with his pants down, and I can't talk with him." Wintermute's
expression hadn't changed except that under his great brows the
shadow was perhaps deeper.

"It's stuffy in here," he said. He moved to the window and
opened it. He sat down in his desk chair again, facing the gathering
twilight beyond the window. "I didn't know it was that bad up at
the Hooker house," he mused. "I've been meaning to get up there,
but I've been busy." Then he wheeled suddenly toward his son.
"Well, what are you leading up to?"

"Your taxes are heavy, you told me."

"Well?"

"An' you said it's a hard job making a living at farming."

"It is."

"But we're so much better off than they are. . . . Dad, would you
—would you fix that house up for Mom—Mrs. Hooker—and the kids
—an' maybe let 'em have it rent free, at least for a while? I thought
you would an' I was going to tell Mrs. Hooker. But when I saw her
I couldn't. She's proud, Dad. She wouldn't take that from a kid. But
she would from you. Look, I'll chip in my allowance."

Wintermute looked for a long moment into the eyes of his son. They met his own steadily and all he could see there was a flaming eagerness.

"God," he said, at length. "I didn't know they were that poor." His eyes turned from Chris to some papers on the desk before him. "Yes," he said, wearily. "Yes, of course. What else can a Christian do? . . . I'll go up there tomorrow. Listen," he turned again to Chris and his great face was coming alive as the beginnings of a smile trickled into all its furrows like a spring rain on parched ground, "suppose we put up a dinner for them tonight? Sarah's got a big ham on—"

"Don't have to—tonight. I gave 'em my six trout—and one of 'em was, well—that long."

"Eh? You gave them the fish you promised to your girl?"

"Would *you* have?"

His father didn't answer. He got up from his chair again, stepped to the door and opened it. He put the cane back in its old place behind the door; then he took it up again suddenly, broke it in half across his knee, tossed the two pieces into the wastebasket beside his desk and sat down again.

"You have grown, Chris," he said. "Hooky is a kid's game and a licking is a kid's punishment. Still, hooky is hooky. I'll take your rod and tackle for the rest of the season. . . . No, that's a kid's punishment too. You may have them—and fish when your conscience, as a man, tells you it's all right. . . . I think perhaps we can swing this Hooker matter, financially, without the aid of your allowance. And new shoes for the kids." His voice trailed off but Chris heard him say, "and perhaps a job for the father. We'll see."

The big knocker on the front door banged three times.

"Go see who it is, Chris, while I—liquidate this matter of the hooky." Wintermute took out his pen and drew a letterhead from the recesses of his desk. "There is still your excuse to write to your teacher."

At the door stood Rosemary Martin, looking worried. Beyond her in the driveway stood Dr. Martin's black coupé with Dr. Martin in it.

"I brought my Dad to plead for you—if it's not too late." Rosemary spoke nervously in a half whisper. "He said *your* Dad would do anything for him."

"You told him I played hooky?"

"Yes." She looked at him sharply as if annoyed that he should question her. "*Is* it too late?"

"Yes—no—I mean, I told Dad myself. An' it's all right."

"Oh . . . wait." She ran down the walk and said something to Dr. Martin. He nodded and backed out of the drive and drove off down the road. Rosemary ran back to Chris and he could see that the anxiousness was out of her face. But she said abruptly, "Where are my trout?"

"If I had kept 'em I'd have brought 'em to you."

"If you'd *kept* them! You mean to say you caught them and—well, where are they?"

"I caught six—one that big. I was going to bring you five an' keep one for myself." He couldn't explain everything to her now. Tomorrow he would. But just now he was tired explaining to others all that was so clear to himself. But he began, weakly: "Did you ever see the Hooker house—how they live—?"

She stepped to his side and surprisingly took his hand in hers. "Never saw it till this afternoon," she said.

"This afternoon?"

"I went up there—with Sticks. He knows you played hooky an' he's going to tell it all over. . . . Look, let's go out to your summerhouse. It's nice there—we can talk." She led him down the steps and back toward the rustic and morning-gloried structure on the lawn.

When they were seated on the old gray boards of the bench she said: "I'm being mean to you, Chris. I know all about the trout. I went up there with Sticks *and* Dad. Sticks came down to our house this afternoon—he ran all the way—to get Dad. His baby sister is awful sick. Poor kid."

"I heard her cry. She sounded awful sick."

"She won't die, Dad said. Listen, I saw that house—I even went inside. It makes *me* cry to think of it—of Sticks living there—"

"Dad said he'd fix it up. He owns it. An' get 'em some shoes maybe."

"Oh. That's wonderful." Then she added, "I saw your trout too."

"What did Sticks think of those fish?"

"He said you were the best fisherman and best feller he knew in the world—an' he wished you liked him. Honest."

"Aw—did Sticks say that, honest?"

"Honest an' truly. An' he's not the only one who thinks so."

"Who else?"

"*I* do—there."

They were silent, pondering the import of that confession. The dusk in the summerhouse deepened a little. The broad lawn spread away, and beyond it the maples stood breathless in the quiet evening.

"You gave up something you wanted, and that's brave. An' you told your Dad you'd played hooky. That was the best way. That was brave, too."

"Look, did you give Miss Spencer that excuse, this morning?"

"No. It takes nerve to do something you know is wrong. An' I'm not brave—like you. But afterwards I wished I had. That's why I brought Dad along, soon's I could, to help you. But this morning it seemed too much like a lie. . . . And besides, I was mad at you then."

"Why?"

"Because you left me so quick—at the bridge—after I'd promised to help you. You didn't kiss me good-bye, even."

He thought that he would never, never know anything about girls as long as he lived.

"Can I make that up to you now?" he asked after a moment.

"If you don't, I might still be mad," she said.

Outpost 11

On the final night of the season the bitter-enders who were left on the March Brown water fished down from the Random Rocks to the Outpost Pool in the dusk and hauled out at dark to spend the night in the little cabin there. Bunking at the Outpost on this ultimate night has acquired something of the sanctity of tradition.

The Outpost is a plain conceit if not an abject concession to the frailty of human flesh. Built in the third year of the March Brown tenure, at the downstream end of our water, its purpose is to provide a haven for fishermen overtaken by storm or darkness or simple fatigue, far from the main house. And once or twice a season, usually in mayfly time when the traffic is abnormally heavy on our water, it is used for overflow guests.

The idea is attributable to Doctor Hatch, as are certain other accessories to and improvements upon our original plant—such things as the hatchery and the cable bridge over the stream just above the Club Pool. The Doctor's generosity in these additions has ever contrived to disguise itself as good business sense. An investment, he called the Outpost, and that was what he had called the hatchery and the cable bridge. Though we might not have followed his fiscal reasoning we didn't object. In such things there is no use denying the Doctor his whims. In others, such as stream improvement, he defers to our judgment, contenting himself with remarking that when better snags are built Doc Hatch will get hung up in 'em, or something of that sort.

A simple one-room structure of peeled spruce logs (imported from more northerly regions) with a stone fireplace and a low-pitched shingle roof, the Outpost seems at home among the boulders and hemlocks on the north bank of our lowest pool. In its second year the Doctor wanted to add a screened porch on the front elevation, facing the water. Win Stokes called this an architectural excrescence and a vulgarization of the classic log-cabin spirit, but we gave in to the Doctor as usual, and as usual we were glad we had. Now on the summer nights we can sit there in peace, unlathered by mosquito dope, and watch the Big Stony flow out of our preserve under the cable at the line.

Inside, it has a bare, ascetic, utilitarian aspect such as monks are wont to cultivate in their cells. Four bunks are built into the walls; a table and four straight chairs complete the furniture. On each side of the fireplace are shelves for tackle and miscellaneous gear and on the long wall, opposite, wooden pegs for supporting our fly rods. After the addition of the porch the Doctor got rocking chairs in his mind, being unable to think of one without the other, and on one of his trips he unloaded four of them, the inevitable Outpost number. That, he asserted, was positively his final concession to Outpost luxury.

One or two female guests who, at odd times, have bunked overnight there, have deplored our lack of the decorative touch. They have threatened us with window curtains, a table cover to match, and pretty ornaments for our mantelpiece to replace the nice assortment of tobacco tins, coffee cans and the like which repose on the great slab above the hearth and are good containers for items useful to trout fishermen. Also they have been curious about the only picture that hangs on our walls. That happens to be a portrait of one Andrew Volstead, a man of just fame in his time and a kind of patron saint, in reverse, of the Doctor's. Had they taken that picture down for a closer inspection they had perhaps discovered a niche sawed and chiseled out of the stout logs behind it, just large enough for two bottles and four glasses. This handy cache is thus hidden from any chance intruder but available to March Brown members in good standing who find themselves, for one reason or another, incarcerated overnight at the Outpost.

That final evening was breathless and hot. Late summer brooded over the low and quiet stream. There had been no visible hatch and no definite rise of trout. I had hooked three below the Random Rocks on a Badger Spider, lost one and creeled the other two, a brown and a rainbow of undistinguished proportions. Tom brought in two from the Outpost Pool; the Doctor found one just where that pool tails into the last murmuring riffle of our water. The Professor was on the screened porch with his waders off before any of us came in but he had four trout in his creel, the least of which was close to a pound. Victims of small wet flies, these.

The season was thus ending with everything true to form, the normal ratios and the champion setting the pace. It was well. A season should end that way, not with any violent upset. It is all right for the beginner to be high rod on opening day whose character is unpredictable and haphazard: lucky breaks may add fish to the creel then while the skilled hand may not. But at the close most of the luck is washed out of the season. In the months since April your water has run off to a low and mercilessly clear pitch, the best of the fly season has come and gone, and trout appetites have passed through all the stages of hunger, satisfaction and surfeit. But the expert's skill has remained constant, indeed it has perhaps developed an extra notch in the long days since April. By the close it is operating in a deadly way, and this last day of the season is the day of all days when form will tell.

I am content to let the trout season end on that orthodox note—like the peaceful death of a man who dies calmly at a ripe age with his family around him and his affairs in order—rather than on any discordant or unexpected key. I like to see the Professor, who knows better how to fish than any of us ever shall, assume his modest ascendancy as the rods are taken down for the last time. It is just and fitting; it augurs well for the following year.

I put those nine fish in a long covered pan and took it, plus a glass pitcher, out into the darkness. A barred owl was tuning up across the river. I sank the pan in our refrigerator, a wired enclosure in a pocket of a spring rill that enters the Big Stony at the Outpost.

I filled the pitcher from the same rill and returned to the cabin. Lamplight was in the windows and the open door.

"Next year, Doc," Tom was saying, adjusting the wick of the kerosene lamp, "you'll have to install an icebox here. Not only to keep our trout better, but—"

The Doctor was tilting up the portrait of Andrew Volstead and drawing down the treasure from its niche in the log wall. "No," he said. "This stuff is ruined by ice. Spring water gives the right chill and holds the nostalgic bouquet. This is a melancholy potion, gentlemen, a valedictory to a trout season. . . . Besides, the Outpost ought to *be* an outpost, what? With an electric gadget—would we have an outpost any longer? To hell with your icebox, my boy.

"To the winter," he said, raising his glass. "To the ice—not in any damned icebox but on the water of the March Browns—and to its breaking up in the spring—"

"And to the water under it," added the Professor.

"And to the trout under the water," I said.

"And to the leader which may hold one of 'em—next time," said Tom, recalling an outsize fish he had lost in the Top Pool one day in June.

"You ought to rig for him," the Doctor said. "Put on a 1-X and go after him in the dark with something big—a marabou, say. Don't be piddling around the Top Pool with 4-X tippets when you think he's ready. Am I right, Professor, for once?"

"I don't know. It's too far ahead. I'm thinking of that damned ice you were drinking to."

"Me too," said Tom. "All that's got to happen before I can have another go at that lunker. Almost nine months to the opening—from the conception to the birth—"

We hung the rods on the pegs and went out on the porch. And the talk slatted back and forth in that little enclosure like the bats out there over the Outpost Pool. It was bent on fishing: we had had to give up the flesh but we would keep alive the spirit. All through the early and middle season our talk had touched all manner of topics but now, at the end, it clung to fishing as a man clings to the loved one he is about to leave.

After a while the Doctor and Tom turned in. The Professor sat with me for some time and we smoked in silence. Between us there wasn't much left to talk about. There was only the profound finality of the season's end. And the Professor and I could sit there and think about it and listen to what little we had left of the river and the nocturnal undertone of the woods, and let our thoughts reach out toward that remote and shrouded April which was too far off to be believed.

The Professor got up at length and knocked his pipe out and stood at the screen door a moment, looking out into the warm darkness before he turned to go in. The barred owl, in full voice, boomed its diminishing eight notes across the stream.

"I'm staying a while," I said.

"Okay. Of us all, you're the hardest to kill."

The night held a stillness that was balanced and fragile. The trees stood in a perfection of immobility, massed dark against the faintly lighter sky, stood as if in a vacuum, as if there never had been and never would be such a thing as wind. Only the river told of life and movement in the world. It ran alive and murmuring under the stage set of the forest night. You could tune your ears to its infinite wavelengths, pick it up as it spilled over the lip of the Outpost Pool and chuckled softly among the rocks of the riffle and shouldered deep and swift into the foreign stretch below our line.

It would do the same tomorrow, and the next day, and the next, and for days that would be countless beyond the last sight or sound any of us here in this cabin would have of it. That sense of its fabulous permanence was comforting, for in such an eternity the stretch between now and next April was but a moment after all.

Tomorrow the Big Stony would revert to its own: it would know solitude and beauty and a quiet unscratched by men. It would perhaps be glad that our little interlude was over, for its natural state is a state empty of humankind. In past years our departures hadn't left the river completely to itself. But Lank Starbuck was gone now; the river had outlived even him and could have at last an absolute peace. And yet Lank had never disturbed it much; if his ghost still stalked upon the pools and eddies there would be no less commotion than Lank had ever made in the flesh. Lank's ghost, haunting the Big Stony to the end of time, might be his ultimate victory.

There was something to the Doctor's remark that the Outpost

ought to *be* an outpost. In spirit if not in miles this place is about as far from the heart of what is called civilization as any of us ever fare. And in that intimate simplicity lies the essence of its goodness.

But in a sense this little cabin could be called the Inpost. For it is closest to something big in us, perhaps the biggest thing we have. It expresses a major concern of all of us, feeds a major hunger. In its spirit, its countenance, is the reason we come up here in the spring and through the summer, whenever we can get away.

I am satisfied as to what that reason is. Fishing is its symptom or its natural manifestation. At best, fishing is an applied force to enliven a static principle. But fishing isn't the principle. I can tire of fishing: infrequently it can be too good, frequently too poor. On exceptional days trout can come so fast that one becomes surfeited with strikes. On other days—and they are many—trout come so slowly that the fishing resolves itself to a mere routine of casting, and keenness is lost in the long intervals between strikes. A good trout should be rare but not too rare.

But what we are after up here, and what we get, is beyond fish and fishing. The Professor almost always catches trout but on the days when he doesn't he bears no sign of disappointment. He has no sense of championship or the obligation of his fishing talent. The Doctor, on the other hand, has never brought in a trout of distinction. Both love trout fishing, but certainly not for the fish. The Doctor may secretly hope for a great day; the Professor has had that so many times that he scarcely needs it again. His ambition, his hope—if he has one—must be something beyond. Some specialization, perhaps? A season of experimental fishing exclusively with nymphs or dry flies? I doubt it. That kind of crank has as valid a philosophy as anyone else, to be sure. But the Professor is not that kind of a crank. None of us is. We are looking for something else, or perhaps I should say we used to look for it, for I think we found it long ago.

Men have speculated on this before and have found their individual answers. The voice of the stream, going by out there, may have the answer, or the moon breaking over the woods to the southeast, or the barred owl calling again across the river. The answer may be locked up in such as they. Or maybe not locked up at all but as open as daylight, so obvious that men overlook it. For happiness involves no need to speculate or to hunt reasons. Gladness is its own reward. The simplicity of our life on the Big Stony is greater than any problem of casting or any choice of a fly. The larger simplicity contains all the minutiae of fishing problems. Trout fishing has become so complicated that learned men have written fat volumes on how to do it and the tackle business has become a major industry. But the fact that you're fishing is a simple fact, and the mind and heart that you bring to fishing have forgotten for the moment the complexities and animosities of men. They can look at fishing and, beyond the pool and the cast, look at life in the same terms.

The river and the moon and that barred owl express that sort of simplicity to me. And in a way which is less than perfect only because the hand of man is involved in it, this little cabin, this Outpost, does too.